MINNESOTA SYMPOSIA ON
CHILD PSYCHOLOGY, VOLUME 8

MINNESOTA SYMPOSIA ON CHILD PSYCHOLOGY
Volume 8

ANNE D. PICK, EDITOR

THE UNIVERSITY OF MINNESOTA PRESS · MINNEAPOLIS

Library of Congress Catalog Card Number: 67-30520
ISBN 0-8166-0722-2

PUBLISHED IN THE UNITED KINGDOM AND INDIA BY THE OXFORD
UNIVERSITY PRESS, LONDON AND DELHI, AND IN
CANADA BY BURNS & MACEACHERN LIMITED, DON MILLS, ONTARIO

Preface

EACH YEAR scholars who are prominent in their own fields are asked to come to the University of Minnesota to participate in the Minnesota Symposia on Child Psychology. These participants are invited by the Institute of Child Development, which hosts the event, because the results of their research are advancing significantly our understanding of the basic processes of human development. The papers prepared for the eighth symposium, which occurred in October, 1973, are published in this volume. The variety of topics and contents among these papers illustrates that behavioral scientists use many approaches in their study. There are also, however, ideas which appear in a number of the papers, though in different forms, and such ideas reflect the common concerns of these leading students of development. For instance, the point is made in several contexts that productive inquiry depends on adopting a comprehensive rather than a limited perspective. In at least two papers such a perspective means recognizing the value of procedures from disciplines related to one's own. In another paper, such a perspective means identifying the effects of cultural practices which may not be universal. And in still another paper such a perspective appears with the argument that theory plays a crucial role in generating important problems for investigation.

Beatrice and Allen Gardner describe Project Washoe in which young chimpanzees learn a human language in order that their two-way communication can be observed and compared with that of young humans. The language learned by the chimps is based upon gestures instead of on speech, and it is a language used by deaf humans. It is taught to the chimps by human speakers who are the chimps' companions and who provide an intellectually stimulating setting for their linguistic development. Extensive comparisons of young

v

chimps and young children indicate similarities in the course of their linguistic development.The procedures used by the Gardners to ensure that comparisons across species can indeed be made and interpreted sensibly are important models also for making comparisons among members of the same species who vary in such features as age or cultural background.

For more than a decade, Eleanor Gibson has been investigating the processes of perception and perceptual learning which are fundamental to reading. In her paper she first identifies three general trends in perceptual development: increasing specificity of correspondence between stimulation and perceptual differentiation, increasing optimization of attention, and increasing economy of perception. Then she reviews evidence from her own extensive program of research and demonstrates that the details of these trends are useful in understanding reading — of what it consists and how it is learned. Gibson also documents how theory and empirical inquiry must interact for a systematic and thorough attack on a problem. The theory helps define the particular questions to be asked, and the answers to the questions help refine the theory itself as well as provide new information about the problem being studied.

Irving Gottesman describes an emerging discipline of developmental behavioral genetics, an inquiry which combines the perspectives of developmental psychology and developmental genetics. It is not sufficient for understanding developmental processes and behavioral outcomes to identify the genotype for a specific phenotype, nor to describe the variety of environmental influences on a developing organism. Gottesman's concept of the reaction range helps one to think about the many concurrent contributors to phenotypic variation. The perspective of this new discipline of developmental behavioral genetics has already been useful in describing such diverse phenomena as variation in the eyes of Drosophila, variation in height of human adolescents, and variation in the liability and age of onset of behavior disorders such as schizophrenia.

The paper by Herbert and Gloria Leiderman also demonstrates the importance of a perspective which is not fixed if we are to understand processes of human development. They point out that much theorizing about early social development is based on observations made in cultures in which the norm is for the mother alone to be the primary caretaker for young infants. Unless our theories are to be culture-specific, we must establish their validity by investigating their applicability in many settings. The Leidermans studied the development during the first year of life of infants in an East African com-

PREFACE

munity in which both monomatric and polymatric caretaking arrangements are acceptable and typical. The behavior of these babies toward their mothers, caretakers, and strangers, as well as the babies' performance on standardized tests, suggest some effects of social stimulation on early affective and cognitive development.

Another aspect of human social development is discussed by Ross Parke, who for a number of years has studied how punishment controls young children's behavior. The discovery that if the children in his experiments were given reasons for prohibitions, the effect of punishment was enhanced, led to changes in the direction of Parke's research. He turned to the study of how different types of rationale help children to inhibit proscribed behavior, and he found that the effect of the rationale depends on the age of the child and on opportunities available to children to observe other people inhibiting their own behavior. Parents' choices of disciplinary techniques are probably influenced by characteristics of the children themselves, e.g., their age and sex. Further, the disciplinarian's own behavior is affected by the types of techniques he uses — documenting that socialization need not cease at age 18 or 21 years.

The final paper in this volume, by David Zeaman and Betty House, provides a detailed account of some issues of interest to investigators of children's learning. They evaluate evidence for three hypotheses about the bases for developmental trends in children's discrimination learning and the transfer of that learning. The three hypotheses have to do with how learning occurs — whether or not it is based on mediation, how quickly children differing in age can learn, and what is learned by children of different ages. Zeaman and House suggest that there may be developmental changes in all three aspects of learning, but that the most significant changes occur in what children learn. The authors demonstrate the utility of their own theory about what is learned by confirming a prediction about transfer of learning based on attention.

This eighth symposium was supported financially by a Public Health Service grant from the National Institute of Child Health and Human Development (HD-01765), and by the Institute of Child Development of the University of Minnesota. Also, the early planning for this symposium occurred while the editor was a Fellow at the Center for Advanced Study in the Behavioral Sciences, and the support from that institution is appreciated.

As in previous years, many persons shared responsibility for the symposium event itself and for preparing this volume. The assistance of Judith

MINNESOTA SYMPOSIA ON CHILD PSYCHOLOGY

Allen, Helen Dickison, John Drozdal, Virginia Eaton, Robert Gordon, Elizabeth Haugen, and Melynda Mason is acknowledged with special appreciation. Of course, the primary responsibility for this symposium was taken by the distinguished investigators who participated in it, and whose contributed papers are contained in this volume. It is to them that gratitude is given for demonstrating, both personally and in their papers, how progress in our science occurs.

ANNE D. PICK

Goose Rocks Beach, Maine
August, 1974

Table of Contents

MINNESOTA SYMPOSIA ON
CHILD PSYCHOLOGY, VOLUME 8

+ BEATRICE T. GARDNER AND R. ALLEN GARDNER +

Comparing the Early Utterances of Child and Chimpanzee

PROJECT WASHOE (Gardner & Gardner, 1969, 1971a, 1973) is best understood as a pilot study in a program aimed at establishing a truly comparative psychology of two-way communication. When we started, a large body of data was already available (French, 1965; Miles, 1965; Riopelle, 1967), which indicated to us that chimpanzees must have the requisite intellectual capacities. Apparently this was not a popular or even a common opinion at that time (cf. Premack, 1971), so it is important for us to emphasize our basic assumption. We saw no need for further demonstrations of the fact that chimpanzees can solve problems which, according to one or another current theory of linguistics might be interpreted as analogous to the problems involved in the human use of human languages. Rather, we set out to demonstrate that a chimpanzee could achieve a significant degree of two-way communication by using a genuine form of human language.

All of our procedures are governed by one principle: the observations obtained of the actual linguistic performance of an infant chimpanzee must be compared with the actual linguistic performance of human children. This requirement immediately cut us off from a large body of the technical literature in linguistics which we found to be concerned with the ideal performance of theoretical human beings, with little or no acknowledgement of the differences in ccmpetence between toddlers and college professors. Fortunately for us, modern students of child development have been similarly disillusioned with theoretical linguistics. A rapidly growing body of data has appeared that is concerned with the actual utterances of actual children (Brown, 1973).

3

To obtain data on the chimpanzee, we had to find a suitable human language and to provide an infant chimpanzee with conditions that would be favorable for the development of a significant level of two-way communication. The language that we chose was Ameslan, American Sign Language, the gestural language used by the deaf in North America. Previous attempts to teach chimpanzees to use vocal languages such as English (e.g., Hayes & Hayes, 1951), had produced disappointing results. A great deal of evidence based on observation of chimpanzees in the wild and in the laboratory suggested to us that a language based on gestures would be far more suitable for chimpanzees than a language based on speech.

Here we will describe Ameslan, the laboratory conditions, and some of the results obtained in Project Washoe; we will also indicate certain features of procedure that have been improved in our current project on teaching sign language to several chimpanzees.

AMESLAN

Linguistic Character of Ameslan. It is important to stress certain characteristics of Ameslan as a language because the use of Ameslan is a critical feature of the methodology of a Washoe-type project and also because there are so few persons who have first-hand experience with sign languages and their use among the deaf.

A sign language consists of a system of manually produced visual symbols, called signs, that are analogous to words in a spoken language. Stokoe (1960) has shown that just as words can be analyzed into phonemes, so signs can be analyzed into what have been called cheremes. Carroll (1961, p. 114) comments on this analysis:

To isolate cheremes . . . (Stokoe) . . . proceeded as any linguist would in identifying the phonemes of a new language—by noticing recurrent and discriminating features of utterances—or the analogue of utterances—in sign language. The sign-morphemes, like syllables, were seen to be composed of cheremes. Three varieties of cheremes are distinguished, corresponding to three aspects of the formation of a hand-sign; its position (i.e., location relative to other parts of the body), its configuration, and its motion. . . . The total number of cheremes is roughly comparable to the number of phonemes in natural languages—somewhere between 20 and 60 in most languages.

Because of the cheremic and morphemic construction of signs, a very large number of signs are possible; new signs are continually introduced into Ameslan and old signs drop out, just as with spoken languages (Benson, 1962). Some signs are highly iconic, and others are quite arbitrary; but all are

4

arbitrary to some degree. Even for highly iconic signs different iconic attributes of the same referent are often arbitrarily selected for representation by the conventions of different sign languages (Schlesinger, 1970). Consequently, there are regional and national differences in sign languages as in spoken languages. Deaf persons report that except for a limited number of basic symbols they experience considerable difficulty in conversing with the deaf of another country (Fusfeld, 1958).

The formal analysis of the structure of Ameslan has only recently been attempted, but as more and more studies are performed by competent linguists who are also fluent in Ameslan, the parallels between Ameslan and spoken languages are increasingly evident (see especially Stokoe, 1970).

It is certainly reasonable to suppose that Ameslan is a sufficiently powerful linguistic system to test the capacities of chimpanzees. There is no known limit on the size of vocabulary that can be constructed legitimately within the rules of Ameslan, nor is there a known limit to the number or length of messages that can be communicated by legitimate combinations of signs of Ameslan. Ameslan is used by a large community of human beings as a system of face-to-face communication in much the same way as spoken languages are used in face-to-face communication.

Comparison with Deaf Children. The existence of a community of human beings who use Ameslan as a face-to-face language has a crucial bearing on a Washoe-type project beyond the pragmatic validation of Ameslan as a language. The deaf children of deaf parents comprise an essential control group for evaluating the progress of young chimpanzees that have acquired some facility in Ameslan. If we were to teach an artificial language to our chimpanzee subjects, it probably would not be possible to obtain any suitable human subjects for comparison. For to do so, we would not only have to provide the human children with as much training in the artificial language as the chimpanzees receive but we would have to find parents or guardians who would agree to expose the children to the artificial language only to the exclusion of all other linguistic experience.

The need for comparisons of chimpanzees with human children can be illustrated by considering a hypothetical project in which some rudimentary form of English was successfully taught to young chimpanzees. The fact that these hypothetical subjects could speak some words of English would not in itself be evidence for the mastery of the English language. Nor would failure to speak English as well as the idealized speaker of the transformational linguists prove that the young chimpanzees had failed to master language. It is

5

easy to show that the English spoken by very young children is a far simpler language than the English spoken by their parents (cf. Brown, 1973). To interpret the results of the chimpanzee study, we must have the yardsticks provided by tests of the linguistic performance of immature humans and by careful descriptions of their linguistic development.

As in the case of the linguistic analysis of Ameslan, it is only recently that studies of children learning Ameslan as a first language have been attempted; the pioneering studies are still in progress (Bellugi & Klima, 1972; Schlesinger & Meadow, 1972). In time we expect that developmental norms will become available on the number and types of signs that are acquired and on the sentences constructed by young signers. In the future, norms for immature signers will provide the most appropriate comparative data for evaluating the linguistic achievements of the chimpanzees. For the present we have used data on the performance of immature human speakers for these comparisons.

Exposure to "Native Speakers" of Ameslan. Another important advantage of Ameslan for the purpose of our research is that our subjects can be exposed to adult human beings who are "native speakers." Perhaps the greatest discrepancy between Project Washoe as we originally conceived it and as we were able to execute it was our inability to provide Washoe with a sufficient number of adult models of the language she was to acquire. One high-school-age deaf boy worked with us for two summers, and two recent graduates of Gallaudet College worked with us during a part of the last summer of the project. And occasionally there were visitors who were fluent in Ameslan. But for the most part, Washoe's human companions and adult models for signing could be described as hearing people who recently had acquired Ameslan and whose fluency, diction, and grammar were limited because they had very little practice except with each other and with Washoe.

One of the significant improvements in the procedure of the current project is the use of deaf fluent signers as research personnel. The news of the success of Project Washoe was received most warmly in the deaf community. There have been at least two enthusiastic articles on the project in the *Deaf American* (Swain, 1968, 1970), the most widely circulated publication among the deaf. When we presented an invited lecture and film demonstration at Gallaudet College (the national college for the deaf in Washington, D.C.) in October, 1970, we were told that our audience was the largest that had turned out for a lecture in the history of the college. Many channels of communication with

6

the deaf community were opened for us and as a consequence it has been much easier for us to recruit deaf persons to participate in the current project.

ENRICHED ENVIRONMENT FOR DEVELOPMENT OF TWO-WAY COMMUNICATION

Comparison with Human Children. If chimpanzees are to be compared with some other species of laboratory animal, then there is a great deal that could be accomplished by providing comparable laboratory environments for both species. But there can be no question of keeping human children in laboratory cages, restricting their linguistic training to an hour or so a day (on weekdays only), and confining their practice to laboratory sessions. Therefore, since we cannot put our human controls in cages, we must enrich the environment of our chimpanzee subjects as far as possible.

In addition to humanitarian considerations which make it impossible to consider placing a control group of children in cages, there are most cogent scientific reasons for rejecting such an approach. No one, not even the most extreme Chomskian nativist, could expect normal linguistic development under such impoverished conditions. Consequently, it would be impossible to interpret any linguistic similarities or differences between caged chimpanzees and caged children. Whether the purpose of the project is seen as the demonstration of how close a chimpanzee can come to a child or how far apart they must remain, it is crucial that the chimpanzees be maintained in an environment that is as intellectually stimulating as possible.

Laboratory Environment for Chimpanzee Subjects. The environment that we are trying to provide for the subjects is best characterized by describing Washoe's maintenance conditions (Gardner & Gardner, 1974a). Washoe lived in a furnished house trailer which was located in a large backyard of a suburban home. The living areas were well stocked with furniture, tools, and toys of all kinds, and there were frequent excursions to other interesting places—a pond, a meadow, and various university buildings.

Whenever Washoe was awake, one or more human companions were present. Washoe's companions used Ameslan to communicate with her and with each other so that linguistic training would be an integral part of daily life and not an activity restricted to special training sessions. The companions' function was to see that Washoe's environment was maximally stimulating and maximally associated with Ameslan. They demonstrated the uses and extolled the virtues of the many interesting objects in her world. They anticipated the routine activities of the day and described these with appropriate signs. They invented games, introduced novel objects, showed pictures in books and magazines, and made special scrapbooks of her favorite pictures, all to demonstrate the use of Ameslan. All participants in the project had to be something more than laboratory technicians; they had to be good friends and amusing playmates with whom Washoe would communicate.

PROGRAM OF TESTING AND DATA COLLECTION

Integrating two-way communication by Ameslan into the daily life of a chimpanzee is a distinctive feature of a Washoe-type project. Equally distinctive and equally important is the systematic program of data collection and testing (Gardner & Gardner, 1969, 1971a, 1971b, 1971c, 1974b). Indeed, we may have overdone this aspect of the first project; the continual testing that Washoe endured may have inhibited the free growth of her two-way communication. Yet it was imperative to keep records that were as comprehensive as possible about the course of Washoe's acquisition of sign language. In particular, we needed to obtain developmental data that could be compared with the available data for human children, and we needed to provide evidence for the meaningful use of sign language by our subject under rigorous testing conditions.

Naturalistic Methods of Observation. The methods of data collection most frequently used by developmental psycholinguists consist of longitudinal diary records, inventories of phrases, and repeated samples of all verbal output within a brief period of time. Such methods are as applicable to young chimpanzees as to young children, and in Project Washoe we took pains to use these techniques so that her sign language progress could be evaluated by developmental psycholinguists. Of course, we were able to maintain a far more complete record of her development than has ever been maintained for a child because of the continuous presence of trained observers whose main task was the recording of Washoe's signing.

Brown, Bellugi, and other investigators of the language of children have commented on the many ways in which Washoe's performance in our early records parallels the performance of children—for example, in Washoe's generalization of the meanings of signs, in the gradual increase in length of her sign combinations, and in the types of semantic relations expressed by her earliest combinations (Klima & Bellugi, 1970; Brown, 1970). "As matters now stand," Roger Brown (1973) states, "the evidence that Washoe has Stage I language is about the same as it is for children" [p. 43].

As with human verbal behavior, Washoe's signs were used for classes of referents rather than for specific objects or events. Thus the sign *dog* was used to refer to live dogs and pictures of dogs of any breed, size, or color, and for the sound of barking by an unseeen dog as well; the sign *open* was used to ask for the opening of any door (e.g., to houses, rooms, cupboards) or container (e.g., boxes, bottles, jars) and even—an invention of Washoe's—turning on a water faucet. Within 51 months of training, Washoe came to use 132 signs. In addition, there were several hundred signs of Ameslan that Washoe learned to understand during this period.

As soon as Washoe had about eight signs in her vocabulary, she began to use them in combinations of two or more, and soon combinations such as *You me hide* and *You me go out there hurry* became very common. Washoe's use of combinations was very similar to that of the very young children studied by Brown and others (Brown, 1970, 1973). In Table 1 we followed Brown's analysis of children's combinations (1970, p. 220). Two-word combinations that he observed during the developmental period he calls Stage I have been placed side-by-side with two-sign combinations that we observed during the first 36 months of Project Washoe. The similarities between the types of combinations produced early by children and by the chimpanzee are striking.

Following the procedures used by Bloom, we analyzed the two-sign constructions that appeared in comprehensive samples of Washoe's signing for evidence of the consistent use of order. We found further similarities between Washoe and young children. For example, in the Washoe records there are parallels for all the pivot constructions and substantive constructions reported for Kathryn I (Bloom, 1970). The pivot constructions with *this* and *that*, which Bloom has interpreted as constructions "indicating a particular instance of the referent which she named," appeared 17 times in Kathryn's record, and in each case *this* or *that* was in sentence initial position. In comparable records for Washoe there were 20 instances of constructions with *this* or *that*, all in the context of spontaneous naming of magazine pictures. In 19 of the 20 cases the demonstrative occupied the sentence initial position; the exception was the construction *Food that food*.

The tape recording sessions that provide samples of children's speech contain a great many questions by adults and replies by children. On the basis of appropriate replies to Wh-questions—those containing interrogatives such as Who, What, or Where—Brown (1968) and Ervin-Tripp (1970) claim that young children have mastered grammatical markers and sentence constituents. Using a similar, though more systematic, sample of Washoe's replies to Wh-questions, we were able to compare the types of questions that

9

Table 1. Parallel Descriptive Schemes for the Earliest Combinations of Children and Washoe

Brown's (1970) Scheme for Children		Our Scheme for Washoe	
Types	Examples	Types	Examples
Attributive: Ad + N	big train, red book	Object-attribute[a]	drink red, comb black
		Agent-attribute	Washoe sorry, Naomi good
Possessive: N + N	Adam checker, mommy lunch	Agent-object	clothes Mrs. G., you hat
		Object-attribute[a]	baby mine, clothes yours
Locative		Action-location	go in, look out
N + V	walk street, go store	Action-object[b]	go flower, pants tickle[c]
N + N	sweater chair, book table	Object-location	baby down, in hat[d]
		(not applicable, see text)	
Agent-action: N + V	Adam put, Eve read	Agent-action	Roger tickle, you drink
Action-object: V + N	put book, hit ball	Action-object[b]	tickle Washoe, open blanket
Agent-object: N + N	mommy sock, mommy lunch	(not applicable, see text)	
		Appeal-action	please tickle, hug hurry
(not applicable, see text)		Appeal-object	gimme flower, more fruit

SOURCE: Gardner, B. T. & Gardner, R. A. Two-way communication with an infant chimpanzee. In A. Schrier & F. Stollnitz (Eds.), *Behavior of nonhuman primates*. New York: Academic Press, 1971. (a)
[a,b] Indicate types classified two ways in Brown's scheme and only one way in our scheme.
[c] Answer to the question, "Where tickle?"
[d] Answer to the question, "Where brush?"

BEATRICE T. GARDNER

children and the young chimpanzee answer appropriately and to show that, in terms of this aspect of language acquisition, Washoe's performance at age five exceeded that of Level III children (Gardner & Gardner, 1971c). Some of these results are presented in Table 2. Here we have listed a subset of the replies in the sample, consisting of all instances in which the questioners asked different types of questions while indicating the same type of object (or a member of the same object class, such as a shoe that the questioner was wearing and a shoe that belonged to Washoe). In the current project, we are again recording developmental data, and certainly more can be learned about the acquisition of concepts, vocabulary, and grammar when there are several chimpanzee subjects.

Double-Blind Evaluative Tests. It is necessary to isolate and measure the

Table 2. Replies to Different Types of Question about the Same Type of Object

Object Indicated	Question Type		
	Whose Demonstrative?	What Demonstrative?	What Color?
Bed	*Mine*	*Bed*	*Red*
Berry	. . .[a]	*Food fruit*	*Red black*
Blanket	*Mine*	. . .	*Red*
Book	*Mine*	*Book*	*Black*
Candy	. . .	*Sweet*	*Red black*
Chair	. . .	*Chair*	*Man*
Cheese	. . .	*Cheese*	*Fruit cheese*
Clothes	*Mine*	. . .	*White clothes*
Cube of ice	*Mine*	. . .	*Red white green*
Cup	*Mine yours*	*Drink*	*Red*
Doll	*Mine*	*Baby*	*Black cow*
Flower	. . .	*Flower*	*Red*
Fruit	*Mine*	*Fruit*	*Red black*
Keys	*Yours*	*Key*	. . .
Nut	*Mine*	*Nut*	. . .
Pencil	*Mine*	*Pencil*	. . .
Shoes	*Yours*	*Window*	*White black*
Swallow-game blocks	*Your swallow*	. . .	*Red*
Wristwatch	*Yours*	*Listen*	. . .

[a]Leaders indicate that this type of question was not asked of this type of object during the sampling period.

Classification of replies:			
Possessive	13	0	0
Object + possessive	1	0	0
Object	0	15	2
Object + attribute	0	0	2
Attribute	0	0	11

11

communicative behavior of our subjects under rigorous testing conditions. Any evaluation of the effectiveness of different teaching methods, of the role of individual differences, and of age limits for sign language acquisition requires rigorous measurement.

We were successful in developing rigorous procedures for testing the nouns in Washoe's vocabulary (Gardner & Gardner, 1971b, 1974b) and Fouts (1972) was able to compare three methods of teaching such signs to Washoe. In the current project we plan to expand the test materials to cover other vocabulary categories as well as rules of grammar.

The tests required our subject to communicate information about objects that she alone could see. If we define a vocabulary item as a class of referents that can be correctly named by the use of a given sign and we define an exemplar as a member of one of the item classes, the essential features of the procedure were (1) that exemplars be presented trial by trial in a sequence that could not be predicted either by Washoe or by the observers and (2) that the sign that Washoe made would be the only information available to the observers.

In our most versatile and successful testing procedure we made use of 35mm. color transparencies to present exemplars. The use of photographic slides rather than actual objects allows a wide range of exemplars to be presented. It became possible to produce exemplars for most of the nouns in Washoe's vocabulary, and it became easy to produce many different exemplars for a given item so that the tests could consist of exemplars that were entirely new. Thus we could photograph the entomological collection at the Biology Department and produce exemplars of the item *bug*, or we could go down to the parking lot and produce abundant exemplars of the item *car*.

The apparatus used in the slide test is shown in Figure 1. For this test we used a cabinet built into the wall between two rooms (R_1, R_2) of the laboratory. The slides were back-projected on a screen (P.S.) that was mounted inside the cabinet. A plastic barrier (P.B.) prevented Washoe from touching the projection screen. The cabinet and the screen were flush with the floor, and O_1, standing beside the cabinet, could observe Washoe's signing without seeing the pictures. The test was self-paced: Washoe herself began a trial by unlatching the sliding door (S.D.) of the cabinet. When she opened the door, O_1 asked her (in signs) what she saw and wrote down her reply on a slip of paper which was passed to E_1 through a message slit (M.S.) in the wall. In the other room E_1 operated a carousel projector, presenting the slides in a prearranged random order. A one-way vision screen (1-w.G.) was set into

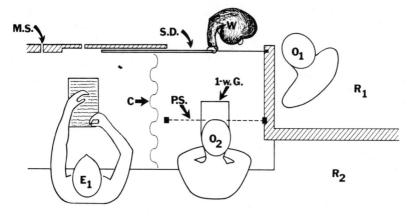

Figure 1. Double-blind testing apparatus used in Project Washoe. The top view is above, the side view, below.

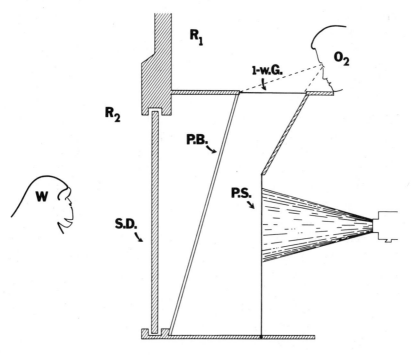

the top of the cabinet which permitted a second person, O_2, to observe Washoe without being seen by her and without being able to see the projection screen. Thus O_2 could confirm the signs reported by O_1.

The slide test proved to be a very efficient means of testing vocabulary. We found that we could administer test sessions with as many as 40 trials in less than 35 minutes, and two such sessions could take place within a week with no apparent loss of interest on Washoe's part.

The slide test was also a very sensitive test of vocabulary. In a two-choice test, such as the WGTA, the subject's expected chance score is 50 percent correct. Such tests require very high scores or a very large number of trials to differentiate the subject's performance from chance responding. In our tests the subject could make many different responses, and hence the chance expectation of obtaining the correct response (that is, the correct sign) for a given exemplar was extremely low. For a test involving N items, Washoe's expected chance score was 1/N items correct, if her responses were confined to the items of the test. Since other signs (extralist intrusions) were also reported, the expected chance score was actually lower than 1/N. For example, the longest test that we administered to Washoe involved 32 different items with 4 exemplars of each. This 128 trial test was administered in four sessions at the rate of two sessions per week. Washoe's expected chance score was 1/32 or 4 trials correct. In fact, according to the record of replies produced by O_1 Washoe named 92 of the exemplars correctly, and according to the records of the second blind observer, O_2, Washoe's score was 91.

The sensitivity of our testing procedure made it possible to learn a great deal from Washoe's errors as well as from her correct naming. A particular form of error could occur infrequently and still be detectably different from chance responding to the exemplar. The analysis of errors showed that incorrect responses reflected conceptual relations among signs: the common error for a photograph of a dog would be a sign for another animal such as *cat* or *cow*, and the common error for pictures of fruit would be another type of food, such as *meat* or *cheese* (Gardner & Gardner, 1971a, 1971b).

Evaluation by Deaf Observers. As has been mentioned, two independent blind observers participated in the vocabulary tests. Usually both O_1 and O_2 were members of the research staff. Their records were in substantial agreement, both on trials in which Washoe replied correctly and on trials in which she made an error. Since O_2 did not have to interact with Washoe in any way, persons who were fluent in Ameslan but strangers to Washoe could

14

serve as observers of her signing. In this important control condition, there was also substantial agreement between the reports of the two blind observers, and their agreement increased from one test session to the next. Two deaf observers, whose previous contact with Washoe had been minimal, participated in the tests. For one, agreement with O_1 was 67 percent during the first test session that he observed and rose to 89 percent during the second test. For the other, agreement with O_1 was 71 percent during the first test and also rose to 89 percent during the second one. The degree of agreement between the deaf observer and the project assistant during the second test was well within the range of agreement found between O_1 and O_2, when they were both project assistants who were thoroughly familiar with Washoe's signing. This implies that Washoe was using very standard sign language and that her accent could be learned readily by persons fluent in Ameslan.

In summary, we were able to administer rigorous tests of vocabulary and to demonstrate that Washoe could use the nouns in her vocabulary to name appropriate new instances of the referent category. Almost certainly, the maintenance conditions that we provided for Washoe—her enriched environment and her friendly relations with her testers—were critical to the success of the testing procedure. The basic requirement of the procedure was that Washoe inform her tester of events that she alone had witnessed. Washoe accepted this requirement readily, probably because the testers were her social companions to whom she reported such events spontaneously in the course of daily life. By contrast, Premack reported that he was unable to devise blind-testing procedures for the cage-maintained chimpanzee, Sarah (Ploog & Melnuchek, 1971).

Tests of Combinations. The data that have been offered as empirical support for claims about the control of grammar by young children fall into two categories. First there are naturalistic observations in which the investigator describes the situation in which the child's utterances occur as well as the words themselves. Then the investigator uses his context notes to interpret and analyze the structure of the utterance, e.g., deciding whether *mommy lunch* is a possessive or an agent-object construction (Brown, 1970). Such data have also been obtained for Washoe and appear comparable to those for young children. Second, specific tests of grammatical comprehension are administered to young children. Typically these are two-choice tests with no double-blind controls. Thus the young child is shown two pictures illustrating a grammatical contrast (*The train bumps the car* and *The car bumps the train*). The experimenter then speaks each of the relevant sentences, and the child is asked to point to the picture named by the sentence (Fraser, Bellugi, & Brown, 1963).

To provide evidence for control of grammar that could be accepted by comparative psychologists, different procedures must be used. By an expansion of our testing materials, the procedures that were used for testing vocabulary in Project Washoe can be used for tests of combined forms in the current project.

The next steps, then, will involve expansions of the test material so that subjects are required to tell us more about the exemplars than just their names. For example, combinations of names with color or numerical modifiers can be illustrated and tested. The use of locative constructions can be tested with a set of photographs illustrating spatial relations between pairs of objects, such as 'X behind Y', 'X in Y', 'X under Y', and so on, for which O_1 would ask the subjects, 'Where X'? or 'Where Y'? The use of order to communicate meaning can also be tested with our procedures. This especially important extension of the test requires the use of short loops of motion picture film. By showing reversible relations between pairs of animate nouns, such as 'A chases B', 'A kisses B', 'A feeds B', and so on, we can require our subjects to use rules of order in their descriptions of the scenes.

SPONTANEOUS UTTERANCES

As comparative psychologists we concentrated much of our effort in Project Washoe on the development of a rigorous program of quantitative evaluation. Yet interpretive discussions of our results tend to focus on Washoe's spontaneous use of Ameslan rather than on her replies to questions (e.g., Gardner & Gardner, 1972; Ploog & Melnuchek, 1971). Only part of Washoe's time was spent in formal lessons or in tests, but the use of Ameslan was a common feature of her social interactions all day and every day. Thus Washoe had abundant opportunity to produce spontaneous comments and questions and to initiate and maintain conversational exchanges. Trained observers were always present and a comprehensive daily log was kept so that the developmental aspects of Washoe's spontaneous utterances can be traced in the record.

Because signing became so much a part of Washoe's social interactions, it was fairly easy to demonstrate Washoe's use of Ameslan to observers who were strangers to her and who could provide an independent evaluation of her signing. Indeed, Washoe seemed to expect everyone to know Ameslan, and signed to every being that she met, including, at first, cats and dogs.

16

Gradually, she came to understand that some people were pretty dense about Ameslan. New research assistants have commented on the singular humiliation of having Washoe sign to them ever so slowly and carefully when they were only beginners at Ameslan.

The use of Ameslan was so well integrated into Washoe's daily life that she was able to learn many signs merely from observing our usage (cf. discussion of *smoke* in Gardner & Gardner, 1971a, 136–137). She also attempted to introduce her own invented signs (cf. discussion of *bib* in Gardner & Gardner, 1971a, 137–140).

Combinations. We made no direct attempt to teach Washoe the important linguistic process of combining signs, other than by modeling combinations in our normal use of Ameslan. In this way, we hoped to observe the spontaneous developments in Washoe's use of combinations. Washoe began to use two-sign combinations quite early. Her first combination, *gimme sweet*, was observed in the 10th month of the project when she was about 21 months old. This is very close to the age at which human infants have been reported to form their first two-word combinations. The types of combinations used early by Washoe are particularly interesting because they are so similar to those of children (Table 1).

We were able to observe the spontaneous emergence of the use of order in combinations. To a large extent, of course, Washoe's preferred orders were the same as ours (for example, agent-action and agent-object). Since an unlimited number of agents, actions, and objects were combined in this way, we can say that it is unlikely that Washoe was copying particular combinations produced by her models, even though we can only be certain of this for a few combinations that we, ourselves, had never used, e.g., the request *Tickle me*. (This phrase of Washoe's appeared long before we found out that she would tickle us.) In other ordered combinations, we can be sure that Washoe was not imitating her companions because she deviated from their usage. For example, Washoe's early attributive constructions followed the order of noun-modifier, as in *clothes white* and *baby mine*, even though her human companions used the normal English order of modifier-noun. This is interesting because the noun-modifier order is fairly common in the earliest combinations of English-speaking children and for young signers as well.

Questions. In human children the earliest questions are formed by speaking one or two words with a questioning intonation (Leopold, 1953–54). The use of interrogative words such as *what*, *who*, *where*, comes later, and the use of the inverted question forms, such as *Will you go?* occurs much later still. In

17

Ameslan, and indeed in all sign languages, there is a gestural equivalent to the questioning intonation that is as common and important in this means of face-to-face communication as it is in speech (Stokoe et al., 1965). Washoe developed the gestural equivalent of the questioning intonation very early; the first recorded observation of this kind of questioning was reported during the 9th month of the project. An interesting and common occasion for Washoe's use of questions was requesting names for pictures in magazines (Gardner & Gardner, 1974a). Washoe was very fond of magazines, especially if they were new; and she would leaf through them for a half hour at a time, looking at pictures, and naming them (*That flower* or *That toothbrush*) either spontaneously or in reply to our questions. Sometimes with a distinct question juncture she would verify the name for the picture by asking, *That food?* As for human children, the Wh-questions were more difficult; by the 51st month of the project, Washoe was producing reliably only questions containing the interrogative *Who*.

Negative Terms. In a formal language such as the Boolean Algebra, negative terms such as the tilde (˜) can be combined with other symbols and expressions to form a negative combination. The result is a set of pairs of expressions, such as P and $˜P$ (not-P) which are precisely symmetrical opposites of each other. Many nonhuman species have been shown to have the ability to solve conditional discriminations in which the values of $S+$ and $S-$ are reversed when a conditional cue is presented. The conditional discrimination is equivalent to the P/not-P type of negative contrast in a logical formula. Since we tend to think that formal, logical languages are more precise and powerful than ordinary languages, it is tempting to use the success of a nonhuman species in solving a conditional discrimination as evidence for the capacity of that species to deal with linguistic negatives.

But it is ordinary language that human beings actually use in their normal two-way communication. In ordinary languages the negative terms have many effects and it is seldom that a negative expression can be created that is precisely or even nearly the symmetrical opposite of a positive expression (cf. *He is a student* versus *He is not a student*). Similarly, even in laboratory tasks negatively defined concepts are not symmetrically equal in difficulty to positively defined concepts either for adult human beings (Hovland & Weiss, 1953) or for children (Bourne et al., 1971); this is true even when the experimenter has used concepts which are symmetrically opposite in their logical definition. Thus it is easy for Brown and others to argue that the performance of animals on conditional discriminations may be analogous to

18

the use of negative terms in formal logic but that it is not "nearly so abstract as is linguistic negation" (Brown, 1958, p. 185).

In teaching Ameslan to Washoe, we soon became sensitive to the asymmetry between the referents of positive and negative expressions. The problem arises because a free-living subject can seldom be forced into a situation with only two alternatives. Most of the time there are several alternatives, A, B, C, . . . N, so that the disjunction A versus not-A is necessarily asymmetrical.

The earliest negative term that we were able to teach Washoe was *enough*, which could be used as a way of terminating an activity. Thus at the end of a meal Washoe could be asked, *You finished?* or *You want more?* and an appropriate reply on her part would be either *enough* or *more*. The negative *enough* transferred from this end-of-meal situation to a variety of situations in which either the formula *more X* or the formula *enough X* was appropriate, as in *enough toothbrush(ing)* or *enough bath*. The sign also appeared quite spontaneously as a way of asking to be excused from lessons.

The Ameslan sign *can't* proved to be a highly useful negative term so that the history of its spontaneous transfer to new referents is of considerable interest. The sign *can't* was first taught to Washoe as a way to be allowed to leave the toilet. Washoe was toilet trained by the 22nd month of the project (Gardner & Gardner, 1968) and would regularly and voluntarily use her nursery chairs. As a precaution, we would make her sit on a nursery chair at bedtime, before taking her for a ride in the car, and before some other activities. Washoe could get excused from the nursery chair without defecating or voiding by signing *can't* or *I can't*. This training transferred spontaneously to testing and lesson situations in which she would sign *can't* when asked for a difficult sign and to situations in which we would ask her to do something beyond her ability, such as breaking a metal rod or a thick branch (Gardner & Gardner, 1973).

There is a special sign in Ameslan for *no*, although headshaking is also acceptable. The special sign for *no* requires more digital dexterity than we were ready to insist on with Washoe, so we permitted headshaking. By the rules that we followed in establishing the reliability of signs, each sign that was counted as part of Washoe's vocabulary had to be used by her spontaneously and appropriately at least once daily on each of 15 consecutive days (Gardner & Gardner, 1971a, p. 141). After that, there were systematic probes for signs that were not being used frequently and daily.

The sign *no* proved to be very difficult to elicit for test purposes, though the

19

successful techniques demonstrate once again the importance of integrating linguistic training into our subject's daily life. It would have been confusing to ask for the strictly informative use of the sign *no* very often as in *Is this black?* (for a red object) or *Is this a dog?* (for a tree). Similarly, although *no* could have been used as a way of refusing the many demands we made of Washoe in the course of a day, we certainly did not want to teach her to be obstinate. We tried clearly unreasonable demands, such as ordering her to bed in the middle of afternoon play or offering her a bowl of rocks at mealtime. But this strategy suffered from the combination of Washoe's good nature (she sometimes allowed herself to be marched off to bed or tried to lick the rocks) and her ability to evade us without verbalizing (she sometimes climbed a tree or spilled the rocks on the floor). Fortunately, there was a stratagem that worked very well without interfering with any aspect of our routine procedures. We capitalized on Washoe's good faith by telling her a variety of tales, of which the following is a typical example: It is late in the day, and getting dark outside. Washoe and a companion are inside her house trailer, and he peers out the window and comes back to initiate the following interchange:

Person: "Washoe, there is a big black dog outside—with big teeth. It is a dog that eats little chimps. You want to go out, now?"

Washoe: (prolonged and emphatic) "Nooooooooo."

Signing to Herself. Washoe often signed to herself in play, particularly in places that afforded her privacy, i.e., when she was high in the tree or alone in her bedroom before going to sleep. While we sat quietly in the next room waiting for Washoe to fall asleep, we frequently saw her practicing signs, just as Ruth Weir (1966) has reported for young children. Washoe would stop if she noticed that we were watching.

Washoe also signed to herself when leafing through magazines and picture books, and she resented our attempts to join in this activity. If we did try to join her or if we watched her too closely, she often abandoned the magazine, or picked it up and moved away. Our records show that Washoe not only named pictures to herself in this situation, but that she also corrected herself. On one occasion, she indicated a certain advertisement, signed *That food*, then looked at her hand closely and changed the phrase to *That drink*, which was correct.

Washoe also signed to herself about her own ongoing or impending actions. We have often seen Washoe moving stealthily to a forbidden part of the yard,

20

signing *quiet* to herself, or running pell-mell for the potty chair while signing *hurry*. On one occasion, Washoe was near a ladder, scribbling on a piece of paper, while her companion was otherwise occupied. Suddenly she signed *Up hurry* to herself and rushed up the ladder. When she climbed down, she resumed her play with the pencil and paper, then once again signed to herself *More up* and did what she had told herself to do.

Project Washoe was the first attempt to teach sign language to a chimpanzee. We were able to integrate Ameslan into Washoe's behavioral repertoire so that spontaneous communication by means of sign language became a common feature of her interactions with human companions. Throughout the project we kept records on Washoe's use of sign language that were as comprehensive as possible, with systematic samples of spontaneous output and with rigorous double-blind vocabulary tests. Our procedures for recording the use of sign language by Washoe were fashioned on those developed for recording the use of vocal language by children, for, as we have argued throughout this paper, the linguistic achievements of a young chimpanzee must be evaluated by comparisons with linguistic performance and linguistic development of children.

The objective of Project Washoe was to demonstrate that Ameslan is a suitable medium of communication for a chimpanzee and that, given a suitable medium, a significant level of two-way communication could be achieved. We hoped to demonstrate the feasibility and promise of our method for studies on the relation between animal and human intelligence, the process of language acquisition, and the basic nature of language.

References

Bellugi, U., & Klima, E. S. The roots of language in the sign talk of the deaf. *Psychology Today*, 1972, (June), 61–76.

Benson. E. Manual signs. *American Annals of the Deaf*, 1962, 107, 501–502.

Bloom, L. *Language development.* Cambridge, Mass.: M.I.T. Press, 1970.

Bourne, L. E., Ekstrand, B. R., & Dominowski, R. L. *The psychology of thinking.* Englewood Cliffs, N.J.: Prentice-Hall, 1971.

Brown, R. *Words and things.* New York: Free Press, 1958.

————. The development of wh questions in child speech. *Journal of Verbal Learning and Verbal Behavior*, 1968, 7, 277–290.

————. The first sentences of child and chimpanzee. In Roger Brown, *Psycholinguistics: Selected papers by Roger Brown.* New York: Free Press, 1970, Ch. 8.

————. *A first language.* Cambridge, Mass.: Harvard University Press, 1973.

Carroll, J. B. Review of 'Sign language structure' by W. C. Stokoe, Jr. *Exceptional Children*, 1961, 28, 113–116.

Ervin-Tripp, S. Discourse agreement: how children answer questions. In J. R. Hayes (Ed.), *Cognition and the development of language.* New York: Wiley, 1970.

21

Fouts, R. S. The use of guidance in teaching sign language to a chimpanzee. *Journal of Comparative and Physiological Psychology*, 1972, 80, 515–522.

Fraser, C., Bellugi, U., & Brown, R. Control of grammar in imitation, comprehension and production. *Journal of Verbal Learning and Verbal Behavior*, 1963, 2, 121–135.

French, G. M. Associative problems. In A. Schrier, H. Harlow, and F. Stollnitz (Eds.), *Behavior of nonhuman primates*. New York: Academic Press, 1965.

Fusfeld, I. S. How the deaf communicate—manual language. *American Annals of the Deaf*, 1958, 103, 264–282.

Gardner, B. T., & Gardner, R. A. How a young chimpanzee was toilet trained. *Laboratory Primate Newsletter*, 1968, 7, 1–3.

Gardner, R. A., & Gardner, B. T. Teaching sign language to a chimpanzee. *Science*, 1969, 165, 664–672.

Gardner, B. T., & Gardner, R. A. Two-way communication with an infant chimpanzee. In A. Schrier & F. Stollnitz (Eds.), *Behavior of nonhuman primates*. New York: Academic Press, 1971. (a)

Gardner, R. A., & Gardner, B. T. Teaching sign language to a chimpanzee. V. A practical vocabulary test for young primates. *Psychonomic Science*, 1971, 25, 49. (b)

Gardner, B. T., & Gardner, R. A. Teaching sign language to a chimpanzee, VI. Replies to wh questions. *Psychonomic Science*, 1971, 25, 49. (c)

Gardner, R. A., & Gardner, B. T. Communication with a young chimpanzee: Washoe's vocabulary. In R. Chauvin (Ed.), *Modeles animaux du comportement humain*. Paris: C. N. R. S., 1972.

Gardner, R. A., & Gardner, B. T. Teaching sign language to the chimpanzee Washoe (16mm. sound film). State College, Pa.: Psychological Cinema Register, 1973.

Gardner, B. T., & Gardner, R. A. Behavioral development in the chimpanzee Washoe (16mm. sound film). State College, Pa.: Psychological Cinema Register, 1974. (a)

Gardner, R. A., & Gardner, B. T. Testing the vocabulary of the chimpanzee Washoe (16mm. sound film). State College, Pa.: Psychological Cinema Register, 1974. (b)

Hayes, K. J., & Hayes, C. The intellectual development of a home raised chimpanzee. *Proceedings of the American Philosophical Society*, 1951, 95, 105–109.

Hovland, C. I., & Weiss, W. Transmission of information concerning concepts through positive and negative instances. *Journal of Experimental Psychology*, 1953, 45, 175–182.

Klima, E., & Bellugi, U. Teaching apes to communicate. *Forum series on psychology and communication, Voice of America*, 1970.

Leopold, W. F. Patterning in children's language learning. *Language Learning*, 1953–54, 5, 1–14.

Miles, R. C. Discrimination learning sets. In A. Schrier, H. Harlow, and F. Stollnitz (Eds.), *Behavior of nonhuman primates*. New York: Academic Press, 1965.

Ploog, D., & Melnuchek, T. Are apes capable of language? *Neurosciences Research Program Bulletin*, 1971, 9, 600–700.

Premack, D. Language in chimpanzees? *Science*, 1971, 172, 808–822.

Riopelle, A. J. (Ed.) *Animal problem solving*. Harmondsworth, Middlesex, England: Penguin Books, 1967.

Schlesinger, H. S., & Meadow, K. P. *Sound and sign*. Berkeley: University of California Press, 1972.

Schlesinger, I. M., Presser, B., Cohen, E., & Peled, T. Transfer of meaning in sign language. Working Paper 12. The potentialities of visual communication systems for the rehabilitation of the deaf. Hebrew University of Jerusalem, 1970.

Stokoe, W. C. Sign language structure: An outline of the visual communication systems of the American deaf. *Studies in Linguistics*, Occasional Papers 8, University of Buffalo, 1960.

———. The study of sign language. *Educational Resources Information Center*. Washington: CAL, 1970.

Stokoe, W. C., Casterline, D., & Croneberg, C. G. *A dictionary of American sign language*. Washington, D.C.: Gallaudet College Press, 1965.

BEATRICE T. GARDNER

Swain, R. L., Jr. Why the language of signs is being taught to a chimpanzee at the University of Nevada. *Deaf American*, 1968, 21, 5–7.

———. Washoe's advanced training in the language of signs at the University of Nevada. *Deaf American*, 1970, 22, 9–12.

Weir, R. Some questions on the child's learning of phonology. In F. Smith and G. A. Miller (Eds.), *The genesis of language*. Cambridge, Mass.: M.I.T. Press, 1966.

✛ ELEANOR J. GIBSON ✛

Trends in Perceptual Development: Implications for the Reading Process

JUST about 13 years ago I was spending a year at the Institute for Advanced Study in Princeton, New Jersey, working with great determination, but not as great confidence, on a book on perceptual learning and development. I had planned this book, struggled with problems of theory construction and pursued relevant research (not only my own but other people's) ever since my arrival at Cornell in 1949. I had thought of it much earlier when I was a graduate student. Still, it wasn't going as smoothly as I had hoped. One day two of my Cornell colleagues telephoned and said they wanted to come to Princeton and talk about a new joint research proposal to study basic psychological processes involved in reading. I said no, this was the year of the book. But they came anyhow and argued that perceptual development was undoubtedly a major factor in the acquisition of reading skill and that reading was an appropriate as well as a useful area in which to apply the theory I had been developing.

A few weeks of thought convinced me that they were right, and I began planning experiments that were under way less than a year later. For the most part the book lay fallow as far as writing went until 1964, when I started it all over again at the Center for Advanced Study in the Behavioral Sciences. This time I knew where I was going and it pretty much wrote itself. Since 1960 I

NOTE: The writer wishes to acknowledge support from the National Institute of Mental Health and from the United States Office of Education during the period of work covered in this paper. Acknowledgement and deepest appreciation are due to the many (onetime) students who contributed so heavily to the research described. Some of the research was done in collaboration with the author but much of it was done independently as theses and research reports.

24

have had twin projects that seem to dovetail very neatly—seeking to understand the principles of perceptual learning and development and trying to apply them to the reading process.

The purpose of this paper is to explain how the theory and the experiments are related. Since I cannot describe the theory in detail in a brief paper, I have decided to try to show how the experiments are related to the three trends in perceptual development that I discussed in the last chapter of my book. They were generated by a long foregrounding in theoretical concepts and factual descriptions of the development of perception of objects, the spatial layout, events, pictures, and symbols, and so these trends serve as a summary that I find exceedingly useful. The three trends were identified as: (1) increasing specificity of correspondence between information in stimulation and the differentiation of perception; (2) increasing optimization of attention; (3) increasing economy in the perceptual process of information pickup.

Other trends in cognitive development, in a wider sense, could be pointed out, and they might be equally or nearly as relevant for understanding the process of learning to read. One that seems to me especially important is the increasing ability to be *aware* of one's own cognitive processes, from the segmentation of the phonetic stream all the way up to the understanding of strategies of learning and problem solving. There seems to be a kind of consciousness-raising that goes along with many aspects of cognitive development, and it turns out, I think, to be associated with attaining mature reading skills. But I shall confine myself to the three trends I mentioned and to some of the research associated with them.

Increasing Specificity

Perceptual learning, as I see it, is characterized by an increased specificity of correspondence between stimulation and the precision of the responding organism's discrimination. My husband and I argued many years ago that the essence of perceptual learning was differentiation rather than enrichment and that this kind of learning was not adding something like a response or an image to sensations but rather was a change in *what* was responded *to* uniquely and specifically (Gibson & Gibson, 1955). Early experiments with Dr. Anne Pick and Dr. Harry Osser (Gibson, Gibson, Pick, & Osser, 1962) pursued this trend and demonstrated the progress of the discrimination of letter-like forms and the way in which confusions decreased and unique identifications increased with age. In later research (Gibson, Osser, Schiff, & Smith, 1963; Gibson, Schapiro, & Yonas, 1968) I sought to specify the distinctive features that are used in letter discrimination and to compare them for several age groups. All of this work was at the perceptual level, and I would of course acknowledge that reading, although based on perception, is a very complex cognitive process.

For this reason I have been speculating further, perhaps overboldly, about the role of differentiation in reading. I am inclined to think that the problem of perceptual differentiation is accompanied by the growth of meaning, first at a perceptual level and later at a more abstract semantic level. The process of differentiating things and events in the world requires the abstraction of contrastive distinctive features and invariants. Objects, events, and their functional relations in the world are differentiated so that perceptions of them come to correspond with information in stimulation at a pretty early age. But the symbolic notations for these objects, events, and relations (*words* both spoken and written) come into more specific correspondence with their referents only later and more gradually. I propose the hypothesis that the meanings of words, like the meanings of things and events, are gradually differentiated and *converge*, eventually, with the meanings of things (and pictures of things, which are also differentiated very early [Hochberg & Brooks, 1962; Ryle, 1966]).

The meaning itself, I think, is *abstract*—neither imagistic nor linguistic. Semantic meaning may in its origins be an abstraction from the distinctive features (themselves abstracted) that permit perceptual differentiation (cf. Clark, 1973). Lexical features of words must in some sense correspond with distinctive features of things and of the events in which they are constituents, but the lexical features presumably are arrived at later. I believe that only much later are they *accessed* as immediately as are distinctive features of perceived objects, especially when the word is written. These arguments are consistent with and may help to explain the observation that immediacy of access to meaning from written verbal input is a characteristic of developmental progress in reading.

An experiment was designed on the basis of the argument just presented (Gibson, Barron, & Garber, 1972). The method was to compare over a wide range of ages the judgments of sameness or difference of a pair of pictures, a pair of words, and a pair consisting of a word and a picture. We predicted that the reaction time of the younger subjects especially would be faster when the items they were judging were presented in the same mode than when the modes were mixed (picture with word). We further predicted a developmental decline in the difference between single mode and mixed mode latencies, with

26

the mixed mode latency converging toward the single mode conditions. The reasoning was that if matching can only be done on the basis of meaning and if the meanings of the word and the thing gradually come to have the same abstract representation with the same access time, then the difference between single mode and dual mode comparisons should progressively decline with age.

Since we wished our subjects to make a comparison on the level of meaning rather than on physical match, sets of words were prepared in two kinds of type (upper and lower case), a condition that has been found to discourage the processing of only graphic features (Posner & Mitchell, 1967), although processing could still stop at a naming stage. Two versions of each picture were also prepared representing similar, but not physically identical, objects—for instance two fish pictured from different angles or differing in a few noncritical details. Simple outline drawings of 12 objects (fish, bird, dog, cup, sock, boat, frog, lamb, cat, key, iron, plane), each in two versions, were prepared on slides, and the names of the objects were set in two kinds of type. The slides were combined appropriately in three conditions: PP, in which pairs of pictures of the same object or two different objects were to be compared; WW, in which pairs of words, either the same word or two different words, were to be compared; and WP, in which a picture and a word indicating the same object or two different ones were to be compared.

The experiment thus had three display conditions, with types of display presented in random order. Half of the displays required a same judgment and half required a different judgment. Each S saw all three types of display, prepared on slides and projected simultaneously with position (right or left) counterbalanced. Subjects were drawn from the second, fourth, and sixth grades and from a college group of summer school students.

Median latencies for each display condition and for each type of response (same or different) were computed for each subject. Means of these medians for the different age groups are presented in Table 1. An analysis of variance showed that the main effects of age and display conditions were significant, but there was not a significant difference overall between same and different responses. It should be noted, however, that *same* responses are shorter in seven out of eight cases for the *unimodal* displays. This trend is in accord with the typical finding in many previous experiments (cf. for example, Gibson, Schapiro, & Yonas, 1968).

The interaction between grade and display, the result of particular interest to us, was significant ($p < .025$). There was a relative decline with age in the

Table 1. Mean Latencies for Each Grade as a Function of Display
Condition and Type of Response (in msec)

Grade	Picture-Picture Display		Word-Word Display		Word-Picture Display	
	Same	Different	Same	Different	Same	Different
Two	1,957	1,987	2,044	2,133	2,141	2,281
Four	1,364	1,343	1,318	1,330	1,479	1,418
Six	1,114	1,194	1,132	1,162	1,224	1,221
College	821	856	783	842	939	893

difference between the dual mode (WP) condition and the other two. A difference score was calculated by the formula $WP - \frac{WW + PP}{2}$ and is plotted for the three age groups in Figure 1. The rationale of this formula was that bimodal comparison would take longer than unimodal in either mode but that as meaning of a word and its pictured counterpart converged toward the same abstract semantic features the difference would decrease. From the second to the sixth grade the predicted downward trend is evident in the responses of different. The trend is absent, however, for the responses of same.

A second interaction, a triple interaction of grade, display, and type of response (same or different), was also significant ($p < .001$). An interpretation of this interaction was suggested in a comparison of some first-order effects at different grade levels. For the second-grade subjects the PP condition had a shorter latency than the WW condition. Fourth and sixth graders did not differ in latency for the PP and WW conditions; but the adults had a longer latency

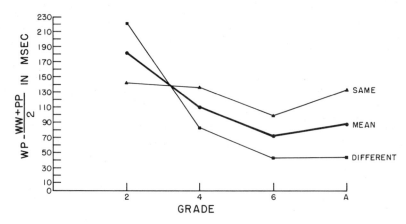

Figure 1. Difference in latency between the WP condition and the mean of the PP and WW conditions across grades.

28

on the PP comparison than on the WW comparison. When same responses and different responses were compared for the WP condition, an age difference again appeared. The responses of same were shorter for second graders but the responses of different were shorter for college students. (The apparent difference for fourth graders was not significant.) There appears to be a radical difference in the processing of WP displays by second graders, and by adults.

What can we say about these differences that might throw light on the development of processing the meaning of written words? The speculation is as follows. Perhaps for the second grader the WW condition elicits the naming of words. When the second grader is faced with a WP display, he looks at the picture first, since pictures are salient and highly meaningful for him but written words are less so. He names the picture to himself in order to compare the name with the word. If the word coincides with the name, his reading will be facilitated and thus the same judgments will be faster (as they were, by 140 msec.).* But for adults words have become highly salient; they arouse a meaning before the word is spoken. The abstract meaning of the word can be compared directly with the abstract meaning of the picture. If they are different, no further processing is necessary. The picture need not be named because the meaning was accessed before the name (Moore, 1919).

What sort of process might the hypothesized comparison entail for the adult? The meaning of a word, I assume, is a set of abstract lexical features, such as animate, nonhuman, house pet, furry, etc., derived from earlier comparisons of real things. These features for the word could be compared with semantic features for the picture. In the WP condition of the present experiment, this comparison might take place serially. Template or "wholistic" processing seems implausible, if not impossible, with two modes of presentation. Thus a mismatch would be identified earlier than a match, and the judgments of different would be faster than the judgments of same. The other features need not be checked out, nor need the *name* of the picture even be processed for a judgment of different. Why should same judgments, on the other hand, be faster in the unimodal comparisons? We can only speculate that unimodal same comparisons can be made on a more wholistic or superficial basis, especially when the set of items has become known, because some physical features, like the tails of the fish or the similarity of two letters (e.g., C and c, S and S) might suffice for the making of a match.

*A recent experiment by Garber (personal communication) confirms the fact that reading a word at this age is facilitated if it is preceded by a picture identifiable by the same word.

29

This view of the picture-word comparison of the adult predicts that a different pair would require a greater amount of time for a decision, the more features the members of the pair share (e.g., deciding that *cat* and *dog* are different should take longer than *cat* and *iron*). Insofar as our data afford a comparison, the results are in accord with the prediction, but the data are too few to provide a convincing test. Dr. R. W. Barron is at present replicating the experiment with a proper test of the hypothesis. We should not expect to find this result for children at the second-grade level, for we suspect that they would do an entirely different kind of processing (naming the picture and comparing it with the word) before they have attained a well-developed set of abstract lexical features that is easily accessed by the printed word.

Some of the assumptions we are making are shared by other psychologists. That meaning is abstract, neither imagistic nor linguistic, has been defended not only by the Wurzburg school (cf. Moore, 1919) but more recently as well. Chase and Clark (1972) say for instance: "Our results suggest that the comprehension of both pictures and sentences must ultimately be represented in the same mental symbolic system. We do not mean by this that the ultimate representation of pictures and sentences is identical to linguistic descriptions of deep structure, but rather that there is a deep or conceptual structure that is common to both sentences and pictures. . . . Our conception is that meaning is to be found in a modality-free symbolic memory, but can be converted into modality-specific images when this is wanted" [p. 225].

The assumption that denotative meaning can be analyzed as a set of lexical features or abstract "semantic markers" was proposed by Katz and Fodor (1963). The notion of abstract semantic features is thus not new, nor is the notion that there is a correspondence between distinctive features of objects and the set of semantic features that comprise lexical meanings. That idea was suggested by Rubenstein (1971) as follows: "If they are the same, we would have a single set of features which would serve as locators for lexical entries both when the input is conceptual as well as when it is perceptual. To play both these roles these features would have to be abstract, that is, not lexical entries themselves . . ." [p. 50]. A similar view has been proposed by Clark (1973), who was particularly interested in the development in children of the semantic features of words.

Now we have come full circle to the hypothesis with which I started: that meanings of words converge developmentally toward a more specific correspondence with the meanings of things and events. I conceive of the meanings of both as sets of abstract features, but they are abstracted for objects early in life, while the development of abstract meanings for words progresses later as language and then reading skills are acquired. The immature reader does not access the abstract meanings directly from the word as he reads it. He probably decodes it to a phonetic representation and matches words (the name of this object and the word he has decoded), in contrast to the adult who has become capable of matching word and picture meanings directly via comparison of amodal, abstract features that have progressed to a high degree of correspondence. These ideas as presently formulated are doubtless more provocative than convincing, but I think the time has come to grope with the problem of how the printed word elicits meaning.

Optimization of Attention

One of the most striking aspects of perceptual development is the improvement of strategies for extracting the relevant and wanted information. Selection of critical features improves progressively, as does the apparent ability to ignore noisy, irrelevant information. The descriptive applicability of this trend to the acquisition of reading skill is so obvious that I hardly need argue it. But I would like to be more explicit. To do so it is necessary to talk a little first about what's in a word—what kinds of information it provides. That a written word has *graphic* information is an essential characteristic of a writing system. A written word has potential *acoustic* information too. We can read it aloud or *sotto voce* to ourselves or we can imagine how it sounds. It can carry *syntactic* and *morphological* information: it is a part of speech like a noun or a verb and it may be inflected to indicate that it is a modifier or a particular tense or plural rather than singular. Most important, a word carries *semantic* information. Our interest in communication is to get across our meaning to someone else or to discover the meaning of what the other one is saying or writing.

Optimization of attention in reading is uniquely characterized, I think, by the reader's ability to extract that aspect of the information that is most useful to him and to ignore or give secondary priority to the rest. I do not think the other information is often completely ignored; an example in point would be Rothkopf's (1971) finding that subjects who were instructed to read to learn facts from a text and who knew they were to be tested on their reading, retained some information about where a reference to a given fact had appeared in the text. Nevertheless, an optimal reading strategy usually assigns some priorities to certain aspects of the information which results in selective reading.*

The aspect of the information that should be selectively attended to depends on the reader's task—the purpose he has assigned himself or the instructions given him by his teacher or perhaps his boss. He may want to get the closing prices at the end of the day for 10 Wall Street stocks, which will result in a scan-and-pause strategy; he may be reading to learn his lines for a play, which will result in alternation of reading and rehearsal, with rather strong attention to phonetic aspects of the material so that he can try out intonations.

One can think of reading tasks which give priority to every one of the aspects of written text that I have mentioned. I have done experiments on only a few of them, but one task I have investigated in detail with the help of my colleagues and students is the task of scanning down a list to find a target such as a letter or a word. The experiments considered as a whole illustrate quite well the highly selective attention of the scanner to one kind of information so as to optimize the efficiency of the scan.

The first of these experiments was carried out in collaboration with Dr. A. Yonas (Gibson & Yonas, 1966a). We used a scan-and-search task modeled on that of Neisser (1963), with a few alterations to make it more feasible for children. Second-grade children and college students scanned down a list for a single letter target randomly inserted in different list positions to cover all positions equally over a series of trials. Although the children had much slower scan rates than the college students, the children did scan quite systematically, as is shown by the correlation between list position and time for scan. The correlation increases for college students, however, so attention in the scanning does become more systematic with age. Scanning rate, as well, becomes enormously faster with development.

There is strong evidence that in this task the subjects attend with high priority to graphic information. Gibson and Yonas (1966a) compared the effect of high and low graphic similarity of context letters to a target letter. Embedding a target letter in a context of letters containing many of the same distinctive features slows the scanning rate greatly, compared to the rate for finding the same letter embedded in a set with different features. This effect

*Compare this idea with a statement by Luria: "The characteristic feature of the adult's verbal meanings is that *the word preserves in itself all systems of connections inherent in it*, beginning with the very elementary and visual and ending with the very complex and abstract. Depending on the task, any one of the systems of connections can become dominant. Without this ability, flexible thinking is impossible" (Luria, 1969, p. 137).

holds for both seven-year-old children and adults, but the interference in one experiment was relatively greater for the children, suggesting that adults may have developed greater efficiency in attending to minimal, optimal distinctive features in this task. Given an opportunity for practice, subjects learn to scan for a single very economical graphic feature as Yonas (1969) and Schapiro (1970) showed in appropriate transfer experiments.

Gibson and Yonas (1966b) also investigated the effect of extra-modal auditory interference on the scanning task. While scanning the list visually, the subject heard over earphones a voice pronouncing letters with names similar in sound to the target letter. Somewhat to our surprise there was no effect at all on the scanning rate of adults or even of seven-year-old children. Acoustic features of letters, or the sound of their names at least, appeared to be virtually ignored in this task. Obviously pronouncing all the letters subvocally while scanning for the target would slow the scanning rate, so this attentive strategy is highly economical. Kaplan, Yonas, and Shurcliff (1966) provided confirmation for this conclusion in a different experiment in which they compared the effect of high and low acoustic similarity of context letter names to the name of the target letter. The target was embedded in a context of letters that rhymed with it (e.g., B, V, D, T) or in a context of nonrhyming letters. Unlike graphic similarity of context, there was no effect on rate of scan of rhyming similarity. Acoustic similarity can, however, produce confusion and interference in another task, notably short-term memory, in which the subject attends particularly to the acoustic information, presumably as an aid to rehearsal.

The lack of interference from competing auditory stimulation in the second-grade children might seem to argue against developing optimization of attentional strategies. But in another thesis experiment, performed by Shepela (1971), improvement of attentional strategies with bimodal input was found when somewhat younger age groups were compared. She performed a detection experiment, a developmental study of "bimodal vigilance," with kindergarten and second-grade children. They detected a given target presented at intervals within a rapid succession of other items under both unimodal and bimodal conditions. The unimodal condition consisted of either a succession of pictures accompanied by the instruction to press a key whenever a picture of a bird appeared or a succession of spoken words presented over earphones with the instruction to press the key whenever the word "bird" was heard. The bimodal condition combined the two types of presentation but target occurrence for the two modes was not redundant. For the kindergarten children, target detection was significantly impaired under the bimodal condition, but for the second-grade children there was no impairment at all compared to unimodal presentation at the same rates. These children were able to attend successfully to both modes of input when the task required it.

It is interesting to ask whether semantic information is picked up in a scanning task. That it *can* be is suggested by findings from experiments in which the subject is required to search for a target *word* which is embedded in a list of other words. Neisser and Beller (1965) asked *S*s to search for a word naming a member of a category, such as an animal (e.g., cat, dog, tiger). They were not given a specific target and the target item shifted from trial to trial. The scanning rate was fast, even though the *S* presumably had to examine each word individually for meaning. The rate, about 300 words per minute, is almost identical to the speed of scan found in a comparable experiment by Gibson, Tenney, and Zaslow (1971) and compares very favorably with the rate of scanning for a single letter. The rate of scan for a single letter tends, in fact, to be considerably slower, depending of course on the type of context, whether the target is repeated or changed, and on practice. Does this comparison imply that in scanning meaning is picked up faster than graphic information? Probably not. A word can be picked up as a whole, but random strings of letters must be scanned letter by letter. In a thesis by Clare (1969) it was shown that pronounceability (orthographic acceptability) of a target item significantly facilitated the search for the item as compared to a random string of letters; so the strategy of searching for a "whole" item, a string of letters that can be picked up as a unit, appears to be the important factor. The fact that context words were poorly remembered perhaps bears this out, but context letters in letter search are poorly remembered too. Unfortunately we have no data at present on children's rate of scan for words as compared with letters, so we do not know how early this attentive strategy develops.

Gibson, Tenney, and Zaslow (1971) investigated the effect on search rate of common categorical meaning in context items (e.g., all items are names of fruit) as opposed to a different category of meaning for target items (e.g., all targets are names of animals). The question was whether semantic structure would facilitate the rate of search for a target word. The target word was embedded in a set of categorically related words. In a preliminary experiment, the *S* was presented with the specific target word before each scan began, but this procedure resulted in *S*'s resorting to graphic information (scanning for the first two letters of the target, for instance), which was (or was considered to be by the Ss) more economical than processing meaning. The procedure was changed to Neisser and Beller's, and the subject was instructed to look for a target belonging to a category, either a name of an animal or a part of the body. (Only one category was used for a subject.) We hoped that this procedure would force S to process for meaning and would allow the categorical structure of the context, when present, to influence the search rate. It did not, however. Categorical structure among context words afforded no faster rate of scan than did randomly selected words carefully matched for word length, initial letters, word frequency, and so on. We were forced to conclude that meaning plays a minor role in a scanning task. "Wholeness" of the items results in fewer units for S to process, but apparently the presence of meaning is not the source of facilitation.

Other tasks, in contrast to search and scanning, are characterized by high utility for meaning, especially categorical meaning. A well-known example of such a task is relatively long-term, as opposed to short-term, memory. Findings from numerous experiments attest to the utility of a common category or categories in a list of words to be remembered. Subjects remember more and tend to cluster by category. In a number of experiments the development with age of attention to common categories and the utilization of them for improved recall has been investigated. Children are not as adept at using categories for this purpose as are adults, but findings about age and categorizing vary with a number of parameters in the experiments.

I would like to summarize one study concerning the development of the use of categories, a very recent Ph.D. thesis by Tenney (1973). Tenney's problem, specifically, was to study the development of strategies of cognitive organization. She wanted to relate the development of the awareness of categories to the spontaneous adaptive use of them. She employed a task designed for this purpose, asking her subjects to tell her words that would be easy to remember along with one (a "key word") that she would give them. She told them that she would write down the words and that she would ask them to remember the words later. Therefore the child could choose what material he would recall, even making use of idiosyncratic strategies if he appreciated the importance of organizational principles and could select and attend to them.

There were three experimental conditions but the subjects took part in only one. One was the *category* condition in which subjects were given a key word such as "blue" by the E and were told to give three words belonging to the same category, which was defined for them. There were 12 categories (such as colors, days of the week, names), all of which had previously been shown to be known by young children. The second condition was the self-directed condition in which the Ss freely generated lists specifically for the purpose of easy recall, again having been given the same 12 key words by E but without any suggestion of a category or strategy. In the third condition, the *incidental* condition, the Ss were never informed of the purpose of the task; instead they generated the lists by free-associating to the 12 key words. The subjects were drawn from kindergarten and from the third and sixth grades. They participated in two sessions scheduled a week apart. During the first session they generated their lists of words (36 words in all for each S, including the key words). In the second session they were tested for recall. The S was read a list of 12 words drawn from the lists he had generated before being asked to recall this selected list. Half of the Ss were asked to recall a clusterable list and the other half a nonclusterable list.

Tenney's experiment was so rich in results that I can only present the gist of them. When the *self-directed* condition was compared with the *incidental* condition, there was a significant age interaction. The older children used deliberate strategies for selecting words for recall, but the younger children settled for the first three words that occurred to them. Sound relationships were very apparent in the lists they generated in both conditions. The use of sound relationships declined significantly with age. The older children made greater use of categories than did the younger children no matter what the condition, although there was category structure in the younger children's lists in the *category* condition.

As for recall, the effect of age on clustering was especially interesting in light of its interaction with condition. There was no significant difference with age in clustering in the category condition. The kindergarten children were helped by the instruction to categorize and were able to make use of it. Nor was there a significant difference among children of different ages in the incidental condition. Clustering by incidental free associations was insignificant at all ages. But in the *self-directed* condition, organization by structural principle—some kind of spontaneous categorizing—increased steadily with age. The kindergarteners showed no more clustering in this condition than in the *incidental* condition, but the older children clustered well above chance. The sixth graders clustered significantly more in this condition than when they were instructed to categorize. There was a strong developmental trend from ease of organization by category structure in response to *E*'s suggestion to ease of organization by a self-directed structure. This seems to me to be a prime example of optimization of attentional strategies with increasing age. The younger children had little insight into how things could be remembered easily, although they could use categorical structure when it was presented to them. But the older subjects deliberately selected words according to a plan of their own, in this case one based on meaningful categorical relationships.

Tenney's results not only illustrate the optimization of attentional strategies with development, they also illustrate the third developmental trend, the trend in perceptual development that I called the increasing economy of information pickup. In the present case, the wording might be broadened to read the increasing economy of cognitive processing. The experiments to be discussed in the following section range, again, from what would ordinarily be termed perceptual tasks to cognitive tasks of presumably greater complexity such as problem solving.

Increasing Economy of Information Pickup and Cognitive Processing

There are two important and contrasting ways of increasing the economy of extracting information. The way that has the greatest utility depends on the task. One is the detection and use of the *smallest possible distinctive feature* that will permit a decision. This strategy is particularly efficient in a scanning task or in a task requiring perceptual categorizing of the Sternberg type. For instance, if there is a positive and a negative set to be distinguished in a reaction time experiment, an *S* will learn with practice to make his decision on the basis of the *minimal* feature difference that separates the two sets into unique categories. This type of learning has been documented in Ph.D. theses by Yonas (1969) and by Barron (1971). Evidence that the tendency to find the minimal most economical feature for perceptual categorizing increases with development is nonexistent, so far as I know. One reason for this lack may be that the tendency to make decisions on the basis of minimal useful information is present as early as we can make reliable observations of the behavior. Yonas (1969) observed children as well as adults in his experiment and found an enormous quantitative difference in reaction time for categorizing letters but found no interaction between age and the reduction of time with a minimal feature distinction. When the condition permitted greater economy of processing, the children exhibited the trend. One is tempted to

37

conclude that cognitive processing tends toward the "least cost" at any age. What develops, I think, is S's ability to select minimal distinctive features that are of increasing validity and subtlety; but the research remains to be done.

The second way of increasing economy is the use of superordinate structure and rule systems to create increasingly larger units. The detection of higher-order structure in the stimulus array is the essence of efficient cognitive processing, and a skilled reader makes use of the rule systems available in written language at many levels—the orthographic level, the syntactic and morphological levels, and the semantic level. Redundancy and constraints within words and between words provide the rules for unit formation, and a reader learns to process textual information in the *largest possible units that are appropriate for his task*. I am not the first to say this, although I believe I have worked longer than most trying to document the trend and find out how it works. Huey remarked on it in 1908 as follows: "We are brought back to the conclusion of Goldscheider and Müller that we read by phrases, words, or letters as may serve our purpose best. But we see, too, that the reader's acquirement of ease and power in reading comes through increasing ability to read in larger units" [p. 116].

Huey might have mentioned Cattell as well. Although Cattell did not note that the reader chooses the unit that serves his purpose best, he showed (Cattell, 1885) that it takes longer to read a letter than to read a word and that a word is recognized in at least as short an exposure interval as is a letter. Since then it has been demonstrated that a letter embedded in a word can be identified at shorter exposure durations than a letter exposed alone (Baron & Thurston, 1973; Reicher, 1969; Wheeler, 1970). Words can be recognized at a distance in type too small to permit the recognition of an individual letter (Erdmann & Dodge, 1898). And detection of a word target in a search-and-scanning task is faster than detection of a letter target (Gibson, Tenney, & Zaslow, 1971; Neisser & Beller, 1965).

It is the principle of extracting and processing higher-order structure that is particularly applicable to the reading process. I would like to show how work of mine and my students relates to this principle and how we have tried to locate the relevant structural variables. What are the structural principles for unit formation? Cattell thought that the "word-superiority effect," as it is often referred to, was the result of the word's familiarity and meaning. But there are other possibilities that, as it turns out, deserve even more serious consideration. There are rules or predictable relations within words and there are relations, syntactical rules, and meaningful relations between words in

38

phrases, sentences, and passages of discourse. It is these relations with which I am concerned in this section.

English has conditional rule systems for spelling that are morphophonemic in nature. Syllables may be morphemic units, but whether a syllable is a morpheme or not, it is a unit with some describable rules. It must have a vocalic center, which may or may not be preceded or followed by a consonant or a consonant cluster. The consonants, and especially the consonant clusters, are often constrained as to whether they can appear in initial or final position. English, compared to many other languages, makes wide use of consonant clusters, and these are nearly always constrained. According to Fries (1963) of the more than 150 consonant clusters in frequent use in English, all but three are constrained to initial or final position. Consider such examples as *script*, *strict*, *cling*, *twelfth*. Other vowels can be inserted in the center of the monosyllable and it retains legal English orthography as long as a vowel is present. But in no case can the final and initial consonant cluster be exchanged without violating English spelling patterns. This feature of English spelling provides enormous redundancy of a useful nature in the sense that there is more than one source of information (beyond the single letter) for what the word can be.

There is also redundancy of a different kind in sets of English spelling patterns that are easily classified and contrasted, thus yielding useful rule-like systems. Fries (1963) has categorized these and the following are examples:

bat → bate	bit → bite	cot → cote
cat → cate	fit → fite	dot → dote
fat → fate	kit → kite	got → gote
mat → mate	mit → mite	mot → mote

There are many such repetitive patterns in English and they provide for easy generalization in reading new English words, once the youthful reader has learned the principle. According to Garner (1962), there is more redundancy within words than between them, so it is not a waste of time to study the development of pickup of higher-order structure at the word level, even though we ordinarily read in larger units like phrases and clauses. I will describe research from our laboratory on intraword redundancy which is grouped by four experimental paradigms that supplement one another.

Tachistoscopic Word Recognition. The first of these experiments was performed by Gibson, Pick, Osser, and Hammond in 1962. Nonwords, termed pseudowords, were generated using constrained initial and terminal consonant clusters with a vowel between to provide two contrasting lists called (at that time) pronounceable and unpronounceable, respectively. The pronounceable items were monosyllabic (e.g., SLAND) and orthographically legal but they did not have referential meaning. The unpronounceable items were constructed by exchanging the initial and final consonant clusters (e.g., NDASL). The items, 25 of each, were presented to Ss tachistoscopically in a mixed order. Numerous replications of the experiment in which parameters such as exposure time, repetition, type of judgment (e.g., identification, recognition in a multiple choice set), and method of scoring were varied have yielded the same result as did the original experiment. The legal pseudowords are perceived better than the illegal ones.

The original experiment was performed on adults. We followed it up with an experiment on children who had just finished first or third grade (Gibson, Osser, & Pick, 1963). Sets of three-letter words and nonsense syllables were constructed to yield a real word in the first grader's reading vocabulary, a legal nonword made by permuting the letters of the word, and an illegal nonword (e.g., ran, nar, rna). The words and legal nonwords were all of the CVC pattern. Twenty four- and five-letter nonwords, ten of them legal ones and ten their illegal counterparts, were added. The items were presented tachistoscopically in a randomized sequence and the children spelled out what they saw (an undesirable way of getting the response, since it could encourage letter-by-letter looking, but seemingly unavoidable). For the three-letter items, words were read best overall, legal pseudowords next best, and illegal pseudowords least well. The two types of longer pseudowords were not differentiated from each other by first graders. All of them, whether legal or illegal, were read poorly. But the third graders read the legal combinations of longer pseudowords better than illegal ones. Accuracy did not approach that of adult Ss, but the difference between the two types was discriminated by some of the third graders.

We began by calling the legal pseudowords "pronounceable," implying thereby that ease of pronunciation had something to do with their superiority. Later when we recast our thinking in terms of an orthographic rule system, with all of its potential constraints and regularities, the pronounceability of the items became a less appealing choice and it certainly was not the only possible facilitator. An experiment was therefore run comparing deaf and hearing Ss of college age (Gibson, Shurcliff, & Yonas, 1970). The subjects were given instructions in sign language and wrote down what they saw. A new comparison group of hearing Ss of similar age was run. The deaf Ss, chosen for maximal and congenital or extremely early hearing loss, perceived fewer words correctly overall than did the hearing Ss, but the difference between the two sets of words was just as significant and just as striking for the deaf as for the hearing, suggesting that orthographic rules, rather than ease of pronouncing, accounted for the difference.

Each deaf S wrote a paragraph about how he had learned to read. We gained little from the factual content of these paragraphs, but the almost total absence of spelling errors was notable, although there were frequent grammatical and morphological errors. Evidently generalized spelling patterns and rules can be learned without the benefit of hearing accompanying sound mappings.

In an attempt to compare the roles of meaning and of pronounceability (as we were still calling it) on recognition and on recall, Gibson, Bishop, Schiff, and Smith (1964) prepared sets of nonword trigrams that varied in both meaningfulness and pronounceability. There were three types: one had referential meaning and formed a set of well-known initials (e.g., IBM); the second was a reordering of the initials in a CVC pronounceable arrangement (e.g., BIM); and the third was a reordering of the initials in a non-CVC unpronounceable arrangement (e.g., MBI). Recognition thresholds for the three types of items were obtained by increasing the brightness contrast of an item until it was read correctly. The lowest threshold was obtained for the pronounceable items. The difference was highly significant compared to both of the other types. The meaningful items did have an advantage, however, over the unpronounceable meaningless items; therefore meaningfulness of an item was apparently effective, even though its utility for this method of reading was not as great as was the unit structure of the spelling pattern. When the same items were tested for recall, the utility of the two features (meaningfulness and structure) was reversed; meaningfulness was more effective for enhancing recall.

Morphological features of a word such as classes of morpheme provide another system that might assist in forming structural units. I thought at first, naively it now seems, that adding a well-known inflectional ending to a base word would create a subordinate unit and thus make it easier to read and afford a longer letter span than a noninflected word of equal total length. Gibson and Guinet (1971) investigated the effect of adding a verb inflection (present tense s, past tense ed, or progressive ing) to monosyllabic base words of three kinds—real verbs such as rain, legal permutations such as nair, and illegal ones such as nrai. The bases varied in length from three to six letters.

41

The words were presented tachistoscopically to third- and fifth-grade children and to adults. The extension of word length by inflection did not increase the length of the word that could be read (e.g., when an inflected word like *trying* was compared with a noninflected word like *listen*, the inflected word had no advantage). The results for nonwords indicated that an inflected ending, per se, was perceived as an intact unit when compared with a segment of the word of equivalent length without morphological significance. Older children noticed and commented on inflections more often than did younger children.

A base morpheme would seem to have priority for the reader; but an inflection also has integrity. These two features of a word, we concluded, provide different kinds of information, and the information is probably extracted independently. That the meaning of the base morpheme is processed separately from that of the tense marker was suggested by the tendency for *S*s to confuse inflected endings and sometimes to substitute one for another. With a fast exposure the *S* in such a case perceived the base morpheme and noted that it was inflected but did not have time to process the inflection accurately. Thus there may be two kinds of meaning within the word, each with its own rules.

Scanning Experiments. Scanning experiments—searching for a word or letter target—have provided a small amount of evidence for the use of intraword structural constraints. As we remarked earlier, word-search is faster than letter-search and a pronounceable legal nonword is a better target than an illegal one (Clare, 1969). Gibson, Tenney, Barron, and Zaslow (1972) sought to determine whether or not context letter strings that were well structured orthographically would permit a faster search rate than poorly structured strings of context letters. The *S*s scanned for a single-letter target embedded in lists with or without good orthographic structure in the context items (e.g., *sland* versus *ndasl; clept* versus *ptecl*). The identical target letter was assigned to all lists. Subjects were fifth-grade children and adults. In neither age group did orthographically well-structured context facilitate the discovery of the target letter. Apparently any advantage of a structured background that could be processed in units larger than a letter was cancelled by the necessity of further processing for a specific target letter. The pickup of orthographic structure was apparently not the most economical strategy in this high-speed scanning task and was not used; the *S*s settled for graphic features.

If built-in structure were made economical for a search task, it should, according to our view, be used. Zaslow (1972), in a senior honors thesis, designed a search task in which a structural feature of orthography had potential utility. She selected consonant clusters constrained as to position within the word (e.g., *CL* would be a possible initial cluster only, whereas *PT* would be a possible final cluster only) and assigned such clusters (half initial and half final) as targets for search, using a different target for each list. In one condition the target was in its legal constrained position in a pronounceable five-letter string (e.g., *CLEPT*); the target assigned might be either CL or PT. The 29 context items were also five-letter pronounceable strings, all different but formed in the same way (e.g., *GLINK*, *FRAND*, etc.). In the other condition unpronounceable target and context items were constructed by reversing the consonant clusters (e.g., *PTECL*) and the same targets were assigned. Thus in one condition a given target item was located in a legal position in a string embedded in similarly formed strings. In the other condition the identical target was located in the reverse, illegal position in a string embedded in similar orthographically illegal strings. The subjects were unaware of the method of list construction.

The *S*s (college students) located the targets faster when they were in their properly constrained positions. They thus generalized this knowledge of consonant constraint to advantage, even though the letter strings were not words. The experiment bears out the previous findings that good orthographic structure is a critical factor in the word-superiority effect, and it also confirms the notion that consonant constraint is an important feature of orthographic structure.

Judging Word-Likeness. Word recognition under enforced, very brief exposure is not a usual condition of reading, so it is interesting to ask whether other types of judgment will reveal the generalizability of the word-superiority effect. A method employed by several of my students has proved successful in extending some of the conclusions stated above. The *S* is presented with a pair of nonwords, one orthographically regular and one not, and asked to judge "which is more like a real word." Rosinski and Wheeler (1972) presented pairs of nonwords taken from the lists of Gibson et al. (1962, 1963) to children from the first, third, and fifth grade. The words varied in length from three to six letters. The first graders performed at chance level, but the third and fifth graders ranged from 69 to 80 percent correct in their choices. Word length in this experiment did not have a significant effect. Nine of the 16 first graders were located the following year and retested. They still did not discriminate between the word types.

Golinkoff (1972) repeated this experiment with several changes. The pairs of nonwords used by Rosinski and Wheeler had not been matched in the sense of being counterparts of one another; for instance a pair might be CLATS versus SPIGR. We thought that contrasting arrangements of the same letters would provide better control and would also be more likely to elicit a discrimination. Pairs of nonsense words ranged from three to six letters each in length. The poorly structured item in the four- to six-letter pairs had a consonant cluster illegally placed in either initial or final position (e.g., TARB - RBAT; GRET - TEGR). There were three conditions of the experiment, two of them adding redundant auditory information to the visually presented items. In one of them, the S heard the word pronounced over a tape recorder as he looked at the printed item. In the other he was asked to read the words aloud as he looked at them. All the S s were drawn from second grade, toward the end of the school year. The children, over all conditions, discriminated the two types of nonword better than chance (74 percent correct), but neither of the auditory conditions differed from the nonauditory condition. Redundant sound did not facilitate judgment, either because the children pronounced the word subvocally when they were told only to look at it or because judgment of orthographic legality is based on purely visual information. Word length, as in the Rosinski and Wheeler experiment, made no difference, but there was some tendency to make more accurate judgments when the misplaced cluster appeared at the beginning of the word rather than at the end.

Golinkoff (1973) repeated her experiment, with modifications, with S s from first and second grade (late in the school year). There were three conditions of word presentation: visual, auditory, and redundant visual and auditory. The results revealed an interaction of age with condition. First-grade children performed only slightly better than chance with visual or auditory presentation alone, but they performed significantly better (72 percent correct) when the presentation was bimodal. But the second graders were significantly better with visual presentation alone (82.5 percent correct, as compared to 65 percent for auditory presentation and 70 percent for bimodal presentation). Thus combining auditory and visual presentation appeared to help in the beginning stages of learning to read, but toward the end of second grade, visual information for word-likeness had become of predominant importance. Golinkoff correlated performance on the word-likeness test with reading scores on the Metropolitan Achievement Test (given at the end of the year) and found a significant relationship ($r = .50$). We infer that ability to generalize knowledge of English orthography does reflect reading ability measured in other ways.

Learning Experiments. Taken together, the preceding experiments suggest that normally children are learning and generalizing at least some aspects of the orthographic rule system in the second grade. How are they doing it? The research strategy by which I attempted to answer this question was a combination of training with a series of small problems requiring abstraction of a common spelling pattern and a learning set procedure. A typical problem consisted of eight words or word-like letter strings, each printed on a card, which the child was to sort into two piles. Half of the words had two letters in common in a given position; the other four contained the two letters but they were never arranged in the same way. When the common pattern was present, the other letters always differed. A typical sorting problem might be:

mean	name
beat	belt
leap	laep
read	road

The words were presented in random order and E corrected sorting errors, but the child made the abstraction for himself as in a concept learning experiment. He was not required to proceed for more than a specified number of trials (four trials in the first experiment) if he did not succeed in sorting correctly, but he was given a new problem. One problem followed another, six a day over five days of training in the first experiment (Gibson, Farber, & Shepela, 1968). The first children tested were in kindergarten and the experiment was not only grueling both for experimenters and for children, but it was a monumental failure. Only one child developed a learning set, showing gradually increasing success over problems. The next year we tried a slightly modified procedure with first-grade children with only a little more success. The patterns that stood out maddeningly to the experimenter seemed to have no salience at all for the children.

An answer frequently suggested by kindly critics was "why don't you just tell them?" So we did. Lowenstein (1969) ran a sorting experiment with the same problems over three days with children nearing the completion of first grade. There were three groups of children, and each group was given different instructions. The control group was run like the earlier experiments; the only instructions given were to "sort the mail, and put all yours here." A card for each pile was laid out for him and the procedure went on as before. The full-information group was told by the experimenter, "You will always know your mail because it will have these two letters in it, in this place." The common feature (constrained letter pair) was pointed out for each problem for the first two days. The third group was told, "You will know your mail because it will have the same two letters in the same place," but they were never shown the letter pair. The full-information group performed significantly better than the other two groups for the first two days, nearly everyone doing perfect sorts on the second day. On the third day, no further instructions were given. The group given the partial hint continued to improve, greatly exceeding the control group. But the full-information group deteriorated to the level of the control group. They had learned nothing from "being told." Apparently, S had to search actively and think for himself in order to learn something generalizable. Other psychologists, including Vygotsky and Piaget have emphasized that concepts are not "the sum of certain associative bonds formed by memory" and that they cannot be taught by drilling. To quote Vygotsky: "Practical experience also shows that direct teaching of concepts is impossible and fruitless. A teacher who tries to do this usually accomplishes nothing but empty verbalism, a parrotlike repetition of words by the child, simulating a knowledge of the corresponding concepts but actually covering up a vacuum" (Vygotsky, 1962, p. 83).

It occurred to me at this point that the sorting task might not make clear enough the economy of using a common feature or "collative principle." I decided to try another learning task, a simple one in which the economy of using a common feature is very obvious. We (Gibson, Poag, & Rader, 1972) set up a two-stage verbal discrimination task, comparing discrimination learning and generalization when there was or was *not* a common feature useful for learning the task in stage 1. All Ss were to learn which of two buttons to press for each of four words when the words were presented one at a time. They were given feedback on each trial. They were run to a criterion of 10 perfect trials or stopped after 60 trials. One group of Ss was presented with two rhyming pairs of words (king and ring; yarn and barn). The members of a rhyming pair were assigned the same button by E, so S had only two associations to learn if he noticed and used the rhyme or common spelling pattern. The other group of Ss had four words that had no obvious common feature (nose, king, bell, yarn), and therefore they had to learn four associations.

Stage 2 was identical for the two groups. Four new words were presented, consisting of two rhyming pairs (boat and coat; cake and rake). It was predicted that an S who had the opportunity to use rhyme in stage 1 would learn to do so and would generalize the principle to stage 2, starting a criterion run of 10 perfect trials on trial 5. The other group, by comparison would be handicapped. The Ss were second- and fifth-grade children.

46

| | Grade 2 | | Grade 5 | |
Condition	Stage 1	Stage 2	Stage 1	Stage 2
GrE (common feature)	20.0%	26.6%	53.0%	60.0%
GrC (no common feature)	0.0	13.0	6.6	53.0

The results are summarized in the accompanying tabulation. When a common feature was present, grade five Ss performed significantly better in both stages than did grade two Ss; but they did not perform better when there was no common feature (GrC, stage 1). There was development with age of an ability to perceive and to use the economical principle, but there was no improvement in associative learning as such. What was the effect of training within the experiment? Did anyone *learn* to use the common feature in the course of stage 1 and then generalize the principle to stage 2? The answer is no. There was no significant change from stage 1 to stage 2 for either of the age groups having a common feature in stage 1; nor did those groups excel significantly compared to the other groups in stage 2. Put another way, the S either applied the rule at once in the training stage or he never did. In terms of development, the ability to do this increases; but apparently it does not increase by virtue of the kind of training given in this experiment. Massed practice with differential reinforcement, even in this simple task, did not help to disclose a principle.

It seems to me now that abstraction of spelling patterns with consequent transfer is the result of much exposure to them and takes place slowly over time. I think that this process is mainly one of perceptual abstraction which occurs with as little awareness on the learner's part as is the case with learning grammar and with as little dependence on external reinforcement. The Ss in the word-likeness experiments were seldom able to justify their choices in any intelligible way, even when the majority were correct. The successful Ss in the discrimination learning experiment, especially the fifth graders, did frequently remark on the common features of the word pairs. The question is, did the learning experiments just described test the same ability as did the tachistoscopic and word-likeness experiments? The Ss in the verbal discrimination learning task could have been given a follow-up test in which they would have been asked to judge word-likeness; the results of the two methods could then have been correlated. Unfortunately when the idea occurred to me, it was too late to retrieve the Ss.

I now see this work as needing to proceed in two directions: one, to continue to attempt to enhance experiences of observing spelling patterns, since I still think there must be ways of helping the abstraction to "roll out" of its diverse contexts; and two, to pin down more carefully the patterns and the rules that are actually effective in creating the "word-superiority" effect and its generalization in adult readers. Without the latter knowledge we cannot know exactly which features of orthographic structure we should attempt to enhance. It is also possible that there is some optimal developmental progression in internalizing the rule system that could be exploited in presenting reading matter so as to reveal higher-order structure.

USE OF INTERWORD REDUNDANCY IN A VERBAL TASK

Most of my students' and my own experiments on the economical use of structure in reading have been aimed at structure within the word, but I am keenly aware that a skilled reader makes use of syntactic and semantic relations between words. So does an unskilled reader; but I am not sure when he begins to use these relations to extract information, rather than merely to guess at what may follow. Must he perhaps learn to deal with words themselves as units first? It is possible, of course, that learning to use all types of structure goes on at the same time in reading. Adults and children by third grade or so appear to make use of phrase structure and other grammatical relations as tested by the eye-voice span (Levin & Kaplan, 1970). These Ss were reading aloud, of course, and were producing all the words in a sequence; the interpretation of the results is not entirely clear, beyond the fact that the Ss have a knowledge of grammar. I sought for a novel verbal task, therefore, that would reveal the extent to which children who presumably know something about word structure would be able to draw on interword relations to increase their economy of verbal problem solving. The task I chose was anagram solution, since a good deal is known about how adults solve anagrams.

If there is syntactic or semantic order in the array of information in an anagram task, will it be used economically by children in the third and fourth grade when they should be freed from letter-by-letter reading? Gibson, Tenney, and Sharabany (1971) performed experiments with children at this age level, investigating the effect of syntactic and semantic structure on anagram solution. In the first experiment the effect of syntactic structure and sentence meaning on the solution of a set of five anagrams was investigated. The anagrams, when solved, yielded a sentence such as "Sally helps Mom clean house." There were three groups of Ss. The anagrams were presented to one group (SS, for sentence structure) one at a time in proper sentence order. There were six sets of this type, each set was arranged on a board so that one followed another. The letters, taken from a magnetized Scrabble set, could be moved around by the S during solution. One anagram was uncovered at a time and was left uncovered during solution. If an anagram had not been solved at the end of 90 seconds, the *E* arranged it in word order and *S* went on to the next anagram. The question was whether *S* would discover the sentence structure during the first few sets and look for structure in the remaining sets, thus facilitating solution.

A second group (NS, no structure) was given the same anagrams to solve, but they were not presented in sentence order. A third group (SS-NS) was presented with the first four sets in sentence order, but the last two sets were in scrambled order. If the sentence had been discovered during the first four sets, *S* might have been expected to continue to search for sentence structure that was no longer present. This group was given help in finding the sentence structure by being asked to read in order the words they had already solved before they uncovered each new anagram on a given board.

The mean summed times for solution of the first four sets varied for the three groups, being shortest for group SS-NS, next shortest for group SS, and longest for group NS. Only the difference between group SS-NS and the other two groups was significant, however. We were obliged to conclude that for these children the sentence structure was not detected and was not used without the hint given by reading the preceding words aloud. There was no interference for group SS-NS when compared to group NS on the last two scrambled sets, which were identical with those presented to group NS. However, 15 of the 16 *S*s in group SS-NS took longer on board five than they had on board four, whereas the majority of the NS group improved their time, a difference which confirms the evidence that group SS-NS had previously been using the structure to facilitate solution. The fact that members of group SS almost uniformly failed to notice that the words made a sentence may be owing to the nature of the anagram task or to their immaturity. In a pilot experiment with adults in which more complex sentences were used, solution was facilitated when the anagrams were in sentence order. However, further confirmation of this result is needed.

In a second experiment the effect of semantic structure, specifically category membership, on anagram solution was investigated. That the solution of anagram problems by adults is facilitated by categorical relations has long been known (Rees & Israel, 1935). Since *S* must identify a solution as being a meaningful word, it stands to reason that knowing that the word will be an animal or a kind of fruit, etc., will assist solution. Six categories which were known to be familiar to third- and fourth-grade children were used. There were five anagrams for each category, and again five anagrams

49

were presented on a board. There were two groups; in one the anagrams belonging to the same category were presented together on a board (group CS, category structure), whereas in the other the categories were scrambled so that none of the boards contained words of all one category (group NS, no structure).

Group CS had shorter mean times for all six boards, as Figure 2 shows. The curves suggest an increasing effect of category with practice, but the interaction was not significant; the facilitation was present and significant for group CS on the first board. The advantage appeared by the third anagram on a board and increased thereafter (a significant condition by trial interaction). Eleven of the 30 Ss in the CS group commented spontaneously on the presence of the category.

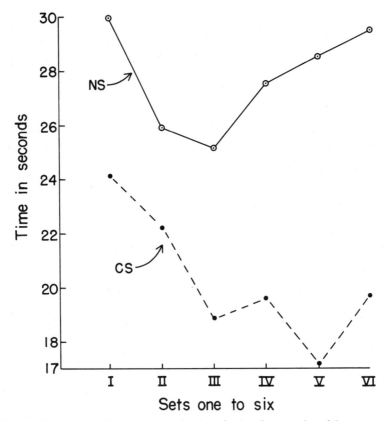

Figure 2. Mean solution time per set as a function of order of presentation of the set.

The results make it plain that the semantic relationship of belonging to a common category can be used by fourth graders for economical solution of a novel verbal problem. But to speculate a bit, we have some reason to think that the children's solution strategies may have differed from the adults' strategies. I would like to indulge in this speculation because it brings me back to meaning and how it is processed—the problem with which I began.

Several strategies for solving anagrams are possible, the simplest being a purely trial-and-error approach of moving the letters about and waiting for a word to pop out by trying to pronounce an arrangement to see if it sounds like a word. The children on the whole appeared to be doing this (admittedly we lack hard evidence, as yet). When an acceptable pronunciation turned up that was not a word (e.g., KLIM when the word was MILK), they were likely to be stuck. How then did presence of a category help them? Safren (1962) suggested that when a set of anagrams is related by meaning, "associative strength activates existing response sets" to facilitate solution. It seemed that something like this did happen with the children; if a child perceived a relation between the first two anagrams, he went through a category list, trying the words in turn on the anagram to see if they would fit, as the following typical comments illustrate: "I'm trying to think of another silverware, but I can't." "It must be another color. I'm trying them." This method of solution, even if not cognitively very sophisticated, did often give results and the strategy would be reinforced.

Adults observed in our laboratory gave comments suggesting quite a different strategy. They deliberately put consonant clusters or consonants at possible places and vowels or vowel clusters in the center to achieve orthographic acceptability, and then they checked for semantic acceptability. Knowledge of a category would facilitate recognition of a word, since much of the processing of lexical features would be eliminated and there would also be no need of going through a whole category list. Word meaning for an adult, as I suggested earlier, may usefully be thought of as the pattern of abstract conceptual features that uniquely characterizes a word.

Whether meaning is more concrete for a child, I do not know; but I infer from the first experiment described in this paper that access to abstract meaning upon reading a word is not so direct for a child as it is for a mature reader, and that the child sounds the word, as he appeared to do with the anagrams, before getting to meaning.

In any case, the children did use category knowledge in a way that facilitated anagram solution. I believe we can conclude that a person will use the most economical cognitive strategy that is possible for his developmental level and that there is progress in developing more sophisticated and higher-order strategies.

This rather lengthy summary of a good deal of the research (my own and a number of my students') of the last ten years or so has forced me to take stock of my successes and my failures and to own up to a fair number of failures and gaps in the evidence. But it leaves me convinced that opportunistic research on unrelated problems is never as rewarding to either the researcher or to the consumer as is research set in a theoretical framework that provides a systematic program. I might have had a better program, but I find that I still see increasing specificity, optimization of attention, and economy of processing the information in stimulation as giving a useful direction to developmental research on problems of reading skill, namely, in determining both what it is and how it is attained.

References

Baron, J., & Thurston, I. An analysis of the word-superiority effect. *Cognitive Psychology*, 1973, 4, 207–228.

Barron, R. W. Transfer of information processing strategies in a choice reaction time task. (Doctoral dissertation, Ohio State University.) Ann Arbor, Mich.: University Microfilms, 1971.

Cattell, J. M. Über die Zeit der Erkennung und Bennenung von Schriftzeichen, Bildern und Farben. *Philosophische Studien*, 1885, 2, 635–650.

Chase, W. G., & Clark, H. H. Mental operations in the comparison of sentences and pictures. In L. W. Gregg (Ed.), *Cognition in learning and memory*. New York: Wiley, 1972. Pp. 205–232.

Clare, D. A. A study of principles of integration in the perception of written verbal items. Unpublished doctoral dissertation, Cornell University, 1969.

Clark, E. V. What's in a word? On the child's acquisition of semantics in his first language. In T. Moore (Ed.), *Cognitive development*. New York: Academic Press, 1973.

Erdmann, B., & Dodge, R. *Psychologische Untersuchungen über das Lesen, auf Experimenteller Grundlage*. Halle: M. Niemeyer, 1898.

Fries, C. C. *Linguistics and reading*. New York: Holt, 1963.

Garner, W. R. *Uncertainty and structure as psychological concepts*. New York: Wiley, 1962.

Gibson, E. J., Barron, R. W., & Garber, E. E. The developmental convergence of meaning for words and pictures. In appendix to final report, *The relationship between perceptual development and the acquisition of reading skill*. Project No. 90046, Grant No. OEG-2-9-420446-1071(010), Cornell University and United States Office of Education, 1972.

Gibson, E. J., Bishop, C. H., Schiff, W., & Smith, J. Comparison of meaningfulness and pronunciability as grouping principles in the perception and retention of verbal material. *Journal of Experimental Psychology*, 1964, 67, 173–182.

Gibson, E. J., Farber, J., & Shepela, S. Test of a learning set procedure for the abstraction of spelling patterns. In *The analysis of reading skill: A program of basic and applied research*. Final report, Project No. 5-1213, Contract No. OE 6-10-156, 1968.

Gibson, E. J., Gibson, J. J., Pick, A. D., & Osser, H. A developmental study of the discrimination of letter-like forms. *Journal of Comparative and Physiological Psychology*, 1962, 55, 897–906.

Gibson, E. J., & Guinet, L. Perception of inflections in brief visual presentations of words. *Journal of Verbal Learning and Verbal Behavior*, 1971, 10, 182–189.

Gibson, E. J., Osser, H., & Pick, A. D. A study in the development of grapheme-phoneme correspondences. *Journal of Verbal Learning and Verbal Behavior*, 1963, 2, 142–146.

Gibson, E. J., Osser, H., Schiff, W., & Smith, J. An analysis of critical features of letters, tested by a confusion matrix. In *final report on a basic research program on reading*, Cooperative Research Project No. 639, Cornell University and United States Office of Education, 1963.

Gibson, E. J., Pick, A. D., Osser, H., & Hammond, M. The role of grapheme-phoneme correspondence in the perception of words. *American Journal of Psychology*, 1962, 75, 554–570.

Gibson, E. J., Poag, K., & Rader, N. The effect of redundant rhyme and spelling patterns on a verbal discrimination task. In appendix to final report on *The relationship between perceptual development and the acquisition of reading skill*. Project No. 90046, Grant No. OEG-2-9-420446-1071(010), Cornell University and United States Office of Education, 1972.

Gibson, E. J., Schapiro, F., & Yonas, A. Confusion matrices for graphic patterns obtained with a latency measure. In *The analysis of reading skilll: A program of basic and applied research*. Final report, Project No. 5-1213, Cornell University and United States Office of Education, 1968. Pp. 76–96.

Gibson, E. J., Shurcliff, A., & Yonas, A. Utilization of spelling patterns by deaf and hearing subjects. In H. Levin & J. P. Williams (Eds.), *Basic studies on reading*. New York: Basic Books, 1970.

Gibson, E. J., Tenney, Y. J., Barron, R. W., & Zaslow, M. The effect of orthographic structure on letter search. *Perception and Psychophysics*, 1972, 11, 183–186.

Gibson, E. J., Tenney, Y. J., & Sharabany, R. Is discovery of structure reinforcing? The role of semantic and syntactic structure in anagram solution. In final report, *The relationship between perceptual development and the acquisition of reading skill*. Project No. 90046, Grant No. OEG-2-9-420446-1071(010), Cornell University and United States Office of Education, 1971. Pp. 48–64.

Gibson, E. J., Tenney, Y. J. & Zaslow, M. Is discovery of structure reinforcing? The effect of categorizable context on scanning for verbal targets. In final report, *The relationship between perceptual development and the acquisition of reading skill*. Project No. 90046, Grant No. OEG-2-9-420446-1071(010), Cornell University and the United States Office of Education, 1971.

Gibson, E. J., & Yonas, A. A developmental study of visual search behavior. *Perception and Psychophysics*, 1966, 1, 169–171. (a)

———. A developmental study of the effects of visual and auditory interference on a visual scanning task. *Psychonomic Science*, 1966, 5, 163–164. (b)

Gibson, J. J., & Gibson, E. J. Perceptual learning: Differentiation or enrichment? *Psychological Review*, 1955, 62, 32–41.

Golinkoff, R. M. Children's use of redundant auditory information in the discrimination of nonsense words. Unpublished paper, Cornell University, December, 1972.

———. Children's discrimination of English spelling patterns with redundant auditory information. Paper presented at the American Educational Research Association, 1974.

Hochberg, J. E., & Brooks, V. Pictorial recognition as an unlearned ability: A study of one child's performance. *American Journal of Psychology*, 1962, 75, 624–628.

Huey, E. B. *The psychology and pedagogy of reading*. New York: Macmillan, 1908. Republished by M.I.T. Press, 1968.

Kaplan, G., Yonas, A., & Shurcliff, A. Visual and acoustic confusability in a visual search task. *Perception and Psychophysics*, 1966, 1, 172–174.

Katz, J. J., & Fodor, J. A. The structure of a semantic theory. *Language*, 1963, 39, 170–210.

Levin, H., & Kaplan, E. L. Grammatical structure and reading. In H. Levin & J. P. Williams (Eds.), *Basic studies on reading*. New York: Basic Books, 1970. Pp. 119–133.

Lowenstein, A. A. Effects of instructions on the abstraction of spelling patterns. Unpublished master's thesis, Cornell University, 1969.

Luria, A. R. Speech development and the formation of mental processes. In M. Cole & I. Maltzman (Eds.), *A handbook of contemporary Soviet psychology.* New York: Basic Books, 1969. Pp. 121–162.

Moore, T. V. Image and meaning in memory and perception. *Psychological Monographs,* 1919, 27 (Whole No. 119).

Neisser, U. Decision time without reaction time: Experiments in visual scanning. *American Journal of Psychology,* 1963, 76, 376–385.

Neisser, U., & Beller, H. K. Searching through word lists. *British Journal of Psychology,* 1965, 56, 349–358.

Posner, M. I., & Mitchell, R. F. Chronometric analysis of classification. *Psychological Review,* 1967, 74, 392–409.

Rees, H. J., & Israel, H. E. An investigation of the establishment and operation of mental sets. In J. J. Gibson (Ed.), *Studies in psychology from Smith College. Psychological Monographs,* 1935, 46 (Whole No. 6). Pp. 1–26.

Reicher, G. M. Perceptual recognition as a function of meaningfulness of stimulus material. *Journal of Experimental Psychology,* 1969, 81, 275–280.

Rosinski, R. R., & Wheeler, K. E. Children's use of orthographic structure in word discrimination. *Psychonomic Science,* 1972, 26, 97–98.

Rothkopf, E. Z. Incidental memory for location of information in text. *Journal of Verbal Learning and Verbal Behavior,* 1971, 10, 608–613.

Rubenstein, H. *An overview of psycholinguistics.* Grant Report, Lehigh University, Bethlehem, Pa., 1971. To be published in *Current Trends in Linguistics,* Vol. 12. The Hague: Mouton.

Ryle, A. L. A study of the interpretation of pictorial styles by young children. Unpublished doctoral dissertation, Harvard School of Education, 1966.

Safren, M. A. Associations, sets, and the solution of word problems. *Journal of Experimental Psychology,* 1962, 64, 40–45.

Schapiro, F. Information extraction and filtering during perceptual learning in visual search. Unpublished doctoral dissertation, Cornell University, 1970.

Shepela, S. T. A developmental study of bimodal vigilance. Unpublished doctoral dissertation, Cornell University, 1971.

Tenney, Y. H. The child's conception of organization and recall: The development of cognitive strategies. Unpublished doctoral dissertation, Cornell University, 1973.

Vygotsky, L. S. *Thought and language.* Cambridge and New York: M.I.T. Press and Wiley, 1962. Edited and translated by Eugenia Hanfmann and Gertrude Vakar.

Wheeler, D. D. Processes in word recognition. *Cognitive Psychology,* 1970, 1, 59–85.

Yonas, A. The acquisition of information-processing strategies in a time-dependent task. Unpublished doctoral dissertation, Cornell University, 1969.

Zaslow, M. The effect of orthographic structure on letter search: A reexamination. Senior Honors Thesis, Cornell University, 1972.

＋ I. I. GOTTESMAN ＋

Developmental Genetics and Ontogenetic Psychology: Overdue Détente and Propositions from a Matchmaker

I HAVE had the experience, while contemplating some of the recent advances in developmental and molecular biology (e.g., Hotta & Benzer, 1972; Ohno, 1972; Brown, 1973), of being so much in awe as to be struck dumb. Such a state obviously is not conducive to writing a paper that has as one of its main objectives the communication of my conviction that we must start now to build a bridge between developmental genetics and ontogenetic psychology. The thesis of the currently popular book *Chariots of the Gods* is that the remarkably precociously advanced levels of culture observed among the ancient Egyptians, Mayans, and Incas were the result of space travelers from distant galaxies landing and imparting their advanced wisdom as well as some of their genes by mating with the Earthlings. Even Nobel Laureate Crick has suggested that panspermia (''seeding'' of life by intelligent beings on other planets) should be considered by those contemplating the origins of life on this planet. Although such a thesis may best be construed as science fiction, it has merit as a parable when applied to the currently great distances (in language, technology, goals) between the planet of ontogenetic psychology and the planet of developmental genetics. My sentiments will be clearer if I paraphrase Paul E. Meehl's (1973) paraphrase of Albert Einstein and say that the trouble with The Concept of Development—the annual organizing theme

NOTE· The author is indebted to D. R. Hanson for his aid in the preparation of this paper and to him, L. L. Heston, and D. J. Merrell for their critical comments on the manuscript.

of these volumes—is that it is too difficult for developmental psychologists and, further, that it is too difficult for developmental biologists. Some of the ideas to be presented in this chapter will be unashamedly conceptual without much, if any, immediate heuristic value. My defense, if I should need any, is that the current apperceptive mass of developmental psychology requires the incorporation of such conceptual ideas if it wishes to avoid a long plateau in its growth curve.

The potentials for genetic individuality and variability of our species are overwhelming (e.g., Brozek, 1966; Harris, 1970). There are some 3.8 billion human beings now alive, but there are some 70 trillion potential human genotypes. Taking only 20 genetic markers for blood group systems, we can calculate that the odds are one in two million that two people (excepting identical twins) would be matched. Fortunately this degree of matching is not required for blood transfusions! It is estimated that our chromosome set contains three to five million genes, but a large number (perhaps 40 to 50 percent) are redundant copies; the probable number of structural genes (see p. 63) that code for an amino acid sequence in a protein is 60,000 to 100,000; the number of these that are polymorphic* is 20,000 to 30,000 (but only some 50 have so far been discovered); and, the number of regulator genes (see p. 64) is unknown and I can find no guesstimates. In the latest edition of McKusick's (1971) catalog of Mendelian phenotypes identified in man are listed 866 definites and 1,010 probables for a total of 1,876 gene loci of which 150 are on the X-chromosome. The extent of our ignorance about the structure and functions of the human genome is obvious; this in no way diminishes my awe at recent advances in molecular biology.

In a beautiful essay entitled "Form, End and Time" in his book *The Strategy of the Genes*, C. H. Waddington (1957) gave an overview of the conceptual framework with which I am grappling in this paper. An adequate picture of any human can only be provided by considering the effects on it of three different types of temporal change, each being effective simultaneously and continuously.

The three time-elements in the biological picture differ in scale. On the largest scale is evolution; any living being must be thought of as the product of a long line of ancestors and itself the potential ancestor of a line of descendants. On the medium scale, an animal . . . must be thought of as something which has a life history. It is not enough to see that horse pulling a cart past the window as the good working horse it is today; the picture must also include

*A polymorphism is defined as the occurrence of two or more alleles at a given gene locus in a population, each allele having frequencies greater than 0.01.

the minute fertilized egg, the embryo in its mother's womb, and the broken-down old nag it will eventually become. Finally, on the shortest time-scale, a living thing keeps itself going only by a rapid turnover of energy or chemical change; it takes in and digests food, it breathes, and so on.

In the biological picture towards which we are finding our way, the three time systems will have to be kept in mind together. That is the feat which common sense still finds difficult. Even in current biology, most of our theories are still only partly formed because they leave one or the other of the time scales out of account. (p. 6)

Therein lies one of the challenges to developmental psychologists who have largely been working within the medium time scale: become aware of large scale time (roughly equated with evolution and population genetics); remind yourselves of the importance of embryology and gerontology; and keep alert to the potential relevance of physiology and developmental genetics. Waddington went on to say:

One might compare an animal with a piece of music. Its short-scale physiology is like the vibrations of the individual notes, its medium-scale life-history is like the melodic phrases into which notes build themselves; and its long-scale evolution is like the structure of the whole musical composition, in which the melodies are repeated and varied. (p. 7)

Simultaneous Contributions of Genotype and Environment to Phenotypes

Throughout its young career behavioral genetics, following in the footsteps of agricultural and medical genetics, has been concerned with identifying the genotypes that correspond to certain behavioral phenotypes. This purpose was fairly well served by a conception of the genes as determiners of the structural end-states of an organism; the single-locus recessive disorder of PKU leading to mental retardation is a classical example of an inborn error of metabolism. The given trait (with implied structure) under investigation, be it intelligence of a rat in a maze, age at which infants walk,* or predisposition to schizophrenia, was observed to be modified in many respects by environmental influences. It then became fairly standard practice to allocate (after appropriate experimental designs involving selection, or strain differences, or twins) proportions of the variance observed in individual differences to heredity, environment, and their interaction (cf. Fuller &

---

*The identical twin concordance rate for onset of walking is 67 percent but it is only 30 percent in fraternals (Stern, 1973, p. 717). Smiling and other indicators of sociability also appear to be under strong genetic control in infants (Reppucci, 1968; Freedman, 1973).

Thompson, 1960; Hirsch, 1967; and McClearn & DeFries, 1973). Such strategies will slowly give way to others suggested by the revolution in molecular biology ushered in by the eras of Watson and Crick (1953) and Jacob and Monod (1961); but they are an important starting point that requires understanding before one moves on to the more dynamic aspects of behavioral regulation and canalization (Fuller, 1964; Meissner, 1965; Waddington, 1957; Thiessen, 1972).

One concept that I have found very useful to explain the simultaneous contributions of genotype and environment to variations in phenotype, thus avoiding a number of pseudoquestions, is the reaction range (Gottesman, 1963a, 1968; Gottesman & Heston, 1972). It will serve to bridge the gap between static and dynamic aspects of structure and function. The explication may also serve to clarify the distinction I am trying to preserve between "interaction" (cf. Erlenmeyer-Kimling, 1972; Bouchard, in press) and simultaneous contribution or co-action. The fundamental points can be made by reference to Figure 1 drawn from data collected by Krafka in 1919 on the effects of Drosophila eye facet number of rearing larvae at different temperatures (incidentally, a concrete example of *very* early experience). Samples of female flies of two genotypes, low-bar and ultra-bar, were examined for eye facet number after the larvae from which they came had been subjected to seven different rearing temperatures (from 15° C to 29° C). Given these ideal circumstances of exquisite control over genotypic *and* environmental variability and given these data, we can make a number of far-reaching statements that have potential application to behavioral phenotypes. Given uniformity of trait-relevant environment, almost all of the observed phenotypic variance in the trait must be attributable to genotypic differences: at 16° the difference is AB, but it is only B'C at 29°, and in fact the genetic difference varies with the environment. Given uniformity in that part of the genome relevant to the trait, almost all of the phenotypic variance is attributable to environmental differences: the low-bar flies have A number of facets at 16°, but the same flies have only B' facets at 29°; the other genotype, the ultra-bars, have only B (= B') facets at the former temperature and C at the latter. The distances (or number of eye facets) AB' and BC are the reaction ranges (R.R.) of these two populations of flies over this particular range of environments; in other words, R.R.L. and R.R.U. are the two different environmental contributions to facet number variability for these two genotypes under these conditions. The different sizes of R.R. suggest that there was differential buffering or environmental sensitivity of the

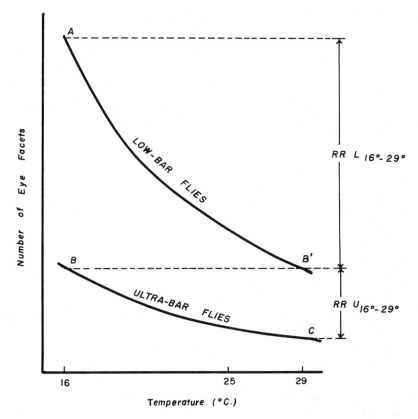

Figure 1. Reaction ranges for *Drosophila* eye facet number as a function of temperatures at which larvae are reared.

developmental reactions of the two genotypes to temperature changes. The differential response of two genotypes to a given environmental change is a 'clean' illustration of one of the meanings of genotype-environment interaction.

From this example we can conclude that the same genotype may have quite different phenotypes and that similar phenotypes may have quite different genotypes. The latter is illustrated by the fact that the overlap in reaction ranges at the point B or B′ would not allow you to distinguish between low-bar and ultra-bar flies from their number of eye facets, unless, of course, you had their *complete* developmental history. Given the usual state of affairs for human experimentation—genetic plus environmental heterogeneity—any

59

observed trait variability must be attributed to some varying combination of genetic and environmental variances.

Figure 2 illustrates the adaptation of the reaction range concept to variation in height for adolescent males and females based on some of the available morphological data (Greulich, 1957; Meredith, 1969; Mørch, 1941). This trait is nearer to the interests of developmental psychologists and provides a shorter leaping distance to such behavioral traits as intelligence. The increased height in Japanese children born to Japanese parents in the United States compared to those born in Japan is well documented (Greulich, 1957). It is a good example (assuming there is no selective migration) of a phenotypic change that is not associated with a genotypic one; it is thus an example of the reaction range for height with the improved pre- and postnatal environment in the American Japanese promoting a changed phenotype. The units for both X and Y axes are only ordinal and are not to scale.

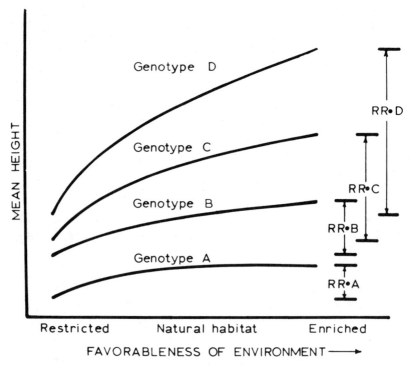

Figure 2. The reaction range concept applied to adolescent height (units for both X and Y axes are only ordinal and are not to scale).

Each curve in the figure can be construed as representing the phenotypic response of samples of individuals homogeneous for four different levels of genetic potential for height who have been reared in various trait-relevant environments (or niches) crudely characterized as restricted, natural habitat, and enriched. Curve Type A could represent a deviant, Mendelizing genotype—for example, the one associated with the dominant gene for classical achondroplastic dwarfism which has an incidence of 1 in 10,000 births. (No connection has been demonstrated between this kind of "growth failure" and that seen in pituitary dwarfs, a condition transmitted as one of a number of recessive loci.) The different environments to which such dwarfs have been exposed thus far do not have much effect on their height; the mean height for 15-year-old cases (sexes combined) is only 120 cm. Curve Type B could represent samples of 13-year-old Japanese girls: in contemporary Japan they average 146.1 cm (= natural habitat); 13-year-old girls measured in postwar Japan (1950) only averaged 139.9 cm (= restricted environment nutritionally); 13-year-old Japanese girls born in the United States to Japanese parents averaged 150.5 cm (= enriched environment). The reaction range (RR B) for the genotype represented by 13-year-old Japanese girls under the range of environments sampled would be the largest value minus the lowest or 10.6 cm. Curve Type C could represent the response of the genotypes of 15-year-old* Japanese boys measured at the same time as the girls in B; we are dealing here with one more example of sexual dimorphism and a different genotype for height (cf. Tanner, 1970). Postwar boys averaged 151.1 cm; contemporary boys in Japan, 158.2 cm; and contemporary Japanese boys born in the United States, 164.5 for a reaction range of 13.4 cm, all of which is attributable to environmental variations. The large difference in reaction ranges of 2.8 cm might suggest that an XY (again) is less buffered than an XX genome. Curve Type D could represent 15-year-old United States white boys who average 168.7 cm (13-year-old white girls average 155.4 cm). Examples of the same phenotype with different genotypes are provided by some data on children of Japanese X United States white matings (fathers always white); the 15-year-old boys averaged 164.7 cm and the 13-year-old girls averaged 151.5. It appears that the hybrids matched the Japanese born in the United States and were about halfway between contemporary Japanese and white children (under natural habitat conditions). Other genotypes could have been

---

*The choice of 13- and 15-year-old girls and boys was dictated by the availability of data, but it does permit a rather close match for *maturity* with girls having a two to three year offset from boys in their velocity curves.

added to Figure 2 for such diverse groups as the Mbuti pygmies and Nuer of Sudan with adult mean heights of 144 cm and 184 cm, respectively. The thrust of the reaction range concept is that both heredity and environment are important in determining trait variation; but they are important in different ways, combinations, and degrees, some of which are amenable to dissection for some traits.

One of the major shortcomings of the reaction range concept is that it is not adequate for the task of encompassing changes observed over time intraindividually or interindividually. Figure 3 presents the growth velocity curves of five boys followed with repeated measurements over the period of their adolescent growth spurts (Tanner, Whitehouse, & Takaishi, 1966; Marshall, 1971). Such a plotting of velocities (rate of growth in cm/yr) rather than of distances (attained height at a point in time) has a number of important advantages: (1) it maximizes the picture of individual differences in a dramatic fashion; (2) it shows the gross kinds of distortion obtained from cross-sectional data compared to longitudinal observation and from averaging compared to individual observation (note that the dashed line represents the average velocity but characterizes not one individual in the group); (3) it forces to the forefront questions about the differential switching on and off of so-called maturational processes and stages; (4) it pinpoints the possibilities for critical or vulnerable periods in ontogeny for dramatically different tissue requirements (cf. Dobbing, 1971; Winick, 1970). If we are to approach an understanding of the phenomena such as those on growth in Figure 3 from a genetic point of view, we must extend our concepts so that regulation and function are included along with end-states.

Regulator Genes and Epigenetic Landscapes

Many attractive, albeit tentative, hypotheses about the processes of development in mammals have been stimulated by the growing understanding of the switching on and off of metabolic processes in the cell of a bacterium. Only a rough-and-ready sketch of the principles involved and their possible extensions to gene expression in mammalian cells (Britten & Davidson, 1969; Tomkins, et al., 1969) can be provided here and the reader is referred to other sources (e.g., Darnell, Jelinek, & Molloy, 1973; Thiessen, 1972; Stern, 1973) for details. Certain pertinent facts should be underscored from among the details. As Thiessen says, "Gene influence on behavior is always indirect. Hence, the regulatory processes of a behavior can be assigned to structural and physiological consequences of gene action and developmental

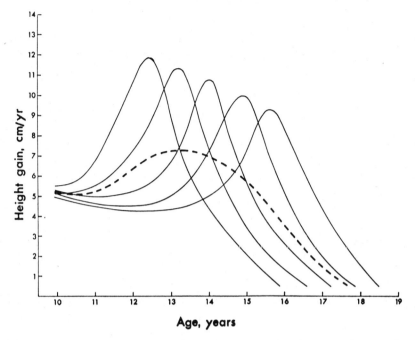

Figure 3. Growth and velocity curves (cm/year) of five males during adolescence; the dashed line represents the average for this sample. (Reprinted by permission from J. M. Tanner, R. H. Whitehouse, and M. Takaishi, "Standards from Birth to Maturity for Height, Weight, Height Velocity, and Weight Velocity: British Children 1965," *Archives of Disease in Childhood*, 1966, 41, 454–471, 613–635.)

canalization. The blueprint for behavior may be a heritable characteristic of DNA, but its ultimate architecture is a problem for biochemistry and physiology" [p. 87]. The basic elements in one version of the Jacob-Monod operon model of the regulation of protein synthesis is given in Figure 4 in its *off* and *on* states with the proviso that the switch is a sensitive one under the precise, instantaneous control of various cybernetic elements in the cell's cytoplasm. It cannot be overemphasized that it is *environmental* factors acting through such extracellular metabolic intermediates as hormones, vitamins, and toxins that determine *which* genes get switched on and *how long* they function. Structural genes (X, Y, and Z) specify the types of enzymes* (x, y, z) associated with classical Mendelian gene effects when they are switched on by the adjacent operator gene (O); the operator together with one or more

*Protein synthesis and structure is more complex than is implied by this abbreviated description. See e.g., Harris (1970) for more details.

63

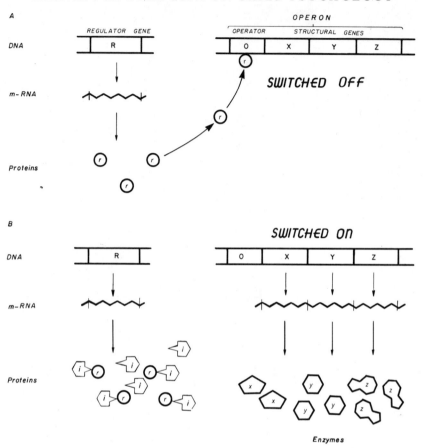

Figure 4. A schematic drawing of the process of Jacob-Monod gene regulation in the off (A) and on (B) states as it occurs in lower organisms (see text for details).

structural genes is called an operon. A regulator gene (R) controls the functioning of the operator and is itself subject to control by elements in the cytoplasm. Regulator genes produce regulator represser protein (r), which combines with the operator to inhibit RNA generation by the structural genes in the off state (Figure 4A). When sufficient quantities of the proper inducer (i) substance become available, it combines with r so it can no longer combine with the operator, thus switching on the X, Y, and Z genes so that transcription of RNA ensues and enzymes can be produced.

Large, some would say radical, changes in the mechanisms involved in gene regulation are required conceptually before the bacterial model can be extrapolated to mammalian cells, but the important message for developmental psychologists is the same. That is, exquisite, precise systems have evolved that provide for qualitative differences in proteins and for quantitative variations in rates of synthesis that are cybernetically related to the needs of the organism. In one extension (Britten & Davidson, 1969) *batteries* of structural genes are regulated by "integrator and receptor" genes with the former under the control of "sensor genes"; this model would permit responses to an external signal, production of a second signal which is transmitted to receptors unresponsive to the original signal, reception of the second signal and a response to it in the form of structural gene transcription. Other points at which mammalian cells may be regulated with "fine tuning" are suggested by the terms *postranscriptional regulation* and *translational modulation* (cf. Darnell, et al., 1973). The thorny problem of what switches on the switches that switch on the switches is tackled by Ohno (1972), who also argues that mammalian regulation involves simplification rather than complication of the bacterial model via changes in the power of regulatory genes versus the acquisition of new structural genes. One of his pertinent and bold conjectures is that maleness and femaleness represent the switched on and switched off state of one and the same regulatory system!

A different but related concept from developmental genetics that should prove an important addition to the apperceptive mass referred to above is Waddington's three-dimensional model for handling phenotypic changes in the states of organs (or organisms) as they develop toward some adult end-state. The top surface of his "epigenetic landscape," together with a peek at what is underneath it—all schematic of course—is given in Figure 5. It allows for the conceptualization of the simultaneous and sequential effects of many genes and many external stimuli influencing the structure and function of an organism. The contour of the landscape is determined by the person's genotype; the surface is tilted so that time of fertilization is in the back plane and end-states are at the bottom of the canals. The location of the ball represents the state of differentiation or development of some part of the fertilized egg, for example that part destined to become the brain. The trajectory of the ball as it rolls toward you analogously represents the developmental history of an egg part. Don't destroy the artistry in the landscape by demanding too much explanatory power from it. You can see though that if, while the system is moving along, environmental or genetic forces push the ball slightly off course it will, with some exceptions, return to its original path. One exception is the "critical period" when the ball is at a fork in the path (T_2); even here individual differences in the depth of the canalization and the steepness of the walls determine the susceptibility to the forces (differential buffering). Underneath the epigenetic landscape you can see pegs representing a sample of structural genes; the wires connecting them to the surface are subject to variable tension as a function of gene expression. (The regulation of the genes is not shown, but see Figure 4 and the discussion above.)

A developmental psychology that incorporates developmental genetics is appropriately complex. The phenotype at any point in time is in a state of dynamic flux with its momentary value determined by all three time-elements (p. 67). Since only a small portion of the genome (perhaps 5 to 20 percent) is activated at any one time, the *effective* genotype upon which environmental forces are acting is constantly changing. As I shall show below, this phenomenon goes a long way toward accounting for the different developmental trajectories of monozygotic (identical) twins with respect to both states and outcomes.

Milk Drinking Habits, Evolution, and Gene Regulation

An informative example of some of the congruences between the ideas in the previous section and reality is provided by a close look at one behavior—milk drinking—in mammals (Gottesman & Heston, 1973; McCracken, 1971; Paige, Bayless, Ferry, & Graham, 1971). Mother's milk or some equivalent provides all the nutrients necessary for the growth of mammals during the early part of infancy. Rarely children are allergic to the protein in milk or have the genetically determined disorder known as galactosemia; such children require a nonmilk food source from the beginning of life. They, however, are not the subject of this section. It is now clear that many adults and older children (after ages two to eight or so) from all races, but especially from non-Caucasian populations, have a considerably lower tolerance than others to the milk sugar, *lactose*, because of low levels of intestinal *lactase* activity. (Lactase, a protein, is the enzyme responsible for the splitting of lactose into soluable sugars which provide 30 to 60 percent of the calories present in milk. Lactose is not absorbed by the small intestine in its unsplit form.) These same individuals with "later onset" lactose intolerance had no difficulties at all using milk as infants. In all mammals that have been studied, with the exception of man, lactase activity is high in infancy and drops to near zero after weaning. This decrease can probably be taken as the normal mammalian pattern; in prevalence studies to be reviewed

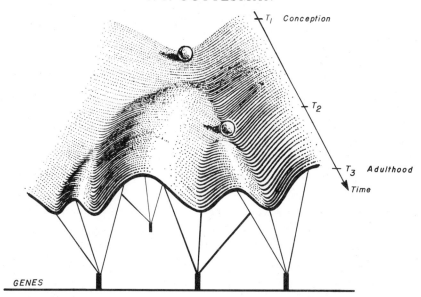

Figure 5. Waddington's epigenetic landscape for conceptualizing genetic and environmental roles in the ontogeny of an organ or organism.

in Figure 7, 60 to 100 percent of many non-Caucasian populations showed this pattern. In contrast, however, only 0 to 20 percent of many North European populations and their descendants showed low levels of lactase activity. The question of whether the populations differ in this respect for genetic reasons after 10,000 years of natural selection or as the result of continuing to drink milk after weaning is probably answered by the evolutionary argument.

A cross-sectional picture of the levels of lactase available to the rat as a function of prenatal and postnatal age (Kretchmer, 1972) is shown in Figure 6. The "wisdom of the body," as it was metaphorically called by the famed W. B. Cannon of a half-century ago is revealed by the evolutionarily optimized regulation of lactase levels which peak just when the rat baby starts to suckle. We can reason that since it would be inefficient for the gene to be switched on too early or to stay on after its product was no longer needed, that was the way the system evolved. A similar developmental pattern for this enzyme is observed in primates other than man and in the majority of humans, with certain informative exceptions.

Since the consequence of low lactase levels is the inability to digest milk followed by such symptoms as diarrhea and gastrointestinal pain, we would expect lactose intolerance to influence patterns of milk consumption among children as the operon turns off. The changes in age (cross-sectional data) in the prevalence of a normal response to a lactose tolerance test in different populations are given in Figure 7. The data lead to the conclusion that it is not the scarcity of milk in the postweaning diet that results in low levels of lactase, although its availability may divert the ball on the epigenetic landscape and delay milk intolerance temporarily. The populations which consume milk as adults are, by and large, of North European origin with exceptions that test the rule; the Masai and pastoral Fulani of Africa, both of whom have raised cattle and consumed milk for thousands of years, are very good milk drinkers without lactase deficiency.

We can speculate that selection for lactose tolerance must have begun 10 to 12 thousand years ago when human populations began domesticating milk-producing animals. Because the adult form of intolerance is not fatal and would only be disadvantageous when food supplies were very marginal,

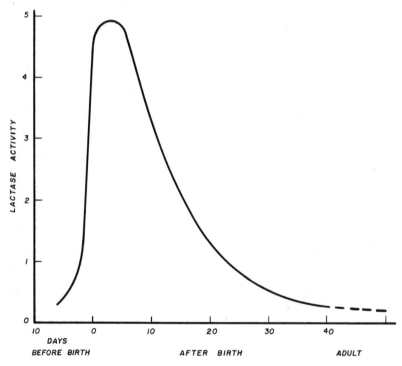

Figure 6. Lactase activity levels in the rat before and after birth. (Reprinted by permission from N. Kretchmer, "Lactose and Lactase," *Scientific American*, 1972, 227, 70–78.)

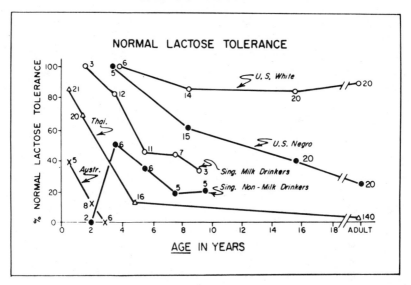

Figure 7. Changes with age (cross-sectional data) in the prevalence of normal lactose tolerance tests in different populations. Sample sizes are indicated by numbers inside the figure. Populations (top to bottom): United States Whites, United States Baltimore Negroes, Singapore milk drinkers, Singapore nonmilk drinkers, Thais in a Bangkok village, and Australian Aboriginal children. Adapted from T. M. Bayless, "Milk Intolerance: Clinical, Developmental,and Epidemiological Aspects," in I. I. Gottesman and L. L. Heston [eds.], *Summary of the Conference on Lactose and Milk Intolerance*. Washington, D.C.: DHEW Publication No. (OCD) 73–19, 1973.

selection pressures must have been gentle. We may also note that selection favoring tolerance must have increased in populations where significant numbers had already become tolerant: the possession of a favorable trait that increases fitness leads to displacement of other phenotypes. Once some members of a population had begun to utilize milk as a food, the remaining members were at a somewhat increased disadvantage.

As in other examples of interaction between environment and genes, the more one understands about this specific phenomenon, the more difficult it becomes to separate genes from environment. In the case of lactase it appears that a cultural-technological advance, domestication of animals, was intermeshed with a change in gene frequency.

As suggested by data on monkeys, primitive man, like all mammals, must have been lactose intolerant after infancy. It is tolerance of lactose that must have evolved. What magnitude of selective advantage would have been required to change the frequency of a favorable dominant mutation to currently observed levels? Accepting the current prevalence of lactase deficiency in contemporary intolerant populations to be 90 percent as opposed to 10 percent in Northwestern Europe, the corresponding frequencies of the gene for adult lactase production would be .05 in intolerant populations and about .60 in tolerant populations. We have worked out the approximate selection intensity against homozygote nonlactase producers required to change the gene frequency from .05 to .60 in the 400 generations since the domestication of sheep and goats. The selection intensity is approximately .01. Literally this number means that if lactose tolerant persons had an average of merely 1 percent more children surviving per generation than had lactose intolerant persons, the observed change in phenotype frequency could occur in the time available. The value .01 is commonly encountered and is of reasonable magnitude.

Developmental Behavioral Genetics and Psychopathology

The area of psychology that has been consuming most of my energy for the past decade has been psychopathology; we are still very much on the frontiers of applying a developmental behavioral genetic point of view to the area, but it has commenced (Gottesman, 1960, 1965, 1966; Gottesman & Shields, 1972; Shields, Heston, & Gottesman, 1974). Genetic disorders of behavior with a variable age of onset provide the most fertile ground for joining developmental psychology and biology. Huntington's disease (HD), caused by a dominant gene, and schizophrenia, a disorder with a well-established genetic component, can be used to illustrate the ontogeny of psychopathology. In a paradigmatic application of the high risk method (Pearson & Kley, 1957), my former student Orcena Lyle (1972) followed up 88 offspring of Huntington's patients some 15 to 20 years after they had been tested with a battery of psychometrics. All 88 were free of clinical signs of HD when they were first tested; 44 would be expected to develop the disease eventually; 28 were found on follow-up to be affected. The results for the children at the time of initial testing on just the Wechsler Performance Scales as a function of their status on follow-up are given in Table 1. Up to this time the use of psychological or other tests to detect the presymptomatic carriers of the dominant gene have not been encouraging. Recently a group of investigators (Klawans, Paulson, Ringel, & Barbeau, 1972) have reported promising results with a provocative test that elicited choreiform movements in 10 of 28 offspring of HD patients (but in none of the controls) after loading with the chemical levodopa; it will take a long term follow-up to determine whether there is a one-to-one correspondence with overt disease.

70

I. I. GOTTESMAN

Table 1. Evidence for Premorbid Effects of Huntington's Disease on Cognition
in the Offspring of Probands

Group	N	Mean Test Age	Mean Wechsler Performance IQ[b]	IQ Range
1. OK at follow-up 15–20 years later	58[a]	30	106	74–134
2. Onset 12.5 years later	17	30	94	74–113
3. Onset within 2 years	10	35	88	73–110
4. Already affected	24	38	86	52–109

SOURCE: Data from Lyle, 1972.

[a] Approximately 13 of these subjects are expected to develop Huntington's disease in the future.

[b] t tests for differences between groups 1 and 2, 1 and 3, and 1 and 4 are significant at .001; 2 and 4 at .05; 2 and 3 at .10; 3 and 4 n.s.

Lyle's analyses of the data from the Wechsler and other cognitive tests (but not the MMPI) can be interpreted to mean that the gene for HD has been having an effect on neural functioning before clear symptoms appear and that the nearer the individual is to overt disease, the greater is the malfunctioning. The age of onset for HD ranges from under 5 to over 75 and from parent-child and MZ twin correlations appears to be under strong genetic control. The variability across families in symptoms and onset ages implicates regulatory genes and their triggers. The practical application to genetic counseling of changes in psychometric status combined with results of a loading test is some way off, but it appears to be promising. Note that performance IQs of 94 or 88 would not ordinarily suggest pathology, and it is only in contrast to the 58 offspring who remained unaffected that suspicions are aroused.

The premorbid detection of schizophrenia has so far met with little success (Shields et al., 1974). The application of the high risk method (cf. Garmezy, 1974) continues to hold promise, but the investigators do not yet have enough affected (with schizophrenia) children of schizophrenics to give definitive findings. A diathesis-stressor model for understanding the etiology of schizophrenia appears to hold the most heuristic promise (Rosenthal, 1963; Gottesman & Shields, 1972) wherein the genes are necessary but not sufficient (Meehl, 1972a, b). While we are waiting for the longitudinal studies of high risk children to "pay off," we can learn a great deal about some of the ontogenetic aspects of schizophrenia by looking at the course of the disorder once it has made its appearance.

Figure 8 shows the MMPI profiles of a pair of female identical twins (MZ 22), age 28, from the Maudsley Schizophrenic Twin Study (Gottesman & Shields, 1972); they both have had repeated admissions since they were first hospitalized at age 19. Both twins were tested in remission (A₁ and B profiles)

71

and showed the kinds of personality resemblance we have come to expect with identical twins (Gottesman, 1963b), but the profiles do not indicate the presence of the kinds of schizophrenic psychoses both had experienced on five previous occasions. The very elevated and typically psychotic profile A_2 in Figure 8 is from Twin A just eight weeks later; she had responded to an accumulation of environmental stressors with another decompensation and was admitted to a day hospital. Twin B was not tested in a psychotic state, since she did not have her next breakdown for another two years; but our data on other MZ pairs tested when both were decompensated suggests that their profiles would be very similar (cf. MZ 13 and MZ 21 in Gottesman & Shields, 1972, p. 274). Despite their identical genotypes and identical predispositions or liabilities to developing schizophrenia, they were capable of showing quite different states because of the differences in their effective genotypes i.e., differences in which genes were activated or inactivated at one point in time.

This phenomenon of environmental determination of effective genotype was ubiquitous as can be seen in Figure 9. The in- and out-of-hospital periods

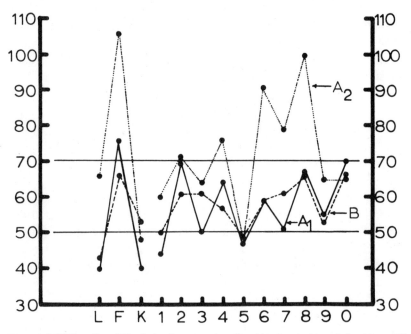

Figure 8. MMPI profiles of identical twins concordant for schizophrenia, in remission (A_1 and B) and after A decompensated (A_2). (Reprinted by permission from I. I. Gottesman and J. Shields, *Schizophrenia and Genetics: A Twin Study Vantage Point.* New York: Academic Press, 1972.)

are shown for all ten pairs of identical twins and three pairs of fraternal twins who were concordant for schizophrenia, using the consensus diagnosis of six judges, in the Maudsley study. It should now be obvious how much information about psychodynamics and about gene regulation may be hidden by the all embracing term "concordant." Ages at first hospitalization are given to the left and the time elapsed since then is indicated by a time line in years at the top and bottom of Figure 9. The longitudinal view of the course of schizophrenia after its onset (cf. Bleuler, 1972) permits the reconciliation of views about the etiology of schizophrenia that lean too heavily in either a genetic or an environmental direction.

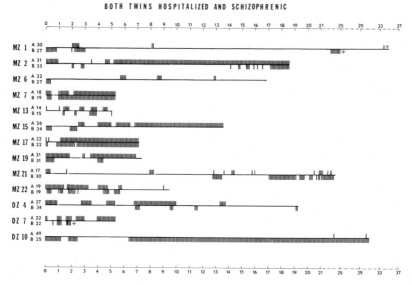

BOTH TWINS HOSPITALIZED AND SCHIZOPHRENIC

Figure 9. Hospitalization periods for concordant identical and fraternal twins in the Maudsley Schizophrenic Twin Study. Intervals of five weeks and less are shown as one vertical bar; death is indicated by a crown (see text). (Reprinted by permission from I. I. Gottesman and J. Shields, *Schizophrenia and Genetics: A Twin Study Vantage Point.* New York: Academic Press, 1972.)

The contribution of specific genetic factors to the genetic liability to schizophrenia suggested by the data from twin, family, and adoptee studies forms only a part of this epigenetic landscape. Comprehension of the *total* liability to schizophrenia requires the concepts schematized in Figures 10 and 11. Figure 10 portrays the various genetic and environmental contributors that combine in some fashion (additively and/or more complexly) to yield a net value on the dimension of combined liability; the concepts are cross-sectional or frozen in time. In addition to specific genetic liability, there are general genetic and general environmental contributors that serve as modifiers or potentiators. Additional axes are shown that provide for genetic and environmental *assets*; the axes have negative values to illustrate the role of factors that may decrease the total liability to schizophrenia, permitting a person to stay compensated or to go into a remission despite high values of genetic and/or environmental liability. The five dimensions in Figure 10 are marked off in liability units of varying length to imply differential weighting effects (Gottesman & Shields, 1972). The curve in the figure depicts the distribution of combined liability units in the general population together with the point defining the threshold value where a diagnosis of schizophrenia is highly probable. If the three liability values plus the two asset values sum to a suprathreshold value for an individual at a point in time, he has reached a schizophrenic state in his epigenetic landscape or in his ontogeny. Of course the concepts are oversimplified and overschematic. There may well turn out to be specific environmental liability to schizophrenia (e.g., ingestion of LSD) in addition to the general one we have shown; but so far the specific candidates proposed have been found wanting (e.g., Schofield & Balian, 1959; Kind, 1966; Scharfetter, 1970; Schuham, 1967; Kohn, 1973).

The dimension of time must be added to Figure 10 to increase the semblance of reality; an effort to represent a more dynamic view of a person's trajectory across the epigenetic landscape and thus to do justice to the concept of a genetic diathesis being influenced by the environment so as to produce a schizophrenic phenotype is given in two-dimensional form in Figure 11. The intention is to incorporate the concepts of changes in effective genotype by gene regulation, critical periods, and environmental inputs into a dynamic system. The time axis starts with the moment of fertilization so that prenatal factors can show their influence on states of combined liability toward schizophrenia. Both chance and ontogenetic constitutional changes will influence the path of the trajectories, leading to both upward and downward inflections. If environmental or genetic contributors to liability occur close together in time, they would be expected to have a cascade effect and be more influential than the same forces spread out in time (think about the ball and the modeling of the landscape).

G_1 is intended to indicate the trajectory of a person with a low (for schizophrenics generally) combined *genetic* liability to schizophrenia; over time environmental contributors to liability, say first the death of a spouse and then the onset of deafness, cause upward deflections of his trajectory to the

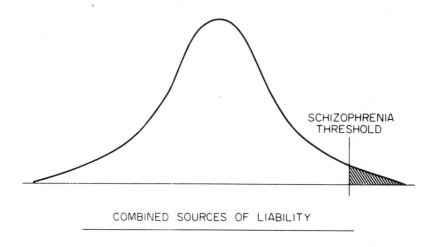

COMBINED SOURCES OF LIABILITY

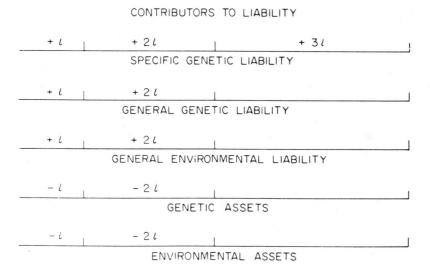

Figure 10. Contributors to the liability to schizophrenia in a diathesis-stressor threshold model. (Reprinted by permission from I. I. Gottesman and J. Shields, *Schizophrenia and Genetics: A Twin Study Vantage Point*. New York: Academic Press, 1972.)

threshold (T), culminating in a late-onset paraphrenia. The line formed by the bottom of the zone of the so-called schizophrenic spectrum disorders (Kety, et al., 1968, 1974; Rosenthal et al., 1968) is intended to convey the idea of a possible need for a second threshold in our model. Wright (1934) invoked a second threshold to account for the imperfectly formed fourth digit seen in crosses between a high and a moderate line of guinea pigs to liabilities to polydactyly.

G_2 could be the divergent trajectories of a pair of MZ twins, only the A-twin encounters over time the sufficient factors leading to schizophrenia for a person with his genotype. The B-twin at the time of observation is discordant for schizophrenia but is close to the threshold of schizophrenic spectrum disorders. Subthreshold values of combined liability make it clear

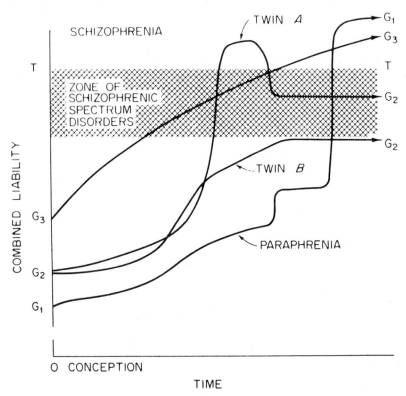

Figure 11. Trajectories over the epigenetic landscape showing the schematic ontogenesis of schizophrenia for different genotypes: (Reprinted by permission from I. I. Gottesman and J. Shields, *Schizophrenia and Genetics: A Twin Study Vantage Point.* New York: Academic Press, 1972.)

why so many first degree relatives can have normal MMPIs (Gottesman & Shields, 1972) and why two phenotypically normal parents are typical for the vast majority of schizophrenics. The A-twin is shown to have an acute onset, an undistinctive premorbid personality, and then a remission from schizophrenia into a chronic schizoid state.

G_3 is the posited trajectory of a person with a high genetic loading needing very little in the way of environmental contributors to make him schizoid; he is shown as having a poor premorbid personality, an insidious onset, and a deteriorating course. Many other life trajectories could have been drawn to illustrate the unfolding of schizophrenia. It is easy to see how the hospitalization data on pairs of twins (Figure 9) and the fascinating histories of the Genain quadruplets (Rosenthal, 1963) would augment the total perspective about the pathogenesis of schizophrenia.

Concluding Remarks

I hope that the diverse subject matter of this paper ranging from Drosophila eye facet number, to height, to milk drinking in rats and in children, to Huntington's disease and schizophrenia will be seen as appropriate for developmental psychology rather than as aimless wandering about the landscape. Heuristic integration is an enormous task and will require teams of scientists who appreciate the contribution each can make to the enterprise of understanding the development of our species. I am pleased that some of my past and present students have chosen to make contributions to the evolving discipline of developmental behavioral genetics (Scarr, 1964; Reppucci, 1968; Nichols, 1970; Arnold, 1971; Lyle, 1972; Hanson, 1974). And soon their present and future students will start to make their presence felt. The opportunities for developmental genetics and developmental psychology to find a happy and fruitful life together are promising. Can I interest you in a match?

References

Arnold, K. Language in schizophrenics and their twins. Unpublished doctoral dissertation, University of Minnesota, 1971.
Bayless, T. M. Milk intolerance: Clinical, developmental, and epidemiological aspects. In I. I. Gottesman & L. L. Heston (Eds.), *Summary of the conference on lactose and milk intolerance*. Washington, D.C.: DHEW publication No. (OCD) 73–19, 1973.
Bleuler, M. *Die schizophrenen Geistesstörungen im Lichte langjähriger Kranken-und Familiengeschichten*. Stuttgart: Thieme, 1972.
Bouchard, T. J. Genetic factors in intelligence. In A. R. Kaplan (Ed.), *Human behavior genetics*. Springfield, Ill.: Thomas, in press.

Britten, R. J., & Davidson, E. H. Gene regulation for higher cells: A theory. *Science*, 1969, 165, 349–357.

Brown, D. D. The isolation of genes. *Scientific American*, 1973, 229, 20–29.

Brozek, J. (Ed.) *The biology of human variation*. New York: New York Academy of Science, 1966.

Darnell, J. E., Jelinek, W. R. & Molloy, G. R. Biogenesis of messenger RNA: Genetic regulation in mammalian cells. *Science*, 1973, 181, 1215–1221.

Dobbing, J. Undernutrition and the developing brain: The use of animal models to elucidate the human problem. In G. B. A. Stoelinga & J. J. Van der Werff ten Bosch (Eds.), *Normal and abnormal development of brain and behavior*. Leiden: Leiden University Press, 1971. Pp. 20–30.

Erlenmeyer-Kimling, L. Gene-environment interactions and the variability of behavior. In L. Ehrman, G. S. Omenn, & E. Caspari, *Genetics, environment, and behavior*. New York: Academic Press, 1972. Pp. 181–208.

Freedman, D. G. *Human infancy: an evolutionary perspective*. New York: Basic Books, 1973.

Fuller, J. L. Physiological and population aspects of behavior genetics. *American Zoologist*, 1964, 4, 101–109.

Fuller, J. L., & Thompson, W. R. *Behavior Genetics*. New York: Wiley, 1960.

Garmezy, N. Children at risk: The search for the antecedents of schizophrenia. *Schizophrenia Bulletin*, 1974, 8, 14–90. (With the collaboration of S. Streitman)

Gottesman, I. I. The psychogenetics of personality. Unpublished doctoral dissertation, University of Minnesota, 1960.

———. Genetic aspects of intelligent behavior. In N. Ellis (Ed.), *The handbook of mental deficiency: Psychological theory and research*. New York: McGraw-Hill, 1963. Pp. 253–296. (a)

———. Heritability of personality: A demonstration. *Psychological Monographs*, 1963, 77 (9, Whole No. 572). Pp. 1–21. (b)

———. Personality and natural selection. In S. Vandenberg (Ed.), *Methods and goals in human behavior genetics*. New York: Academic Press, 1965. Pp. 63–80.

———. Genetic variance in adaptive personality traits. *Journal of Child Psychology and Psychiatry*, 1966, 7, 199–208.

———. Biogenetics of race and class. In M. Deutsch, I. Katz, & A. Jensen (Eds.), *Social class, race, and psychological development*. New York: Holt, 1968. Pp. 11–51.

Gottesman, I. I., & Heston, L. L. Human Behavioral adaptions: Speculations on their genesis. In L. Ehrman, G. S. Omenn, & E. Caspari, *Genetics, environment, and behavior*. New York: Academic Press, 1972. Pp. 106–122.

———. *Summary of the conference on lactose and milk intolerance*. Washington, D.C.: DHEW publication No. (OCD) 73-19, 1973.

Gottesman, I. I., & Shields, J. *Schizophrenia and genetics: A twin study vantage point*. New York: Academic Press, 1972.

Greulich, W. W. A comparison of the physical growth and development of American-born and native Japanese children. *American Journal of Physical Anthropology*, 1957, 15, 489–515.

Hanson, D. R. Children of schizophrenic mothers or fathers compared to children of other psychiatric controls: Their first eight years. Unpublished doctoral dissertation, University of Minnesota, 1974.

Harris, H. *Principles of human biochemical genetics*. Amsterdam: North-Holland, 1970.

Hirsch, J. *Behavior-genetic analysis*. New York: McGraw-Hill, 1967.

Hotta, Y., & Benzer, S. Mapping of behavior in *Drosophila* mosaics. *Nature*, 1972, 240, 527–535.

Jacob, F., & Monod, J. Genetic regulatory mechanisms in the synthesis of proteins. *Journal of Molecular Biology*, 1961, 3, 318–356.

Kety, S. S., Rosenthal, D., Wender, P. H., & Schulsinger, F. The types and prevalence of mental illness in the biological and adoptive families of adopted schizophrenics. In D.

I. I. GOTTESMAN

Rosenthal & S. S. Kety (Eds.), *The transmission of schizophrenia*. Oxford: Pergamon, 1968. Pp. 345–362.

Kety, S. S., Rosenthal, D., Wender, P. H., Schulsinger, F., & Jacobsen, B. Mental illness in the biological and adopted individuals who have become schizophrenic: A preliminary report based upon psychiatric interviews. In R. R. Fieve, H. Brill, & D. Rosenthal (Eds.), *Genetics and psychopathology*. Baltimore: Johns Hopkins Press, 1974.

Kind, H. The psychogenesis of schizophrenia: A review of the literature. *British Journal of Psychiatry*, 1966, 112, 333–349.

Klawans, H. L., Paulson, G. W., Ringel, S. P., & Barbeau, A. Use of l-DOPA in the detection of presymptomatic Huntington's chorea. *New England Journal of Medicine*, 1972, 286, 1332–1334.

Kohn, M. L. Social class and schizophrenia: A critical review and reformulation. *Schizophrenia Bulletin*, 1973, 7, 60–79.

Krafka, J. The effect of temperature upon facet number in the bar-eyed mutant of drosophila. Part I. *Journal of General Physiology*, 1919, 2, 409–432.

Kretchmer, N. Lactose and lactase. *Scientific American*, 1972, 227, 70–78.

Lyle, O. Premorbid psychometric indicators of the gene for Huntington's Disease. Unpublished doctoral dissertation, University of Minnesota, 1972.

Marshall, W. A. Somatic development and the study of the central nervous system. In G. B. A. Stoclinga & J. J. Van der Werff ten Bosch (Eds.), *Normal and abnormal development of brain and behavior*. Leiden: Leiden University Press, 1971. Pp. 1–15.

McClearn, G. E., & DeFries, J. C. *Introduction to behavioral genetics*. San Francisco: Freeman, 1973.

McCracken, R. D. Lactase deficiency: An example of dietary evolution. *Current Anthropology*, 1971, 12, 479–517.

McKusick, V. A. *Mendelian inheritance in man*. (3rd ed.) Baltimore: Johns Hopkins Press, 1971.

Meehl, P. E. A critical afterword. In I. I. Gottesman & J. Shields, *Schizophrenia and genetics: a twin study vantage point*. New York: Academic Press, 1972. Pp. 367–415. (a)

———. Specific genetic etiology, psychodynamics, and therapeutic nihilism. *International Journal of Mental Health*, 1972, 1, 10–27. (b)

———. Why I do not attend case conferences. In P. E. Meehl, *Psychodiagnosis: Selected papers*. Minneapolis: University of Minnesota Press, 1973. Pp. 225–302.

Meissner, W. W. Functional and adaptive aspects of cellular regulatory mechanisms. *Psychological Bulletin*, 1965, 64, 206–216.

Meredith, H. V. Body size of contemporary youth in different parts of the world. *Monographs of the Society for Research in Child Development*, 1969, 34 (7, Ser. No. 131).

Mørch, E. T. Chondrodystrophic dwarfs in Denmark. *Opera Ex Domo Biologiae Hereditarie Humanae Universitatis Hafniensis*, 1941, 3, whole.

Nichols, P. The effects of heredity and environment on intelligence test performance in 4 and 7 year old white and negro sibling pairs. Unpublished doctoral dissertation, University of Minnesota, 1970.

Ohno, S. Gene duplication, mutation load, and mammalian genetic regulatory systems. *Journal of Medical Genetics*, 1972, 9, 254–263.

Paige, D. M., Bayless, T. M., Ferry, G. D., & Graham, G. G. Lactose malabsorption and milk rejection in Negro children. *Johns Hopkins Medical Journal*, 1971, 129, 163–169.

Pearson, J. S., & Kley, I. B. On the application of genetic expectancies as age specific base rates in the study of human behavior disorders. *Psychological Bulletin*, 1957, 54, 406–420.

Repucci, C. M. Hereditary influences upon distribution of attention in infancy. Unpublished doctoral dissertation, Harvard University, 1968.

Rosenthal, D. (Ed.), and Colleagues. *The Genain quadruplets*. New York: Basic Books, 1963.

Rosenthal, D., Wender, P. H., Kety, S. S., Schulsinger, F., Welner, J., & Østergaard, L. Schizophrenics' offspring reared in adoptive homes. In D. Rosenthal & S. S. Kety (Eds.), *The transmission of schizophrenia*. Oxford: Pergamon, 1968. Pp. 377–391.

Scarr, S. Genetics and human motivation. Unpublished doctoral dissertation, Harvard University, 1964.

Scharfetter, C. On the hereditary aspects of symbiontic psychoses—a contribution towards the understanding of the schizophrenia-like psychoses. *Psychiatria Clinica*, 1970, 3, 145–152.

Schofield, W. & Balian, L. A comparative study of the personal histories of schizophrenics and non-psychiatric patients. *Journal of Abnormal and Social Psychology*, 1959, 59, 216–225.

Schuham, A. I. The double-bind hypothesis a decade later. *Psychological Bulletin*, 1967, 68, 409–416.

Shields, J., Heston, L. L., & Gottesman, I. I. Schizophrenia and the schizoid: The problem for genetic analysis. In R. R. Fieve, H. Brill, & D. Rosenthal (Eds.), *Genetics and psychopathology*. Baltimore: Johns Hopkins Press, 1974.

Stern, C. *Principles of human genetics*. (3rd ed.) San Francisco: Freeman, 1973.

Tanner, J. M. Physical growth. In P. H. Mussen (Ed.), *Carmichael's manual of child psychology*. (3rd ed.) New York: Wiley, 1970. Pp. 77–155.

Tanner, J. M., Whitehouse, R. H., & Takaishi, M. Standards from birth to maturity for height, weight, height velocity, and weight velocity: British children 1965. *Archives of Disease in Childhood*, 1966, 41, 454–471, 613–635.

Thiessen, D. D. *Gene organization and behavior*. New York: Random House, 1972.

Tomkins, G. M., Gelehrter, T. D., Granner, D., Martin, D., Jr., Samuels, H. H., & Thompson, E. B. Control of specific gene expression in higher organisms. *Science*, 1969, 166, 1474–1480.

Waddington, C. H. *The Strategy of the Genes*. London: Allen & Unwin, 1957.

Watson, J. D., & Crick, F. H. C. Genetic implications of the structure of deoxyribonucleic acid. *Nature*, 1953, 171, 964–967.

Winick, M. Cellular growth in intrauterine malnutrition. *Pediatric Clinics of North America*, 1970, 17, 69–78.

Wright, S. The results of crosses between inbred strains of guinea pigs, differing in number of digits. *Genetics*, 1934, 19, 537–551.

+ P. HERBERT LEIDERMAN AND GLORIA F. LEIDERMAN +

Affective and Cognitive Consequences of Polymatric Infant Care in the East African Highlands

TO STIMULATE a lively discussion in the field of early child development, mention the topic of mothering. The interchange is certain to range from primate behaviors to day care centers and more recently to cross-cultural comparative studies. Our contribution to this discourse will be to report on the effects of monomatric (single caretaker) and polymatric (multiple caretaker) caretaking systems on the affective and cognitive development of the infant in an East African community where both systems are part of the cultural norm.

In the majority of studies on infant affective development (Gewirtz, 1972) and cognitive development (Freeberg & Payne, 1967) the mother-infant dyad within the nuclear family structure has been assumed to be the primary unit for caretaking and social interaction. Although findings from these studies have greatly elucidated our understanding of infant social development, and to a lesser extent of cognitive development, the implicit attitudinal set has placed the nuclear family as the standard for mother-infant relationships.

NOTE: This research was supported by a Carnegie Foundation grant to Professor John Whiting, Harvard University, and by a Grant Foundation grant to Professor P. H. Leiderman, Stanford University. This paper was written while the first author was a fellow at The Center for Advanced Study in the Behavioral Sciences and a recipient of a Guggenheim fellowship.

We wish to thank Dr. Helena C. Kraemer for statistical analyses, Barbara Andersen, Adrienne Lindstrom, and Rosalind Revell for research assistance, and Tome Tanisawa and Joan Warmbrunn for typing the manuscript. We are particularly grateful to Beatrice Babu for infant testing, Violet Gatheru, Eunice Mutero, Arthur Ngiritta, Florence Mbogua, and Irene Kamau for data collection. Our special appreciation goes to Professors John and Beatrice Whiting who in many ways made this study possible.

81

Other mother care systems are frequently seen as deleterious, perhaps because they are interpreted through the perceptual schema of a behavioral scientist who was reared in a nuclear family. Since the ontogeny of early development plays an important role in many psychological and psychiatric theories, studies of this early period are critical. Given the ethical limitations on experimental manipulations of the family and of the mother in the human infant's earliest years, an obvious alternative is to examine societies where both monomatric and polymatric maternal care systems are part of the cultural norm. This comparative approach, though sacrificing some of the rigor and precision of the laboratory, gains credence through the relevance of the naturalistic setting.

Despite the possible bias among investigators toward a monomatric caretaking system, there is considerable documentation of wide variation in the mother-infant caretaking arrangements in the infant's first year. Minturn and Lambert (1964) described wide variations in the amount of time a mother spends with her infant. For the United States middle-class sample, 92 percent of the mothers usually or always cared for their infants. For the East African agricultural community sample, only 38 percent of the mothers were the usual caretakers of their infants. In social groups such as the hunting and gathering tribe of bushmen reported by Konner (1972), the mother-infant relationship might be extremely close for as long as the infant's first three years of life.

More important than the mother's sheer physical presence with her infant is the question of her role in the caretaking system during the infant's first year. Clearly she is responsible for the infant's physical care—feeding him, cleaning him, and otherwise protecting him from the dangers of the physical and social environment. Beyond this, she is assumed to be the chief agent for establishing social relationships. Undoubtedly she is the first person with whom he establishes a social bond; the intensity of this social bond depends in large part on the rapidity and appropriateness of her ministrations in meeting his physical and social needs. It is further assumed that the infant constructs the schemata of his social world through contact with his mother, although the development of social interactions such as smiling, social vocalizations, and visual attentiveness to familiar figures is not totally dependent upon the mother's physical caretaking.

In the monomatric family the mother is certainly the main purveyor of physical and social stimuli. Her manner of caretaking makes it virtually impossible to separate the physical from the social stimuli; thus she becomes the sole central figure in the life of the infant. If we examine polymatric systems, on the other hand, we may find two or more individuals providing both physical and social care to the infant—for example, in a residential nursery in the United States and Europe. Or we may find that although the mother remains the primary agent for meeting the physical needs of the infant, another individual meets his social needs. It is this latter circumstance, typical of many societies in which the mother has multiple tasks in addition to infant care, that characterizes the polymatric caretaking system described in this study.

This split between physical caretaking and social interaction cannot be absolute. Rather, it is a function of the mother's economic and social responsibilities within the family. In many agricultural communities, especially those in sub-Saharan Africa, the mother has the major responsibility for the physical care of the infant. However, the social and other daytime care is delegated to other individuals while the mother does the farm work essential for providing the family's food supply. Because her contact with the infant is primarily concerned with his physical needs, she has time to devote to satisfying the economic needs of the entire family. The remaining caretaking, frequently done by others, includes some physical care, but primarily involves social relationships with the infant, such as talking to him, carrying him, and distracting or comforting him when he cries.

Much of the theory construction on the development of social relationships assumes that a single person is responsible for the social, emotional, and physical development of the infant, at least in his first year. But what is the effect on the infant if his social needs and physical needs are met by two individuals rather than by a single mother? A society in which these functions are separated naturally allows us the opportunity to establish the relative contribution of each source of caretaking to the affective and cognitive development of the child. Therefore one of the issues that we will examine in this study is the contribution of individuals other than the mother to the infant's social development, i.e., to his social bonding in the first year of life. The second issue we will examine is the effects of these multiple caretaking arrangements on the infant's cognitive development, particularly on his social responsiveness and on his achievement of object permanence.

THE COMMUNITY

The study was conducted over a one-year period, 1969–70, in an East African agricultural village undergoing rapid transition to a modern cash economy. The village is a Kikuyu-speaking community of 4,500 individuals, located about 25 miles from the urban center of Nairobi in the Kenya highlands at an elevation of approximately 7,500 feet. The highlands, extending northward from Nairobi, consist of gently rolling hills and ridges, covered with a luxuriant foliage of trees, shrubs, and grass nourished by 35 inches or more of rain per year. The area, formerly heavily forested, has largely been cleared. Rows of trees or shrubs now mark the limits of rectangular plots of land.

The village covers an area of about ten square miles and is approximately four miles from the nearest paved road which leads to Nairobi. There are clay or dirt roads into the village which are frequently impassable during the two rainy seasons (April through June and October and November). The village center is located about three miles from the area of the Kenya highlands settled by the British. (This proximity has had some influence on the village itself, although the British community has been, and remains, oriented toward Nairobi.) The village center consists of a market and a meeting place, surrounded by a series of small shops in well-constructed stone buildings. A variety of staple goods is sold in most of these shops although specialized services, such as tinsmithing, bicycle repair, and tailoring are offered in some shops. Several small restaurants, selling tea, beer, and food, serve as social centers for the men.

Three sections within the community were identified on the basis of distance from village center, type of family structure, and size of family plots of land. The first section is nearest to the village center and consists of small households on small plots of land usually less than one acre in size. Most of the rectangular houses are made of rough-sawn lumber and have tin roofs: there are, however, some more modern houses and a few traditional Kikuyu houses, circular, thatch-roofed, and made of mud and wattle wood. Households in this central section are located on small lanes and paths running parallel to the larger dirt roads. The homes are partially screened by trees and cannot be seen from the roads, but the families are within hearing distance of one another. Some of the families in this central section have plots of land adjacent to their houses, but many other families have small plots a distance away. The major crops are maize, beans, and millet. A few chickens are kept and, very rarely, a cow.

The second section of the community consists of traditional Kikuyu compounds, typically occupied by polygamous families. Here the traditional circular houses are generally arranged in groups of four or five on two to four acre plots of land. Families in this section have sufficient acreage to keep

84

cows and chickens, and they have more land on which to grow staple crops than those families in the village center.

The third section of the community is made up of families living in rectangular houses of somewhat better construction than the houses in the village center. The plots of land are generally larger than two acres. Like the families in the traditional compounds, several of these families have outbuildings for storing maize. Frequently, adjoining plots belong to members of the same lineage. Most of the individuals in this section, therefore, have extended family relationships, with relatives living in houses on the same plot of land or houses on separate, but contiguous, plots.

The predominant household arrangement was monogamous—there were only nine polygamous families. Monomatric and polymatric caretaking arrangements existed throughout the community regardless of the economic level of the family, the place of residence, or the household arrangement. Although there are economic and status differences within the community,. these differences are not related to place of residence, to educational level of the father, or to the degree of acceptance of modern attitudes.

None of the homes had electricity or cement floors at the time of the study. There were only four private vehicles within the community, none of them owned by individuals in the study. There was one telephone located in the village center. Contact with outside communities was made most frequently by walking, although there was bus service available to Nairobi several times a day from the village center.

Water within the village can be bought at one of two pumps or taken from a nearby river. Families with greater economic resources are able to obtain tin rain barrels in which to collect water from their roofs, thereby saving the cost of water from the pumps. Some families are affluent enough to have taps in their home compounds. Fuel for cooking and heating is the responsibility of the women in the household. Sometimes accompanied by young daughters, they walk from one to five miles several times a week to cut wattle trees and to carry the loads of wood to their homes. However, families with sufficient cash resources can purchase fuel from "charcoal burners" who deliver to the village center or, in some instances, directly to the homes.

The cash crop consists mainly of pyrethrum, which is grown cooperatively within the community. A few families keep enough chickens so that they can sell eggs commercially, although none of the families in the sample did so on a large scale. A few families who have cows are able to sell surplus milk to a milk cooperative.

Health services are provided within the village by a mobile health team which comes once a week from a distant community. More frequently, health care is obtained at a community health center manned by a medical assistant; this center is located five miles away and is reached by walking. Our research project provided medical attention one-half day per week to family members of the infants who constituted the sample.

The sample consisted of 67 infants and their mothers. Originally 90 families were selected from an estimated population of 100 families to whom infants were born during the period of 1 July to 31 December 1969. Eighteen infants were used as controls for another study and will not be described. Five infants were lost to the study either when their families moved away or after they missed two or more tests or interviews.

Information about the families was obtained by two female University of Nairobi undergraduate students, fluent in Kikuyu and English, who interviewed mothers and who made observations in the homes. Ethnographic data were collected about both the mother and father, including age, education, current employment, household density, and economic resources available to the family. In addition, observations were made to determine the presence in the home of modern amenities such as calendars, books, and playthings.

The demographic description in Table 1 shows that the group is relatively diverse in terms of age, education, household arrangements, amount of land, occupation, languages spoken, and contact with urban centers. All individuals in the sample were members of the Kikuyu tribe. Approximately two-thirds of the sample were identified with three lineages residing within the community; all nine of the traditional Kikuyu clans were represented by either the mother or the father of the infant. All of the adults in the sample were acquainted with the senior investigators, were volunteers to the study, and understood that we were interested in how children grow and develop. Most of the men and about half of the women had lived in the community since it moved from a former site one mile away at the end of the "Mau Mau rebellion" in 1958.

It is useful, in understanding the results, to be familiar with a typical day for mother, caretaker, and infant in this village. The activity of the vast majority of women centers on the household, the agricultural fields, the

Table 1. Demographic Description of the Sample

Parent Data			Family Data		
Variable	Mother	Father	Variable		Household
Age	(N = 67)	(N = 57)	*Years married*		(N = 59)
15–19	01%	—	Unmarried		08%
20–29	46	17	1–4		22
30–39	37	39	5–9		25
>39	16	44	10–14		17
Birth order	(N = 66)	(N = 58)	15–19		10
1	11%	23%	20–24		10
2	18	24	>25		08
3	27	17	*Family structure*		(N = 65)
4	18	16	Monogamous		68%
5–6	20	17	Nuclear	32	
7–8	06	03	Paternal	29	
Education:			Maternal	07	
Highest grade completed	(N = 67)	(N = 57)	Polygamous		12
None	42%	19%	Divorced, separated,		
1–3	16	14	widowed		12
4–6	18	14	Unmarried		08
7–8	12	41	*Children in family*		(N = 67)
>8 (Teacher or technical	12	12	Study child only		18%
training)			2		16
Language spoken	(N = 66)	(N = 59)	3		10
Kikuyu only	37%	14%	4		12
Kikuyu and Swahili	29	27	5		12
Kikuyu and English	02	00	6		10
Kikuyu, Swahili and	32	59	7		06
English			>7		16
Church membership	(N = 65)	(N = 59)	*Land owned*		(N = 58)
Presbyterian	44%	29%	None		14%
Baptist	06	05	<1.9 acres		43
Catholic	19	16	2–3.9 acres		29
Anglican	11	13	4–9.9 acres		07
African Greek Orthodox	18	10	>10 acres		07
None	02	27	*Occupation of father*		(N = 58)
Nairobi travel	(N = 63)	(N = 56)	Job with salary (trained)		42%
Daily	03%	55%	Job with salary (nontrained)		09
Weekly	11	11	Business		09
Monthly	38	14	Part-time work		02
Yearly	35	09	Subsistence farmer, <2 acres		14
Never	13	11	Subsistence farmer, 2–4 acres		06
			Subsistence farmer, >4 acres		04
			Unemployed		14
			Educational material:		
			(books, magazines or		
			newspapers)		(N = 67)
			None		24%
			1		12
			2		07
			>2		57

market, and, on weekends, the church. Typically, a woman arises before dawn, kindles the fire, and prepares food for the day. The food consists of ground maize, millet, and occasionally beans, served with hot tea mixed with milk and sweetened with sugar. The food prepared in the morning often satisfies the family's needs for the entire day. In a home with an infant, the mother nurses him while she goes about her household tasks. Frequently by 6:30 or 7:00 A.M. she is on the road, with or without her infant, to fetch water or wood. Usually an older daughter, ranging in age from five to thirteen years, accompanies the mother to cut wood and carry water. If the infant accompanies his mother, he is usually strapped on her back with two towels, and his head is covered or uncovered depending upon the weather. On the return journey the infant is carried against the mother's chest or strapped on the daughter's back.

When the mother goes to the fields to cultivate her crops or to perform other seasonal tasks, young girls, and occasionally young boys, assist her. Whether the mother takes her infant to the field depends upon the infant's age, the season of the year, the availability of a caretaker, and, perhaps, the mother's inclination. Usually the mother regularly takes her infant to the fields until he is three or four months of age. She may have a caretaker with her to watch the infant while she works, but she stops her work to nurse him. In the early afternoons she frequently returns home to manage the affairs of the other children and to proceed with household tasks such as grinding maize, washing clothes, or directing the older children in household chores. On occasion the infant is left at home; if the mother has to work the entire day, she will come home at least once during the day to observe her infant.

At the end of the day, mother and children gather for an early evening meal consisting of maize and millet prepared in the morning, as well as hot tea and milk. In the evening the husband may spend time with the mother and children, or he may prefer to socialize with his male friends in the village center.

Most families retire fairly early, frequently shortly after dusk. The infant sleeps with his mother, and the other young children sleep either in special places within the hut or very near the mother. Depending on the size of the house, the arrangement of the other household buildings, and the observation of traditional practices by the family, the husband may sleep in a separate hut or in a separate room within the family hut. Older boys sleep in separate huts or in their father's room if there are no separate sleeping quarters.

Two days a week the mother visits the central market within the village or, if she has a large amount of produce to sell, she may go to a more distant market. The market, of course, provides the opportunity for socializing with other women as well as for commercial transactions. Frequently the infant accompanies the mother. On journeys to a more distant market, an older sibling accompanies the mother to help carry the infant, or else the infant is left at home with a caretaker.

If the mother holds a position outside the household, the routine is different. Such a woman may be a nursery school teacher or she may work in a shop in the village center. She leaves the infant at home with a caretaker and returns at midday to take care of him. These women tend to be among the more educated women of the community and, hence, are less involved than are older women with the traditional practices of the community. Even though these women are away from home during much of the day, they spend considerable time with their children and husbands when at home. Husbands of these women generally have cash incomes. Although these men may not spend more time with their children during the day than do other fathers, they may very well do so in the evening.

The person who cares for the infant and assists the mother is important for the infant. Typically the mother's principal helper is a young girl aged seven to twelve years; occasionally the helper is a young adolescent, and rarely the helper is a male sibling or a paternal grandmother living in the household. Characteristically the young caretaker is an older sister of the infant, but if no older female siblings are available, children are recruited from the mother's natal family or from other families in the village. Usually the caretaker has completed two years of "nursery school" by the age of about eight years. If fortunate, she might also have had from three to five years of primary school by the age of eleven or twelve years. Her education is typically terminated by lack of funds or lack of family interest in educating its female members. The caretaker is usually old enough to know the responsibilities of the household, yet she is young enough to want to be included in the children's games and activities. On a typical day she gets up with the mother and helps with household activities. She frequently accompanies the mother to collect fuel and water, usually taking responsibility for the infant on the journey. If needed, she accompanies the mother to the fields where she assists in cultivating and planting or cares for the child while the mother performs chores. If the young girl is left at home to care for the infant, she is solely responsible for his care. She provides food if the infant is old enough to take supplemental food, or, if he is still nursing, she carries him to the mother in the fields. The young caretaker may watch the infant extremely carefully, or she may do so in a desultory manner, giving in to the temptation of playing with her friends and siblings while overseeing his activities. However, most caretakers take their responsibilities very seriously, and many are genuinely interested in playing with and caring for the young infants.

For the infant, his first year is the halcyon period of his life. He spends the first four months in almost constant contact with his mother. He is fed on demand; he accompanies her on journeys; he sleeps with her; and he is comforted at night by the warmth of her body. By the time the infant is four months old, he has seen or heard most of the activities in the household and has been stimulated tactually and kinesthetically when he is carried by his mother and by his many siblings. He probably has not had much social interaction with his mother, at least in the form of verbal communication, but has probably had considerable interaction with his siblings and with other children. His father has probably looked at him but has not held him nor played with him, although this pattern may be changing as fathers in the more modern group take a more direct interest in their infants.

By four months of age, the infant has been introduced to his caretaker. By five to six months he may be with her almost half of the day, although for much of that time the caretaker might be distracted by playmates and/or household chores. The mother continues to nurse him on demand but occasionally she will not be available immediately, so he is fed other foods or must wait to be nursed. By six or seven months of age he is allowed greater freedom. He is put on the ground to play, and he usually crawls by seven to eight months and he walks by ten to twelve months. The mother is still an important figure in his life, although she clearly shares his caretaking with other individuals. During the latter part of the infant's first year, his caretaker and other siblings become increasingly important in his social life. Routine caretaking is still the responsibility of the mother, but for many other activities he is cared for by others, under the direct supervision of a caretaker and the indirect supervision of his mother.

There is considerable variation in the amount of time and attention the infant receives from other family members. Generally the father remains only distantly involved. Although children are highly prized both for themselves and for the social status they may bring to their parents, the weight of tradition and outside obligations limit direct contact between father and infant during the first year.

P. HERBERT LEIDERMAN

The Effect of Differential Roles on the
Attachment Behavior of Infants

Since Bowlby first wrote about attachment (1952, 1958), the concept of attachment has intrigued both clinically and experimentally oriented behavioral scientists. The concept was derived from clinical psychoanalysis and from behavioral ethology, but it is relevant also for laboratory studies done by experimental child psychologists. The attachment concept is summarized in several excellent reviews (Ainsworth, 1969; Maccoby & Masters, 1970) and is elaborated in two volumes by Bowlby (1969, 1973). Is there more to say? The reply is yes, if we are to answer questions raised about attachment by Rutter (1972). One such question concerns the primacy of the mother in the initial attachment relationship and in the subsequent development of the infant's attachment to other individuals.

Bowlby and Ainsworth rely on a maturational model in discussing the concept of attachment. Attachment is said to unfold as part of a maturational process which has been biologically selected for in mammals and in certain avian species, thereby insuring the survival of the individual and of the species. To the extent that social learning occurs during this early period, it affects only the details of the fundamental attachment process. Bowlby describes attachment as a species specific response, initially relatively independent of physiological requirements, whose function is to promote social interaction between members of a species. Ainsworth (1972) further elucidated the concept by describing attachment behavior as that behavior promoting proximity to, or interaction with, a particular object of attachment. Thus she implied that the initial attachment is primarily to an individual although there is no reason why attachment cannot occur with more than one individual. It may be that the initial attachment of the infant to his mother is part of a maturational process, whereas attachment to other individuals occurs as a result of learning at an appropriate time in the course of cognitive development. Whatever the mechanism for establishing attachment to the primary and secondary individuals, in the Bowlby and Ainsworth formulations attachment to the primary individual is necessary for subsequent attachment to other individuals. Thus they view the mother as a central figure in attachment formation, and subsidiary attachment by the infant to others occurs in relationship to this primary figure. Support for this proposition comes from observations made of Western European and North American middle-class families in which the mother is the exclusive caretaker and has

91

the opportunity to devote herself almost exclusively to this caretaking relationship. There is also some support for this formulation from observations in societies in which caretaking is shared with others in the infant's first year, for example in the Israeli kibbutz. However, even in that society, the mother probably has a central role in the life of the infant, and her role is supplemented by the daily caretaking provided by the surrogate mother in the nursery.

Sears (1972), in separating attachment from nurturance and dependency, argued that the following conditions are required for attachment formation: maturation of a specific genetic propensity; consistent and definitive expression of love by caretaker; and development of the discrimination of the caretaker from other persons. Although the genetic component is difficult to quantify, this argument follows Bowlby's biologically based thesis that attachment functions as protection (initially from predators and more recently from other dangers that threaten man) since attachment insures proximity to a protecting and caretaking agent. Sears's last two conditions—consistent expression of love by the caretaker and the development of discrimination of the caretaker from other persons—relate to Ainsworth's formulation that the human infant's behavior is adapted to the mother who is continuously nearby and who is responsive to his signals.

According to the above formulations, we might expect an infant's attachment to be different when there are multiple caretakers. Several questions arise. Will the attachment to the mother who shares caretaking differ from attachment to the mother who is the exclusive caretaker? Is attachment different when the caretaking function is undertaken by two individuals, one of whom meets the infant's physical needs and the other who meets his social needs? Will relative inconsistency of care, as might occur with multiple caretakers, influence the infant's response to other, noncaretaking individuals in his environment?

To determine the influence of monomatric and polymatric caretaking arrangements on social development, it was necessary to establish an index of monomatry and polymatry for our sample. All families in the sample were classified as either monomatric, mixed, or polymatric, on the basis of the percentage of observations in which mothers were found to be the principal caretakers of the infant. These observations of caretaking were made periodically during the daylight hours over a nine-month period, following a procedure suggested by Munroe and Munroe (1971). A minimum of 8 and a maximum of 23 observations were made for each family. During these five-minute observations, the presence or absence of the mother and/or other caretaker and the behavior of these individuals in relation to the infant were noted. Observers recorded whether or not the infant was awake or asleep; whether he was being carried or held; whether he was lying down or sitting alone; whether he was being fed, talked to, or played with; and whether he was relatively isolated or was near other individuals.

In the monomatric group, the mother was the principal caretaker in over 75 percent of the observations; in the mixed group, in 50 to 75 percent of the observations; and in the polymatric group, in less than 50 percent of the observations. In the mixed group there was usually one other caretaker in addition to the mother; in the polymatric group there were at least two other caretakers, with one clearly predominant. As is shown in Figure 1, by the time the infants were five months of age, the mothers in the sample carried out about 50 percent of the caretaking, young females 10 to 50 percent, and males about 10 percent.

Although there is no unanimity on the best indexes of attachment, there is consensus that attachment exists when the infant strives to establish or maintain proximity to a single individual. The stage of the infant's development dictates the behaviors that serve as indexes of attachment. For example, before the infant is mobile, behaviors such as smiling, crying, and reaching out are believed to draw the mother or mother surrogate closer to the infant. After the infant is mobile, these behaviors are supplemented by movements of the infant toward the preferred or attached individual.

Since, as Masters and Wellman (1973) have demonstrated, no single set of behaviors can be used to index attachment (especially when these behaviors vary with the age of the infant), we decided to use as an indicator the infant's affective response to his mother, to a caretaker, and to a stranger. By using the affective response, we were able to make comparisons across situations and at various ages, regardless of whether the child was mobile. The affective response also has the advantage of summarizing the positive and negative feelings of the infant in any given situation. However, our index does have disadvantages: individual differences and the fine details of attachment may be obscured. The possibility that some negative affect may actually indicate positive attachment of the infant may also be obscured. This is especially true in older infants after prolonged absence of the mother, though it is a less likely possibility in the age range of the infants in this study.

We assessed two aspects of the strength of attachment. First, we assessed the ability of the infant to differentiate the attachment figure from all other

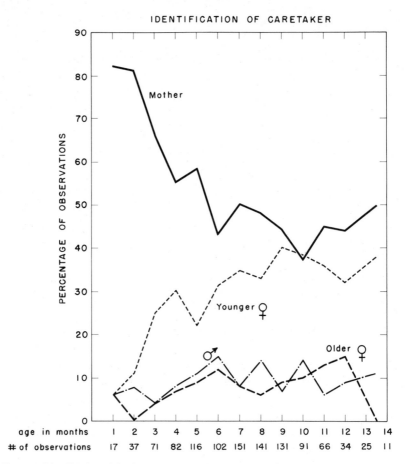

Figure 1. Identification of daytime caretaker during the infant's first year.

nonattached individuals. If the attached object is not discriminated, attachment cannot be presumed. Therefore we assessed attachment to the mother by comparing the infant's response to her, to the caretaker, and to a stranger. This is termed the recognition situation.

The second aspect of attachment we measured was the infant's reaction in a stressful situation. We assumed that a provocative and threatening situation would enable us to distinguish an infant's response more clearly than would his response in a mildly stressful recognition situation (approach reaction). The stressful situation used was the departure and brief absence of the mother,

94

a caretaker, or a stranger. This second situation is termed the absence situation (departure reaction).

Recognition and absence situations were arranged as follows: the initial approach was by a stranger, a college-age Kikuyu woman, while the infant was seated in his mother's lap in front of the homestead. The female stranger slowly approached the infant, making certain that the infant was looking at her. At a distance of approximately ten feet from the infant, she would pause for about ten seconds while an observer recorded the infant's reaction. (The observer was situated so that the infant could not see her.) The stranger then moved closer, stopping immediately in front of the infant, smiling, and calling out his name. The infant's response to this event was recorded. The stranger then touched the infant and continued to talk and smile. Again the infant's reaction was recorded. The stranger then offered to pick up the infant, and the mother presented the infant to the stranger. With the stranger holding the infant, the mother then said good-by and went behind the house out of the infant's sight, where she remained for about two minutes while the infant's responses were recorded. The mother then returned and went through the same series of maneuvers as had the stranger. At the end of the sequence, she received the infant and the stranger departed. At another time, usually one to two weeks later, a different stranger and the caretaker, if one was present in the family, would go through the same sequence.

Comparison of the infant's responses to the stranger, mother, and caretaker in the approach and absence situation constitutes the basic data for the assessment of attachment. The behaviors recorded included smiling, laughing, joyous movements, neutral staring, frowning, turning away, crying, or no reaction. These behaviors were coded into positive and negative scores for each infant in the approach and in the absence situation. These scores were algebraically added across infants for the monomatric and polymatric groups. Each infant was tested at least once during each of two age periods, seven to nine months and ten to twelve months. To simplify the presentation of data, only the scores for the monomatric and polymatric groups are presented here, leaving aside the mixed group.

The results are shown in Figure 2 and Table 2. In the approach situation, we found that mothers and caretakers are reacted to similarly in both the monomatric and polymatric groups by infants at both seven to nine months and ten to twelve months. As measured by their affective responses, infants apparently do not differentiate between two caretaking figures as long as they

95

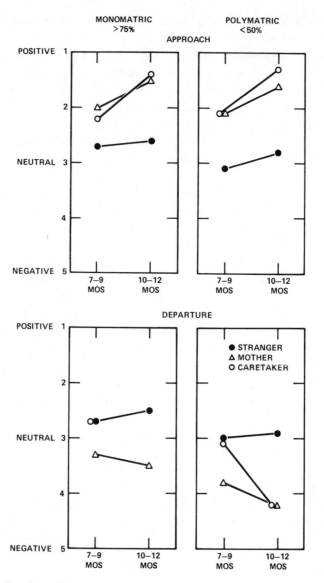

Figure 2. The effect of the caretaking arrangement on the infant's attachment behavior.

Table 2. Reactions of Infants to Stranger, Mother, and Caretaker

| | Aged 7 to 9 months | | Aged 10 to 12 months | |
	Monomatric Group	Polymatric Group	Monomatric Group	Polymatric Group
Approach reaction to:	*Mean*	*Mean*	*Mean*	*Mean*
Stranger	2.8 (N = 15)	3.3 (N = 13)	2.7 (N = 17)	3.0 (N = 19)
Mother	2.1 (N = 14)	2.3 (N = 9)	1.6 (N = 18)	1.8 (N = 18)
Caretaker	2.3 (N = 4)	2.3 (N = 5)	1.5 (N = 5)	1.5 (N = 14)
Departure reaction to:				
Stranger	2.7 (N = 14)	3.0 (N = 10)	2.5 (N = 21)	2.9 (N = 26)
Mother	3.3 (N = 13)	3.8 (N = 10)	3.5 (N = 17)	4.2 (N = 18)
Caretaker	2.7 (N = 3)	3.1 (N = 5)		4.2 (N = 9)

Scale: Lifts arms to be picked up	Smiles, joyous movements	Indifferent or staring	Frowns, restless	Turns away or buries face
1	1	1	1	1
1	2	3	4	5
Positive		Neutral		Negative

have had previous experience with them. We conclude that infants form attachments to more than one individual—a finding that is consistent with the observations of Schaffer and Emerson (1964) and of Ainsworth (1967).

The reactions to the stranger differ for the two groups (p.<.05, Mann-Whitney U-Test, two-tailed) in that infants in the polymatric group react more negatively than do infants in the monomatric group. This result suggests that polymatry is associated with more apprehensive infants. This apprehensiveness, perhaps equivalent to the attachment insecurity described by Ainsworth, provides some support for the position that polymatry leads to greater insecurity in infants. This insecurity is not obvious when the infant is observed with familiar figures but becomes apparent when a potentially threatening stimulus, an adult stranger, comes into the infant's environment.

When the response to a stranger was compared with the response to the caretaker and to the mother, we found the reaction to the stranger to be more negative (p.<.02, Mann-Whitney U-Test, two-tailed). However, the infant's responses on the affect scale were neutral or only slightly negative. The absence of a more negative response should not be surprising, since the stranger was superficially quite similar to the mother and caretaker and since she approached the infant in a manner not likely to alarm him. Although there have been other reports on positive responses to strangers (Greenberg, Hillman, & Rice, 1973) at eight months of age, neutral or positive responses to strangers can best be understood if they are compared with responses to familiar individuals.

The fact that the infant's response to the mother, the caretaker, and the stranger was more positive at the older age for both the monomatric and polymatric groups might suggest that the infant became more comfortable in the test situation with increasing familiarity; he was not necessarily better able to discriminate among the three individuals.

The results for the departure situation are shown in Table 2 and Figure 2. The data on caretakers are incomplete for the monomatric group in which there were too few caretakers to support the data analysis. The infant reacts to the stranger's departure either neutrally or slightly positively in both the monomatric and polymatric groups. Mother absence is reacted to more negatively by the polymatric group than by the monomatric group ($p < .05$, Mann-Whitney U-Test, two-tailed), a finding consistent with that for the approach situations. These findings suggest that the polymatric infants may be less secure than infants in the monomatric group.

In the polymatric group, the comparison of the infant's reactions to the caretaker and to the mother is particularly interesting because his response to the caretaker's absence at seven to nine months was similar to his response to a stranger's absence, whereas at ten to twelve months it was similar to his response to the mother's departure. Since we know from the approach situation that the infant was able to discriminate between the caretaker and the stranger at seven to nine months, his similar response to the absence of the caretaker and of the stranger at seven to nine months indicates that he has interpreted the meaning of the mother's absence to be different from that of the caretaker and the stranger. It appears that the infant has placed the stranger and the caretaker in one category. At ten to twelve months, the infant's response to the caretaker's absence is similar to that of the mother's absence, the mother and the caretaker now being placed in the same category. This result indicates that the infant has assimilated the meaning of absence to include individuals other than the mother, a result entirely consistent with the postulated process of assimilation and accommodation occurring at this stage of development.

The Effect of the Differential Roles on the Cognitive Behavior of Infants

Although there has been considerable interest (Freeberg & Payne, 1967) in the influence of parents on children's cognitive development, there are very few papers (Kohen-Raz, 1968) addressed to the effects of polymatric care on cognitive development.

In the nuclear family with a single caretaker, routine caretaking and social stimulation are normally provided by a single individual. In the polymatric family, routine caretaking and social stimulation are provided by several individuals, though the responsibilities are not equally divided. The mother is likely to be responsible for routine care while others engage in social interaction with the infant. The question then is whether single or multiple forms of caretaking have different effects on the cognitive development of the infant.

According to Piaget (1951, 1969), no initial perceptual behavior—visual or auditory—is a simple act. Each perception is an assimilating activity, susceptible to practice or repetition and, therefore, to recognition and generalization. This formulation suggests that if the mother is consistently the agent of interaction with the infant, recognition and generalization may be more limited than if there were more than one primary caretaker. This would be especially true if the mother involves herself primarily in the feeding and basic physical care of the infant. These interactions would certainly elicit appropriate attachment responses but could have a limiting effect on the infant's cognitive development, especially if the variations and the perceptions of the infant are limited. This perceptual narrowing would be especially heightened if the mother must do many other jobs in addition to infant caretaking. With an additional caretaker, the infant is exposed to greater variation in perceptions and interactions and in the giving and receiving of stimuli. This increased interaction with another individual, we assume, enhances his cognitive development. Therefore, we expect that infants in monomatric homes will perform less well in psychological testing than will infants provided with two or more individual caretakers.

Infant test performance was assessed by the Bayley Test of Infant Development (Bayley, 1969) given in a standardized form by a Kenyan nurse trained for that purpose. Because of the previous finding (Leiderman, Babu, Kagia, Kraemer, & Leiderman, 1973) that the economic level of the family is related to the performance of the infant on mental and motor tests, familial economic level was considered in analyzing the data. Therefore, each of the three groups—polymatric, monomatric and mixed—was further subdivided on the basis of the familial economic level. This level was determined by rating each family on a summary score of the important economic indexes in this community. These indexes are: the amount of land owned by the family, the number of cows and chickens that the family owns, the source of water, and the presence or absence of a cash income. (Designation of families as upper and lower economic level does not imply social class differences as we know them in Western societies. It should be obvious that the Western concept of social class is not directly applicable to non-Western societies.)

The tests were given to the infants at approximately two-month intervals. Reliability of scoring test performance between the investigators and the tester reached 85 percent agreement on the final two of ten pretest infants. Sixty-five of the 67 infants in the study had at least four tests; the other two had three tests. To avoid the possibility of spurious test scores if United States standards were used as a reference, a Kenya standard curve was calculated, based on all tests given to all infants in this study. Each individual infant test score was then related to the Kenya standard with the arbitrary mean set at 100 and a standard deviation of 16. All scores reported in this paper refer to the "Kenya norm." (It has been shown elsewhere, [Leiderman et al., 1973] that this Kenya norm exceeds United States norms for both mental and motor test performance in the infant's first year.) For the 65 infants who were tested four times, the scores on all tests were combined to yield a single score, thus reducing the amount of variability between tests.

The results are shown in Table 3. Birth order and education of the father did not differ statistically between the groups and therefore do not appear in the table. The age of the mother varied from 25.8 years in the monomatric low economic group to 34.9 in the polymatric high economic group. The mothers' education did not differ significantly between groups. The economic level of the family varied, as expected, on the basis of the initial selection of these groups as did the amount of time the mothers spent in caretaking activities.

The lowest mean score on the mental test was found for those infants who were from monomatric families in the low economic group. In the mixed and polymatric low economic groups, the scores for the infants on the mental test were significantly higher (Table 3). Multiple caretaking arrangements appear to shift the low mental test performance for infants of the low economic level families to scores above the mean. In upper economic level families, slightly higher mental test performance is found in the infants of monomatric and mixed families; slightly lower scores are found in the polymatric group. However, since these differences are not statistically significant, we conclude that the main effects of polymatry are to be found in the low economic group and not in the high economic group. A possible explanation for this is evident in the data presented in Table 4. The percentage of social activity of mothers and infants is highest in the monomatric group and lowest in the polymatric group; the opposite is true for the caretaker's social activity, which is higher

Table 3. Infant Test Performance as Related to Maternal Contact and Familial Economic Level

Caretaking System and Economic Level	Maternal Data		Education: Highest Grade Completed	Infant Test Scores					
	% of Time Present	Age		Kenya Mental	Kenya Motor	Goal Direct.	Social Resp.	Vocalization	Object Perm.
Monomatric									
Low Economic (N = 12)	86.6	25.8	2.7	84.9*	89.3*	96.7	90.6**	90.4**	91.7
High Economic (N = 7)	84.6	27.3	3.1	105.7	107.3	108.2	106.2	103.5	105.7
Mixed									
Low Economic (N = 9)	58.1	32.4	2.0	101.5	91.8	98.4	101.5	95.2	100.5
High Economic (N = 8)	55.4	30.8	2.9	106.6	107.6	100.9	102.1	104.8	106.6
Polymatric									
Low Economic (N = 10)	31.5	32.1	3.2	102.9	104.8	97.2	105.2	108.2	102.9
High Economic (N = 12)	31.4	34.9	2.4	98.8	103.2	99.3	97.1	103.5	99.2

*p<.05, One-way analysis of variance (across caretaking type and within economic level)
**p<.10, One-way analysis of variance (across caretaking type and within economic level)

101

Table 4. Percentage of Time Spent in Social Activity with Infant

Caretaking System and Economic Level	Mother	Caretaker	Total
Monomatric			
Low Economic	6.2%	1.9%	8.1%
High Economic	7.6	0.8	8.4
Mixed			
Low Economic	1.4	4.6	6.0
High Economic..............	4.2	15.5	19.7
Polymatric			
Low Economic	2.6	17.9	20.5
High Economic.................	0.4	11.1	11.5

in the polymatric group. If we combine the mother's and the caretaker's social activity scores, we find that a greater amount of social activity is associated with higher test performance except in a single group, the high economic level monomatric group. These results suggest that either nonspecific factors associated with the high economic level or the amount of social activity provided by the caretaker is associated with the higher scores on the mental test. We can conclude that for increased mental test performance of infants, high economic level of the family or high caretaker social activity is necessary and, further, that either one is sufficient.

It might be expected that economic level and social interaction would combine to yield the highest scores in the polymatric high economic group. Since the data do not bear this out, it is possible that there is a threshold for social stimulation that is necessary for adequate cognitive development. When the threshold is exceeded, no further stimulation will enhance that development. Infants in the lower economic level families perhaps require more social stimulation to achieve the level of development that is attained by the higher economic level infants with less stimulation.

The results on the motor test for the low economic group infants indicate that the lowest scores were obtained by infants from mixed and monomatric families (Table 3). However, as in the mental test performance scores, the lower scores are compensated for in polymatric familial arrangements. The higher motor test scores were found in the higher economic group infants, and these scores did not differ by caretaking arrangement.

To elucidate further the relationship between more specific cognitive functioning and the type of caretaking arrangement, we obtained subscores on the Bayley test according to the schema developed by Yarrow (unpublished data, 1968). Four cognitive subscores, relating to social responsiveness, goal directedness, object permanence, and vocalization, were derived from the mental and motor test data. These four were selected from a group of nine such subscores because it was predicted that they would vary with the caretaking arrangements. The Bayley items for each subscore are shown in Table 5. We hypothesized that social responsiveness scores might be increased in multiple caretaking arrangements because of the necessity for the infant to increase his repertoire of proximity-inducing behaviors to involve more than one individual. Goal directedness was expected to be enhanced in infants raised in monomatric families since the contingencies for reinforcement provided by a single figure would be more consistent than those provided by several individuals. We hypothesized that object permanence would be increased in the polymatric infant group because of the opportunity given the infant frequently to experience his mother's departure and return (as well as the caretaker's). According to Piaget's (1969) formulation of cognitive structures and stage development, this regularized disappearance and reappearance of familiar and important adults should enhance the infant's attainment of object permanence. Finally, we hypothesized that vocalization would be enhanced in polymatric families where the mother and the caretaker showed a great amount of social interaction, since those families would probably have a considerable amount of adult vocalization.

Again, because of the association of familial economic level with the infant's test performance, we analyzed the data by dividing the groups into high and low economic families (Figure 3). Goal directedness and object permanence did not significantly differ as a result of caretaking arrangement for either economic group. Social responsiveness and vocalization scores differed by caretaking arrangements in the low economic infants. In the high economic group there was no significant difference in the social responsiveness of children reared in the three caretaking arrangements, despite considerable difference between the mean scores. These mean differences were attenuated by the high variability among the infants on this measure. It is quite possible that a larger sample of subjects and more careful control of testing would yield other statistically significant subscores. Nonetheless, the data provide evidence that caretaking arrangements have an effect on cognitive functions. Specifically a greater amount of social interaction, provided chiefly by the caretaker but additionally by the mother, leads to higher scores on the vocalization and social responsiveness subtests of the Bayley test. The importance of the social environment in enlarging the behavioral repertoire of the infant in the first year is confirmed by these data.

103

Table 5. Bayley Items on which Cognitive Subscores were Derived

Goal Directedness	Social Responsiveness	Vocalization	Object Permanence
Reaches persistently	Social smile	Vocalizes at least 4 times	Reacts to disappearance of face
Pulls string to secure ring (purposeful)	Vocalizes to social stimulus	Vocalizes 2 syllables	Turns head after dropped objects
Pulls string to secure ring	Anticipatory adjustment to lifting	Vocalizes attitudes	Looks for dropped objects
Attempts to secure 3 cubes	Enjoys frolic play	Vocalizes 4 different syllables	Uncovers toys
Unwraps toys	Smiles at mirror image	Listens selectively to familiar words	Picks up cup and secures cube
Attempts to secure pellet	Responds to social play	Says da-da or equivalent	Looks for content of box
		Adjusts to words	
		Uses expressive jargon	

104

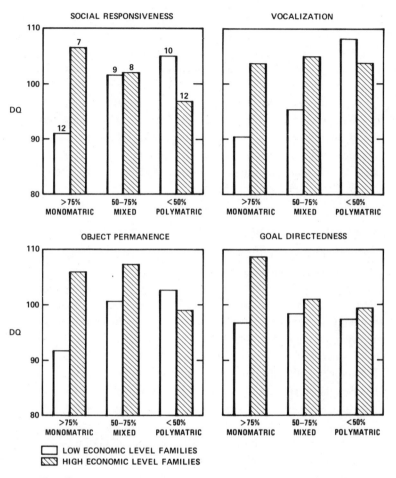

Figure 3. The effect of the caretaking arrangement on the infant's cognitive behavior.

SUMMARY OF FINDINGS

We have attempted to demonstrate how the familial caretaking arrangements influence the infant's social and cognitive development in his first year of life. Where social development is concerned, although the polymatric caretaking system appears to modify an infant's affective response to his mother, this response is about the same as that shown to an alternative caretaker. Strangers are discriminated from familiar individuals to about the same extent in both caretaking arrangements, and there is some indication that

105

strangers are responded to less positively by infants raised in a polymatric family system.

The major effect of the polymatric care system is the enhanced cognitive development of the infant, particularly those infants from lower economic level families. In this group, infants cared for by a mother alone produce the lowest cognitive test scores. The presence of alternative caretakers has the effect of improving an infant's test performance. This improvement was attributed largely to the social stimulation provided by caretakers, which supplements whatever social stimuli are provided by the mother. High economic level infants appear to be less dependent upon this supplemental social stimulation for achieving high scores.

DISCUSSION

The first point to emphasize is that monomatric caretaking systems are not the norm in large parts of the nonindustrial world. Maternal infant caretaking systems have been adapted not only to the biological requirements of the infant and of his mother but also to the social and economic requirements of the particular society and to the environmental pressure confronting the mother and her infant. In many agricultural societies the mother does not have the luxury of arranging her time to provide exclusive attention to an infant. In many of these communities she is responsible for the provision of family nutrition, water, and child care, and for management of the household. Given these tasks, the infant care system has been modified to include alternative caretakers to aid the mother. A by-product of this adaptation (Mead, 1962) is the assurance that the infant will survive if the mother dies. In addition the system provides a training ground for the next generation of mothers through encouraging older daughters to model themselves on the mother through direct experience by the young mother surrogate.

The modified polymatric system described in this paper, in which a mother remains the central figure and is helped substantially by others, should not be confused with a shared maternal system such as that found in Israeli kibbutzim. The kibbutz system was ideologically inspired, relatively isolated from the larger society, and definitely in the minority when compared to the competing systems of the outside society. Most of the evidence (Neubauer, 1965) from the Israeli kibbutzim suggests that this system had no deleterious effects on the development of infants and young children. However, observers report that the kibbutz system has undergone considerable modification (Jarus, Marcus, & Rapaport, 1970), partly owing to the presence

106

of alternative child-rearing systems within Israeli society and because of social and economic changes within the kibbutzim.

In contrast, the modified polymatric system within agricultural communities of sub-Saharan Africa is operating entirely within a cultural norm; there is a new trend, still minor, toward an exclusively monomatric nuclear family system. Neither the Israeli polymatric system nor the African agricultural polymatric system described here bears a close relationship to institutional systems in which there may be no specific individual singled out as the primary maternal figure for the infant. Clearly the social and cognitive effects of such a system on an infant are different from those described in this paper.

Apart from our monomatric cultural bias, an additional push toward idealization of a monomatric system has been implicitly derived from primate studies which frequently have been misinterpreted when extrapolated to the human systems. The long-term exclusive mother-infant relationship described by many observers in such primates as the chimpanzee, baboon, and rhesus monkey (DeVore, 1965) cannot be considered a prototype for humans unless one considers the Western European or North American middle-class monomatric system to be the prototype for the human primate. The anthropological evidence for an exclusive mother-infant relationship for humans, at least during the infant's first year, is sparse indeed, especially when one considers not only the data from this study and other studies from developing countries but also the evidence from British upper-class society (Hardy, 1972) and the variations of infant care systems (Caldwell, 1962) operative in working-class families in the industrial societies of the world.

Caretakers contribute substantially to the infant's social and cognitive development during the first year. Our results show that infants form multiple attachments when given the opportunity under a polymatric system and that these multiple attachments are similar as measured by the techniques used in this study. This finding does not imply that the infant is affectively bonded to a caretaker as he would be toward his mother, since evidence in this study indicates that he does discriminate between them. In addition, there is evidence that the monomatric and polymatric systems are not equivalent because infants raised in the polymatric system react more positively to the approach of their mother and more negatively to her absence than they do to the approach and absence of a caretaker. Despite the possibility that the polymatric infants might be more variable (perhaps interpretable as less secure in their affective responses), they nonetheless develop strong affective

107

bonds to both mother and caretaker. We can conclude that the monomatric care system may be sufficient, but it certainly is not necessary for the formation of multiple attachment relationships in the human infant.

Ainsworth (1967) studied the development of attachment among the Ganda infants. Although she does not report data separately for "caretakers" in the caretaking of infants, it is possible to assess indirectly the caretaker's contribution to the development of the infant's attachment. In the group of infants described as securely attached, only three of sixteen were categorized as having mothers who did not share caretaking with others. The score in total care, which included caretaking by both mothers and caretakers, was high for these three as well as for ten of the remaining thirteen infants. This suggests that caretaking by individuals other than the mothers must have been considerable, and therefore it cannot be ruled out as a factor in accounting for the secure attachment of these infants. Similarly, in Ainsworth's insecure attached group, only one of seven mothers did not share caretaking chores. Of the other six infants, four received high ratings in total care, again suggesting a contribution from the caretaker. For the five nonattached infants, all mothers shared caretaking but the total care score was low. We can conclude from this analysis that the contribution of caretakers cannot be excluded in accounting for the development of attachments in these Ganda infants; this is consistent with the results found in the present study. However findings concerning the effects of multiple caretaking on attachment are more specific than Ainsworth's, and they suggest that the insecure attached group of her study may be equivalent to our mixed and polymatric groups.

Considering the long history of polymatric infant care systems, we may speculate about their function in evolution. When physical and social dangers were considerable for the infant, close relationships with familiar individuals and wariness toward strangers may have had selective benefit for the individual and for his group. For the future, with the probable decrease in danger from external physical and social forces, at least in sub-Saharan African agricultural communities, stranger awareness may have no particular selective advantage. Therefore we may anticipate that a shift to a monomatric system will not particularly threaten the infant's survival and may have the advantage of encouraging social bonding to groups beyond the individual's immediate family.

A major benefit of the polymatric system is the enhancement of the infant's cognitive development. The presence of an individual who aids the mother in the caretaking of an infant, especially an infant from a low economic level family, appears to improve the infant's cognitive and psychomotor performance at least during his first year. This finding supports observations derived from a United States study (Hess, 1970): a) that infants from families in the lowest economic scale are particularly vulnerable to environmental effects, and b) that social stimulation appears to compensate for a relatively impoverished environment, at least for a limited period. Whether the improved test performance found in this study continues in the child's later years is unknown. Findings of Hunt and Bayley (1971) suggest that enhanced performance in the early years of a child's life has some predictive value for performance in later years.

The importance of familial economic level for some aspects of infant test performance, apart from the maternal caretaking arrangements, is clear. Since familial demographic considerations were not a major focus of this paper, suffice it to say that genetic, nutritional, and unmeasured maternal behaviors, varying according to familial economic level, cannot be excluded as explanations for some of these findings. Undoubtedly, further work will be required in this extremely complex area of research. Despite the lack of definitive answers, our findings suggest that a modified polymatric system operating in societies where it is an essential part of the value system and of the socioeconomic requirements of the community, provides an environment for infants conducive to their social and cognitive development.

References

Ainsworth, M. D. S. *Infancy in Uganda*. Baltimore: Johns Hopkins Press, 1967.
———. Object relations, dependency, and attachment: A theoretical review of mother-infant relationship. *Child Development*, 1969, 40, 969–1026.
———. Attachment and dependency: A comparison. In J. Gewirtz (Ed.), *Attachment and dependency*. Washington: Winston, 1972.
Bayley, N. *Bayley scales of infant development*. New York: Psychological Corporation, 1969.
Bowlby, J. *Maternal care and mental health*. Geneva: World Health Organization, 1952.
———. The nature of the child's tie to its mother. *International Journal of Psychoanalysis*, 1958, 39, 350–373.
———. *Attachment and loss*. Vol. I. *Attachment*. London: Hogarth Press, 1969.
———. *Attachment and loss*. Vol. II. *Separation, anxiety and anger*. New York: Basic Books, 1973.
Caldwell, B. M., Hersher, L., Lipton, E. L., Richmond, J. B., Stern, G. A., Eddy, E., Drachman, R., & Rothman, A. Mother-infant interaction in monomatric and polymatric families. *American Journal of Orthopsychiatry*, 1962, 33, 653–664.
DeVore, I. (Ed.). *Primate behavior*. New York: Holt, 1965.
Freeberg, N. E., & Payne, D. T. Parental influence on cognitive development in early childhood: A review. *Child Development*, 1967, 38, 65–87.
Gewirtz, J. (Ed.). *Attachment and dependency*. Washington: Winston, 1972.
Greenberg, D. J., Hillman, D., & Rice, D. Infant and stranger variables related to stranger anxiety in the first year of life. *Developmental Psychology*, 1973, 9, 207–212.

MINNESOTA SYMPOSIA ON CHILD PSYCHOLOGY

Hardy, J. G. *The rise and fall of British nanny*. London: Hodder & Stoughton, 1972.

Hess, R. D. Social class and ethnic influences on socialization. In P. Mussen (Ed.), *Carmichael's manual of child psychology*, Vol. 2. New York: Wiley, 1970.

Hunt, J. V., & Bayley, N. Explorations into patterns of mental development and prediction from Bayley Scales of infant development. In J. P. Hill (Ed.), *Minnesota Symposia on Child Psychology*, Vol. 5. Minneapolis: University of Minnesota Press, 1971.

Jarus, A., Marcus, J., & Rapaport, C. (Eds.). *Children and families in Israel*. New York: Gordon and Breach, 1970.

Kohen-Raz, R. Mental and motor development of kibbutz, institutionalized and home-reared infants in Israel. *Child Development*, 1968, 39, 489–504.

Konner, M. Aspects of the developmental ethology of a foraging people. In N. Blurton Jones (Ed.), *Ethological studies of child behavior*. Cambridge: Cambridge University Press, 1972.

Leiderman, P. H., Babu, B., Kagia, J., Kraemer, H. C., & Leiderman, G. F. African infant precocity and some social influences during the first year. *Nature*, 1973, 242, 247–249.

Maccoby, E., & Masters, J. C. In P. Mussen (Ed.), *Carmichael's manual of child psychology*, Vol. 2, *Attachment and dependency*. New York: Wiley, 1970.

Masters, J. C., & Wellman, H. M. Human infant attachment, a procedural critique. Paper presented at the Society for Research on Child Development, Philadelphia, April, 1973.

Mead, M. A cultural anthropologist's approach to maternal deprivation. In *Deprivation of maternal care. A reassessment of its effects*. Geneva: World Health Organization, 1962.

Minturn, L., & Lambert, W. W. *Mothers of six cultures*. New York: Wiley, 1964.

Munroe, R. N., & Munroe, R. L. Household care and infant care in an East African society. *Journal of Social Psychology*, 1971, 83, 3–13.

Neubauer, P. *Children in collectives*. Springfield, Ill.: Thomas, 1965.

Piaget, J. *Play, dreams and imitation in childhood*. New York: Norton, 1951.

———. *Origins of intelligence in children*. New York: Norton, 1969.

Rutter, M. *Maternal deprivation reassessed*. London: Penguin Books, 1972.

Schaffer, H. R., & Emerson, P. E. The development of social attachment in infancy. *Monographs of the Society for Research in Child Development*, 1964, 29 (Serial No. 94).

Sears, R. Attachment, dependency and frustration. In J. Gewirtz (Ed.), *Attachment and dependency*. Washington: Winston, 1972.

+ ROSS D. PARKE +

Rules, Roles, and Resistance to Deviation: Recent Advances in Punishment, Discipline, and Self-Control

A CONTINUING theme of our research program has been the investigation of the effects of punishment on children's behavior. Findings from earlier research (Parke, 1970, 1973) have indicated that the effects of punishment are complex and depend on a variety of parameters such as the timing, intensity, and consistency of the punishment. However, there is a growing body of evidence that suggests that punitive inhibitory tactics can have deleterious side effects (Parke, 1972b). Although I still believe that punishment plays a role in childhood socialization, our focus has shifted to an examination of the effectiveness of alternative inhibitory techniques which may be effective and may avoid some of the disadvantages of punishment. One theme of this presentation will be a review of some of the research that has led to this shift and a review of some of our recent findings on the effectiveness of cognitively based inhibitory tactics. Accompanying this shift of focus to cognitive strategies has been an increased concern about developmental changes in the effectiveness of different types of control tactics as well as a concern about the modifying impact of social learning on these developmental relationships.

A second purpose of this presentation will be to illustrate our shift from a unidirectional model of inhibition, in which the main issue concerned the

NOTE: The preparation of this chapter and the research that is reported were supported by Grants GS-1847 and GS-31885X from the National Science Foundation. Thanks are extended to Douglas Sawin for his helpful comments and to Frances Hall for her assistance in the preparation of this manuscript.

111

direct effects of exposure to different types of adult inhibitory tactics. That approach seriously curtailed our understanding of the role of punishment and discipline in childhood socialization. Not only have we expanded the range of our inquiry beyond the study of direct effects but, more importantly, we have altered our views concerning the child's own contribution to the socialization process. An examination of the impact of assuming the role of disciplinarian on the disciplinary agent's own rule conformity represents one new direction. A second recent direction concerns the ways in which children modify adult behaviors in disciplinary contexts. Hopefully, addressing these questions will not only move us closer to understanding some neglected facets of childhood discipline but will also move us toward an interactive and bi-directional model of socialization in which the child receives proper recognition as an active participant.

Punishment and Rationale Training as Determinants of Resistance to Deviation

Until 1969 our main effort was to investigate the effectiveness of various punishment parameters for inhibiting children's behavior. Findings from the Parke (1969) study indicating that the effects of punishment could be modified by the provision of a verbal rationale marked a turning point in our research program. A brief description of this study will illustrate the procedures that are typically employed in this series of studies. Two phases can be distinguished: a training phase in which the child was punished or was in some manner trained not to touch certain toys and a test phase in which the child was left alone with a set of prohibited toys. In the first phase the child was presented with pairs of attractive toys for a series of trials. On certain predetermined trials the child was punished by a noxious noise or a verbal rebuke regardless of which toy he chose. On completion of the punishment training session, the subject was seated before a display of the toys that he was previously punished for touching. The resistance-to-deviation test phase consisted of a 15-minute period during which the child was left alone with the prohibited toys. The extent to which the subject touched the toys in the absence of the external agent was recorded by an observer located behind a one-way vision screen. We found that punishment accompanied by a verbal rationale ("the toy is fragile and may break") produced greater inhibition than did punishment without any accompanying rationale. In a later experiment, Parke and Murray (1971) found that a rationale alone is more effective than is punishment alone. A comparison of the results of the two studies indicates that the combination of punishment and a rationale is the most effective procedure (Figure 1).

These results are highly consistent with the findings of a study by LaVoie (1970). He compared the effectiveness of punishment alone, punishment accompanied by a rationale, and rationale alone for producing response inhibition in adolescent boys. The training procedure used in our other studies with children (Parke, 1969; Parke & Murray, 1971) was altered for LaVoie's study to insure that the objects were of interest to boys of this age. Instead of using "professional" experimenters, the subject's mother or father was used as the training agent. A 2 × 2 × 2 design was employed involving three independent variables: (1) sex of parent—mother or father; (2) punishment (104 db. noise) versus no punishment; and (3) presence or absence of a rationale. The no noise, no rationale group served as a control condition. The rationale used was a property rationale: "You don't handle other people's property without their permission." As predicted, the rationale and

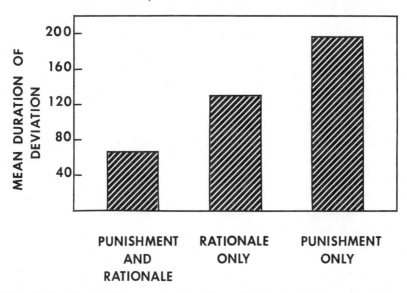

EFFECTIVENESS OF COMBINATIONS OF PUNISHMENT, RATIONALE, AND PUNISHMENT AND RATIONALE

Figure 1. The effect of punishment, rationale and the combination of punishment and rationale on response inhibition. (Reprinted by permission from R. D. Parke, "Explorations in Punishment, Discipline and Self-Control," in P. Elich [ed.], *Social Learning*. Bellingham: Western Washington State Press, 1973.)

113

punishment combination produced the most response inhibition. The subjects who received neither punishment nor rationale training exhibited the greatest amount of deviant behavior. Punishment alone and rationale alone were of intermediate effectiveness. As with the earlier comparisons involving child subjects (Parke, 1969; Parke & Murray, 1971), the rationale alone produced more inhibition than did the punishment alone; however, the differences between these two groups were not significant. The consistency of these results with those of our earlier work—in spite of the change in the age of the subjects and the use of parents as punishing agents—clearly suggests that the provision of a rationale is an effective technique for achieving response inhibition in children. However these experiments suggest that punishment and the provision of an accompanying rationale operate additively to produce a degree of response inhibition that is greater than that resulting from either a rationale alone or from punishment alone.

In addition, the provision of a rationale alters the operation of other punishment parameters, such as the timing and intensity of the punishment and the nature of the agent-child relationship. Although punishment that occurs early in the response sequence is more effective than punishment that occurs late in the sequence (Walters, Parke, & Cane, 1965; Aronfreed & Reber, 1965), when a verbal rationale accompanies the punishment, the effect of the timing of punishment is eliminated; early and late punishments are equally effective inhibitors of the child's behavior (Aronfreed, 1965; Cheyne & Walters, 1969; Parke, 1969). Reasoning manipulations alter the operation of other punishment parameters as well. Parke (1969) examined the impact of reasoning on the effect of intensity and nurturance. When no rationale was provided, the expected effect of intensity of punishment occurred: high intensity punishment produced significantly greater inhibition than did low intensity punishment. However, when a rationale accompanied the punishment, there was no difference between the effect of high and low intensity punishment. Similarly the importance of the agent-child relationship in achieving inhibition by punishment is affected by a rationale. Children who experience nurturant interaction with the punishing agent before punishment training deviate less often than do subjects in a low nurturance condition. However, this effect was present in the Parke (1969) study only when no rationale accompanied the noxious buzzer. When a rationale for not touching certain toys was provided, the children who had experienced the friendly interaction and the children who had had only impersonal contact with the agent were equally inhibited during the resistance-to-deviation test period.

Taken together these experiments constitute impressive evidence of the important role of cognitive variables in modifying the operation of punishment.

Developmental Factors in Rationale Effectiveness

Although a great deal of research has been done on age-related changes in children's moral judgments (Piaget, 1948; Kohlberg, 1964, 1969), relatively little attention has been paid to age-related changes in the effectiveness of different types of prohibitory rationales for inhibiting children's behavior. In part this apparent lack of interest in the contribution of developmental shifts in cognitive development to behavioral conformity stems from the assumption that moral behavior, such as resistance to deviation, is age independent (Grinder, 1964). This assumption was related directly to the parameters that were typically manipulated in studies of resistance to deviation. The demonstration that adherence to adult standards was age related was unlikely to result from continuing to manipulate situational parameters which were not themselves presumed to be age related. For example, punishment parameters such as timing and intensity are unlikely to show marked or interesting relationships to age. Rather, age changes are more likely to be apparent from an analysis of the cognitive and linguistic abilities that are required in different types of test contexts. To the extent that situations vary in the cognitive demands placed upon the child, age changes in behavioral inhibition are likely to be observed. In fact there is substantial evidence that as children develop, motor behavior comes under verbal control. In this context we are particularly interested in the effect of justificatory rationales on response inhibition in children of different ages.

In the results of a recent study (Parke & Murry, 1971) an interaction between age of the child and the effect of different prohibitory rationales was found. There were two age levels—four years and seven years. Similarly there were two rationales that varied in degree of abstractness. The first—an object-oriented appeal—was relatively concrete and focused on the physical consequences of handling the toy (''the toy is fragile and might break''). This emphasis on the physical consequences of an action is similar to the types of justificatory rationales that young children use in their moral judgments (Kohlberg, 1964). The second rationale was a property rule which stressed the ethical norm of ownership. This rationale was more abstract and assumed that children understand the rights of other individuals. In Kohlberg's moral judgment system this understanding represents a more sophisticated level of moral development. It was predicted that the property rationale would be most effective with the older children and that the concrete rationale would be more effective with the younger children. The results were consistent with this prediction. The concrete rationale was significantly more effective than was the property rationale in producing response inhibition in the younger children. At the older age level the effectiveness of the two rationales was approximately equal, the property rule being slightly more effective. In a more recent study (Parke, 1972a) with boys and girls of nursery school age, a similar interaction of age x type of rationale was found (Figure 2). The children in the younger age group (three to four and one-half years) were more inhibited by the object-oriented rationale than by the property rationale; children in the older age group (four and one-half to six years) were inhibited equally by the two types of rationales, although the property rationale was, again, slightly more effective. As in the earlier study, the children at the two age levels differed in their response to the property rationale. The replication increases our confidence in this relationship; moreover the finding suggests

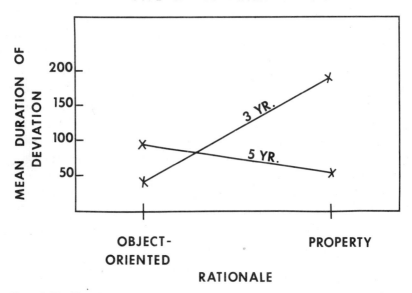

Figure 2. The effect of two types of rationales at different age levels on response inhibition (Parke, 1972b).

that during the latter half of the fourth year the child is showing a significant shift in response to abstract rationales.

These findings are consistent with other data reported by Cheyne (1972) and LaVoie (1973) concerning developmental changes in the effects of different types of prohibitory rationales. Together the findings emphasize the importance of considering developmental factors in studies of different types of control tactics. Finally, by using cognitively based control tactics, age changes in behavioral aspects of moral development are clearly demonstrated. The task of charting in more detail age changes in relation to specific types of prohibitory rationales would appear to be worthwhile.

One important theoretical implication of this pattern of results is the necessity of distinguishing between the developmental course for response inhibition and for moral judgments. The recognition/production distinction that is made in other areas to account for the developmental lag between the processes of recognition and production may be profitable in the moral development area as well. The course of development may be similar for the inhibitory effect of different types of rationales and for the use of these rationales in making moral judgments; however, the child is able to respond to justificatory rationales to control his own behavior earlier than he is able to actively utilize these rationales to justify his moral decisions. In fact, hearing adults use these rationales to control his behavior may not only increase their inhibitory effectiveness, but it may also contribute to his eventual use of these justificatory tactics in moral judgment situations.

Acknowledgment of the existence of suggestive parallels in the development of moral behavior and in moral judgment does not necessarily imply an endorsement of the cognitive-developmentalist (Kohlberg, 1969) view, which places a limited emphasis on situational factors for the promotion of developmental change in the effectiveness of different types of prohibitory rationales or for developmental shifts in moral judgments. From a social learning viewpoint developmental shifts are not conceptualized as inevitable products of the child's cognitive developmental progress, nor do they invariably occur under all circumstances. Social learning theory assumes rather that a variety of situational and subject variables are important for understanding the effect of different types of rationales at different age levels. This theory also assumes that these developmental differences are modifiable. Contextual variables, in short, are seen as modifying factors which may accentuate or depress developmental variables.

Some recent research illustrates the modifiability by situational variables of

117

the developmental effects of different types of rationales. In one study (Parke & Dimiceli, 1973) 60 children at two age levels (three to four and one-half years and four and one-half to six years) were exposed to one of two types of prohibitory rationales that were known to differ in their inhibitory effectiveness, e.g., concrete rationale ("the toy is fragile and might break") or abstract rationale ("the toy belongs to another child"). However, the source of the prohibitory rationale was varied through verbal instructions. Half of the children were told that the peer group had endorsed the rule (e.g., "the other children do not want you to play with those toys because they might break or because they belong to someone else"). The remaining children merely heard the adult deliver the rationale without the additional accompanying peer group endorsement. Of interest is the modifying impact of the peer group endorsement on the interaction of age x type of rationale. The predicted interaction was evident when no peer endorsement accompanied the rationales: the younger children showed significantly less inhibition under the abstract than under the concrete rule, and the older children showed greater inhibition under the abstract than under the concrete rationale. However, the age trends in rationale effectiveness were absent when the rationales were accompanied by peer endorsement. As Figure 3 indicates, the younger children were much more inhibited by the property rule when it was accompanied by the peer endorsement instructions than when it was not. On the assumption that the younger children are responsive to peer pressure and potential peer group disapproval, this influence increased the effectiveness of the property rule for inhibiting the younger subjects. Alternatively, the provision of the peer endorsement may have made this property or ownership rule less abstract by specifying the reference group (peers) to which the property rule referred. Further, the importance of the type of rationale may vary with the presence of other accompanying parameters; specifically, the relative importance of the source (peer versus adult) and of the content of the rule needs attention. Perhaps if a rule is endorsed by peers the specific content of the accompanying rationale is less important than it is if the rule is not endorsed by peers. It remains to be determined whether peer endorsement increases the effectiveness of other types of abstract rationales. In any case, the investigation is illustrative of the modifying impact of situational cues on the developmental relationship between age and the effect of prohibitory rationales. Similar effects have recently been reported by Allen and Newtson (1972) in their studies of developmental changes in peer group conformity.

RATIONALE EFFECTIVENESS: AGE & PEER ENDORSEMENT EFFECTS

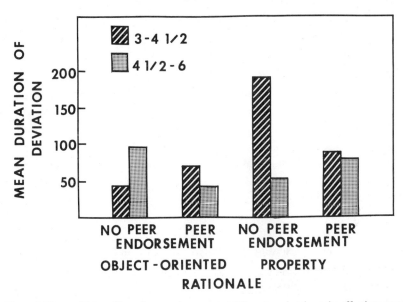

Figure 3. The modifying effect of peer endorsement at different age levels on the effectiveness of two types of rationales (Parke and Dimiceli, 1973).

Some important issues remain. Of central interest is the manner in which verbal rationales acquire their effectiveness. One suggestion (Walters & Parke, 1967) is that verbal rationales initially may acquire their inhibitory capacities by being paired with anxiety-arousing stimuli. Such training may assume a variety of forms. The socializing agent may pair a rationale with punishment, particularly with younger children. Through classical conditioning the child may eventually learn to inhibit when he hears the rationale. Another related possibility is the use of punishment for noncompliance with the rationale-based prohibition. The child learns to anticipate punishment for nonconformity to a verbal rationale. In both cases, once the child has learned the rationale it may produce inhibition with little or no accompanying anxiety. In addition the child may learn to comply with verbal rationales by observing the inhibitory impact of rationales on the behavior of other children. Similarly adults may invoke verbal rationales as justification for certain of their actions and thereby provide further examples for children. Such experience may be particularly important for teaching children to use verbal rationales in regulating their own behavior. Research concerning the role of models in the adoption of self-evaluative standards (e.g., Bandura & Kupers, 1964) is relevant. Finally, adherence to rationale-based prohibitions is probably maintained by avoidance of punishment as well as by direct reinforcement by parents and other socializing agents.

This analysis emphasizes the importance of the child's social learning history as a determinant of the effectiveness of rationale-based prohibitions. It does not deny that differences in the child's level of cognitive and verbal development are relevant predictors of the effects of rationales. Rather, this analysis stresses the importance for prediction of opportunities to become familiar with various rationales and to experience the contingencies necessary for rationales to become inhibitors. Children of different social classes, for example, are exposed to different kinds of control tactics. Kamii (1965) and Hess and Shipman (1967) report that lower-class mothers tend to use power-oriented disciplinary techniques more frequently and to provide rationales and explanations for their prohibitions less often than do middle-class parents. It is predicted that rationale-based control techniques would be less effective with lower-class children than with middle-class children—not only because of class-related differences in cognitive skills but also because of differences in the social learning experiences of children of various social classes.

A similar analysis may facilitate an understanding of the differential effect of rationales at various developmental levels and may point to some neglected determinants of these developmental changes.

Theories of moral development give little credit to the direct contribution made by socialization agents to age-related shifts in responsiveness to different types of rationales. Our social learning position, however, assumes that adults (and possibly a child's peers as well) directly contribute to developmental changes by using rationales that are appropriate for a child at a given age level. For example, adults typically do not use complex rationales with two-year-olds nor do they anticipate compliance by two-year-olds with sophisticated appeals. As the child develops, the adult's prohibitory rationales probably show corresponding changes toward greater complexity.

Direct evidence of how parents and other socializing agents systematically alter their disciplinary tactics as the child becomes older is surprisingly limited. One illustrative exception is a study by Clifford (1959) of the types of disciplinary practices that mothers used with children at three, six, and nine years of age. Noncognitive tactics, such as spanking and forcibly removing the child from a situation, are used more frequently with younger children than they are with older children; cognitive techniques, such as appeals to humor and self-esteem, are used more often with older children. Reasoning, according to Clifford, is used frequently at all ages, but many types of reasoning are hidden under this blanket label. For our purposes it is necessary that we have more information concerning the shifts in the specific types of prohibitory rationales used by parents and other socializing adults in order to elucidate the direct role that shifts in adult input may play in the developmental effectiveness of different types of rationales.

Another source of influence on developmental shifts is the peer group. Piaget (1948) and, more recently, Haviland (1970) have documented developmental shifts in the frequency with which children advocate the use of restitutive versus expiatory types of punitive tactics. To the extent that advocacy predicts actual use, it could be argued that children increasingly practice adult-transmitted types of control in peer situations and may also refine their understanding of differing tactics in peer interactions. In some cultures (USSR) where older peers exercise control over younger children, differential peer utilization of sophisticated inhibitory tactics with children of varying ages may contribute to developmental shifts in the children's responsiveness to different types of prohibitory rules. This type of peer control is probably a less likely contributor in the United States where children interact primarily with children of their own age.

Our approach does not deny the important role played by developmental shifts in the child's cognitive and verbal sophistication in the increasing effectiveness of different types of rationales. Rather, we argue for an interactive model in which developmental changes are viewed as being determined both by the cognitive and verbal capacities of the child and by a variety of social situational cues.

Determinants of Rule Transmission

One recent concern of our research program has been to expand our question about the effect of punishment and rationales for achieving inhibition in order to examine the extent to which different types of training tactics transform the child into a rule transmitter. In other words, will different types of inhibitory tactics result in differing degrees of transmission to other children of adult-established rules? To investigate this issue, we modified the resistance-to-deviation paradigm used in earlier studies. In addition to the training phase in which the prohibition is established, a test phase was added to examine the extent to which the trained child would transmit the prohibitory rule to a second child. During this phase a peer who was given permission to touch the ''prohibited'' toys was introduced into the test setting. By recording the trained child's attempts to influence the peer, the effect of various training tactics for producing rule transmission could be evaluated.

Two factors were examined that were assumed to affect this rule transmission process. First, rationale training was compared with punishment training, and it was anticipated that the prohibition transmission rates would be higher among children who received rationale training than among children who received punishment training. The extent to which a rule is adult or peer group derived provides another determinant of rule transmission. The more children view a rule as endorsed by the peer group, the more likely they are to enforce this rule on their peers. However, the impact of the peer endorsement of prohibitory rules may depend on the child's own relationship with the peer group. The child's history of interaction with his peers probably affects his reaction to the sanctioning of a rule by the peer group—the higher the level of interaction, the greater the degree of rule enforcement. On the other hand, peer group endorsement is unlikely to be effective for children who have had a low rate of peer interaction.

A total of 194 boys and girls, ages three to six, participated in this study; half of the children received the prohibition training and the remaining half served as nontrained peers. A 3 (type of prohibitory content) by 2 (source of rule endorsement) design was used. There were two types of rationale: a property rule (''the toy belongs to another child'') and an object-oriented rule (''the toy might break''). There was also punishment, a buzzer, unaccompanied by a rationale. For half of the children in each of these groups a peer endorsement was included. For example, the children in the property rationale training group were prohibited from touching the toys ''because they belong to another boy (girl) and so some of the other kids here got together and decided no one should play with them.'' The remaining subjects did not hear this additional peer endorsement; they simply heard the rationale and prohibition delivered by the adult agent.

Following the training phase the child was left alone with the prohibited toys for a six-minute period. After this period, a second child (of the same age and sex as the trained subject) who had been given permission to play with the toys appeared on the scene.

Regardless of sex, the children touched the toys for the shortest amounts of time after training with the object-oriented rationale; punishment alone was least effective and the property rationale was of intermediate effectiveness. Of particular interest is the effect of the peer endorsement: children who were trained with a peer-endorsed prohibition deviated less than subjects who did not receive this type of endorsement in the training period. Finally, all subjects, regardless of type of training, deviated significantly more in the presence of the peer than when they were alone.

The effects of the peer endorsement variable, however, are qualified by the typical level of peer interaction in the nursery school setting. In addition to the experimental measures, the rates of peer interaction in the nursery school were obtained by trained observers. Each child was observed for 12 consecutive 15-second intervals on approximately six occasions. Verbal and physical interactions with both teachers and peers were recorded, as were the reactions of the target child. An index of peer participation was obtained by calculating the percentage of intervals in which each child interacted with another child, rather than remaining alone. On the basis of these scores, the children were tricotomized into groups representing high, medium, and low levels of peer-peer interaction. Analyses employing this naturalistically derived measure of peer interaction revealed some interesting results.

There was a significant peer-endorsement x peer-interaction level x test interaction. For the no-peer-endorsement children, those who were low peer interactors deviated equally during the test phase in which they were alone and the phase in which a peer was present. The medium and high interactors increased their deviant behavior in the presence of the tempting peer when there was no peer endorsement. On the other hand, under peer-endorsement conditions the medium and high peer interactors deviated about the same degree in the alone and peer-present conditions. However, the low peer interactors under the peer-endorsement condition increased their deviant behavior when the tempting peer was present.

Rule enforcement by children in the different training conditions is presented in Figure 4. A composite inhibitory index was computed, which includes the following inhibitory tactics: verbal discouragement, physical discouragement, attempts to take away the toy, repeating the rationale used in the training (e.g., "the toy might break"), and using a subject-generated rationale (e.g., "the lady will spank you"). Children trained with the object-oriented rule most frequently attempted to inhibit the second child's toy-touching activities; subjects trained with punishment least frequently tried to enforce the rule. Although the nursery schoolers trained with peer-endorsed

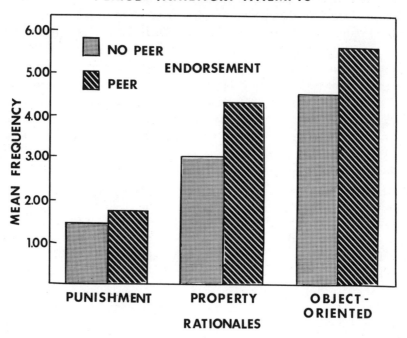

PEER INFLUENCE DURING PEER PRESSURE TEST
PERIOD: INHIBITORY ATTEMPTS

NO PEER
ENDORSEMENT
PEER

MEAN FREQUENCY

PUNISHMENT   PROPERTY   OBJECT-
                         ORIENTED
          RATIONALES

Figure 4. Inhibitory influence attempts by the trained peer during the peer pressure test period (Parke, 1973).

procedures tended to show higher rates of inhibitory attempts than children not so trained, this trend was not significant. However, the importance of peer endorsement becomes clear when the level of peer interaction in the nursery school setting is taken into account. Children who exhibited a high level of peer interaction encouraged deviant behavior more often when the prohibition did not have the endorsement of the peer group than when it did. For low peer interactors, encouragement rates were higher when the prohibition was endorsed by a peer than when there was no peer endorsement (See Figure 5). It is clear that prior level of peer participation is an important variable to be considered in studies of peer influence. Interestingly, there were no age effects for rate of rule transmission.

Did the differential rates of rule transmission affect the extent to which the second child touched the toys? To determine whether the behavior of the child who had been given permission to touch the toys would vary in the presence of children from different training conditions, the toy-touching behavior of the second child was examined. The type of training received by the first child affected the level of toy touching for the second child. A peer who was observed with a child trained with punishment deviated significantly more than did a peer observed with a child trained with a rationale. In addition, peer-endorsement training affected the behavior of the second child as well. A child accompanied by a peer who had received peer-endorsement prohibition training deviated for significantly less time than the child accompanied by a child who had not received this type of peer-endorsement training. Finally, since these levels of inhibition closely parallel the results for the children who received direct training, it is possible that modeling as well as direct peer influence may have contributed to this pattern of findings. An examination of rule transmission from a trained to an untrained peer immediately after training rather than following a response inhibition test period is currently being conducted in order to clarify this issue.

In summary, these findings suggest that the use of rationales as a socializing technique may not only produce a greater degree of inhibition but

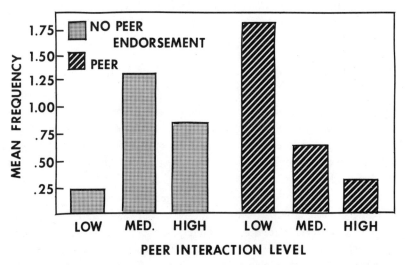

Figure 5. Encouragement of deviant behavior by the trained peer during the peer pressure test period (Parke, 1973).

may result in greater rule transmission. As the earlier studies and this study indicate, not only is the child more likely to inhibit his deviant responses, but he is more likely to attempt to prevent his peers from similar rule violations. Also, the results underline the importance of the source as well as the content of the prohibition in studies of rule conformity and rule transmission.

A number of other issues require attention in future investigations. The behavior of the second peer should be more adequately controlled. The reactions of the peer to the trained child's control attempts could be varied so that the peer confederate either complied with or violated the rule transmitted by the trained child. By introducing another child after the first pair of children have interacted it would be possible to assess the impact of compliance or violation by the first child on the trained child's subsequent rule-transmitting behavior. Thus the impact of feedback on the controlling behavior of a disciplinarian would be examined.

Another issue raised by these studies is the impact of being a rule transmitter on the child's subsequent self-control. Would the child who has transmitted the rule himself subsequently show greater resistance to deviation? Both issues—the effect of feedback on the disciplinarian's behavior and the effect of assuming the role of disciplinarian—are extremely important aspects of socialization. The present paradigm, however, is probably most appropriate for exploring the kinds of training procedures that result in spontaneous rule transmission. In the next section ways of examining the effect of being a rule transmitter on the subject's own self-control will be presented.

The Effects of Assuming the Role of Rule Enforcer on Resistance to Deviation

What effect does being the controlling agent have on the agent's own subsequent behavior? Will those who enforce a set of rules be more likely to follow them? Do children who learn rules by enforcing them learn those rules more effectively and obey them more closely than do children who have had rules imposed on them?

Although there is little empirical knowledge about what effect being a rule enforcer has on children's own rule-following behavior, some of the recent work on the effects of cross-age helping (Gartner, Kohler, & Riesmann, 1971; Lippitt & Lippitt, 1968) is relevant. The purpose of these studies is to examine the effect of teaching a younger child on the learning of an older peer instructor. A recent study by Allen and Feldman (1973) illustrates this approach. These investigators trained low achieving fifth-grade children to teach third graders a series of 10 lessons in a variety of academic subjects including language, science, and reading. The fifth graders learned more when they were tutoring than when they were studying alone—even though they were rated as "low achievers." On the other hand, there was no difference in the performance of the third graders whether they were taught by an older child or whether they studied the material alone. Other evidence (Lippitt & Lippitt, 1968) suggests that placing a child in a position of responsibility may produce change in his school behavior as well as in his academic achievement. Although the situations used in our studies do not involve scholastic skills, the finding that the opportunity to assume responsibility in a teaching situation improves both the scholastic and nonscholastic behavior of the peer instructor is suggestive for our work.

Role playing in peer interaction contexts is probably important for moral development and for the development of self-control. Piaget (1948), for example, has argued that spontaneous rule making and rule enforcing in informal play among children contributes to the development of mature moral judgments. Piaget and other cognitive developmentalists are less clear concerning the impact of this type of peer group experience on the child's moral behavior, particularly on his rule-following behavior. Findings from an experimental investigation (1965) by a Russian, Borishevsky, provide information about this type of behavior. He compared rule-following behavior of children in a checkers game before and after they had had the opportunity to use those rules to control the behavior of peers. One group of first-grade children was matched with superior children players from another first-grade class, so that all members of the first group lost the first game. The games were played according to rules agreed upon by all the children. The "losers" were then matched with inferior players, so that the losers of the first game all won the next game; then they were designated "captains" to oversee a game between two other children and to report all rule infractions. The captains were then matched once again with superior players so that all captains lost their third game. The behaviors compared for the two games lost (before and after the children were designated captains) included the degree to which the players broke the rules, complained of others breaking the rules, referred to the set of rules during the game, and corrected themselves for rule infractions. Significant differences were found for all measures. It is impossible to tell how much of this change reflects imitation of the superior players or how much reflects increased knowledge of the rules from repeated

127

exposure. It would be necessary to test additional control groups before this change could be clearly attributed to the increased relevance of rules for a child after he had used them for controlling the behavior of others. However, this study suggests that further investigation of peers as rule enforcers will be worthwhile.

Bosserman and Parke (1973) recently investigated the effects of assuming the role of rule enforcer on children's self-control. To provide continuity and to permit comparisons with our earlier work, we used a modified version of the resistance-to-deviation paradigm employed in our earlier studies. Two issues were examined: the first was whether children who are given the responsibility of enforcing a set of rules are more likely to follow those rules than are children who do not have responsibility for enforcement. It was predicted that rule-enforcing experience would increase the rule enforcer's own rule-following behavior. The second issue was the effectiveness of the disciplinary tactic in controlling the target child. The question is whether a control agent is more likely to follow a rule that was effective in promoting peer control than a rule that was ineffective.

Forty-eight first- and second-grade boys participated in a study involving high and low rule transmission responsibility and high and low rule effectiveness. A modified resistance-to-deviation situation with three phases was used. First, the subject was shown a set of attractive toys and was informed that these toys were not to be touched. Second, the child went to an adjoining room where he could monitor the toy-touching behavior of another child. Fictitious rule violations (toy touching) were signaled to the subject by a light which was activated at predetermined intervals. The boys in the high rule-enforcement responsibility condition were given five opportunities to ''remind the other boy about the rule'' by pushing a buzzer whenever the light indicated a rule violation. Boys in the low rule-enforcement responsibility condition heard the experimenter activate the buzzer for the same number of rule violations.

To manipulate the rule effectiveness variable, the time interval between successive fictitious rule violations was varied. For half of the subjects in each responsibility condition the rule violations occurred at regular 25-second intervals (low rule-effectiveness); the length of time between violations for boys in the high rule-effectiveness condition gradually lengthened, indicating that the buzzer was increasingly effective. In addition, the experimenter commented on either the effectiveness (''the buzzer really worked'') or the ineffectiveness (''didn't really make any difference'') of the rule-enforcement procedure. The total length of this phase (approximately 2.5 minutes) was equated across the two conditions. To assess the effects of these manipulations on the subject's own rule-following behavior, all children were left alone for 15 minutes with the forbidden toys during the third phase. The frequency and duration of toy touching was observed through a one-way screen and was recorded.

The results in Figure 6 indicate that boys who were given the opportunity to enforce the toy-touching rule for another child touched the toys themselves significantly less frequently and for shorter durations than did boys who were not given this opportunity. Thus, assuming responsibility for controlling the behavior of another individual had an important impact on the controller's own subsequent rule-following behavior. Although the high rule-effectiveness boys touched the toys less than did the low rule-effectiveness boys, the difference was not statistically significant. This finding is similar to the results of peer teaching studies (e.g., Allen & Feldman,

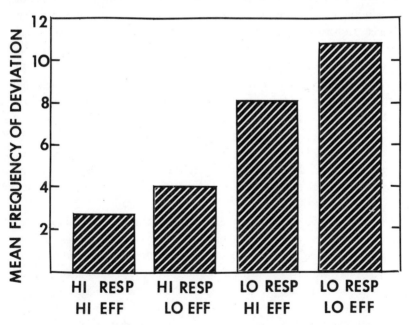

RULE TRANSMISSION RESPONSIBILITY AND INHIBITION

Figure 6. The effect of rule transmission responsibility and rule effectiveness on response inhibition (Bosserman and Parke, 1973).

1973) in which the level of success in executing the assigned task does not appear to be a necessary condition for improving the behavior of the tutor or peer-teacher.

In a subsequent, similar experiment two additional components of rule enforcement by peers were examined. In the original study the type of disciplinary tactic was not varied; a noxious buzzer was used for all subjects. To determine whether the type of discipline used by the peer enforcer altered his own subsequent resistance to deviation, the effects of three types of discipline were compared: (1) a noxious buzzer, (2) a verbal reprimand ("don't touch the toys"), and (3) a verbal rationale in the form of a property rule ("don't touch the toys because they belong to someone else"). We had previously found the rationale to be more effective than punishment (Parke & Murray, 1971) when the discipline was administered directly by the social agent. From these findings we predicted that boys who used or heard the experimenter use the verbal rationale as a method of rule enforcement would later transgress less than would boys who were exposed to the verbal reprimand or the buzzer.

In addition to comparing types of discipline, we examined the effects of responsibility and freedom to choose disciplinary tactics on the child's own subsequent resistance to deviation. There were three levels of responsibility. One group of children (high responsibility-free choice) was allowed to choose the type of discipline (verbal rationale, reprimand, buzzer) by which to enforce rules. A second group (high responsibility-no choice) actively participated in the rule-enforcement phase but was not given a choice of disciplinary tactic. Instead, through a yoked control procedure the type of discipline used by children in this second condition was determined by the prior choice of a yoked partner in the free-choice group. A third group of children (low responsibility-no choice) merely heard the experimenter deliver one of the three disciplinary procedures for the rule violations of the fictitious peer.

There are a number of bases for predicting that if one is given increasing freedom to choose a type of disciplinary tactic it will enhance one's own subsequent adherence to rules. Role theorists (Sarbin & Allen, 1968) argue that increasing role involvement promotes greater behavior change in the direction of the role behavior. Similarly, reactance theorists (Brehm, 1966) predict that children who are not allowed to choose their own means of rule enforcement will resent the experimenter's restriction of their freedom. This resentment might be expected to lead the child in subsequent choice situations

130

to exert his freedom by behaving contrary to the experimenter's stated restriction. Such effects would be reflected in the resistance-to-deviation test phase where restricted subjects would be expected to violate the toy-touching prohibition more than would subjects who had been allowed to choose their means of rule enforcement. This array of conditions resulted in a 3 (type of discipline) x 3 (level of responsibility) design. Eighty-one boys from the first, second, and third grades participated in the study with nine subjects in each of the nine groups. As Figure 7 indicates, the type of responsibility was an important determinant of subsequent subject self-control. Subjects who actively participated in rule enforcement and who chose the type of discipline showed less deviation subsequently than did subjects who had responsibility but no choice in the type of discipline. The low participation-low choice group showed the lowest level of subsequent self-control. As Figure 8 illustrates, the type of rule enforcement also was a significant factor in

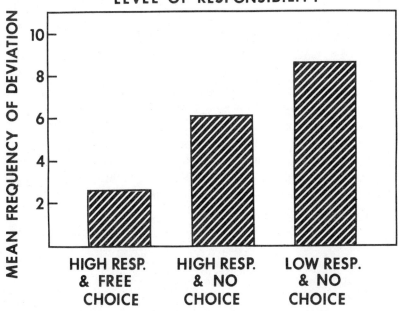

Figure 7. The effect of level of rule transmission responsibility on response inhibition (Bosserman and Parke, 1973).

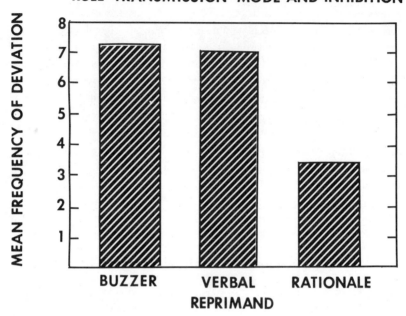

Figure 8. The effect of the type of disciplinary tactic employed during rule enforcement on response inhibition (Bosserman and Parke, 1973).

promoting subsequent self-control. Children who either used (high responsibility) or heard E use (low responsibility) the rationale deviated less than did children who used or who heard either the verbal reprimand or the buzzer. Children in the latter two conditions did not differ. In summary, both the level of responsibility afforded the rule-enforcing peer and the type of disciplinary tactic contribute to the impact of training on children's subsequent self-control. The finding for type of tactic parallels previous findings in which rationales and punishment (noxious buzzer) were used as training techniques by adults (Parke, 1973).

Although the interactions were not significant statistically, inspection of Figure 9 reveals some interesting effects. The clearest difference among the three responsibility conditions occurs when the buzzer is the disciplinary tactic; the difference is less clear when the verbal reprimand is used; and there is no difference among the responsibility groups when the verbal rationale is used. Introducing the verbal rationale attenuates the differences previously found between high responsibility and low responsibility conditions.

132

ROSS D. PARKE

Moreover, the modifying effect of a cognitive rationale is reminiscent of earlier findings that a rationale weakened the effects of timing and of intensity of punishment (Parke, 1969). Finally, the high degree of response inhibition by children who heard the experimenter use the rationale, but who did not themselves participate in enforcing the rule, suggests that mere exposure to rationales directed toward other children may facilitate the child's ability to use rules and rationales to control his own behavior.

These studies suggest that the impact of discipline on the disciplinarian, as well as on his target, needs to be examined closely. An analogue of naturalistic disciplinary practices would include an assessment of the effects of rule enforcement by adults on subsequent rule-following behavior by those

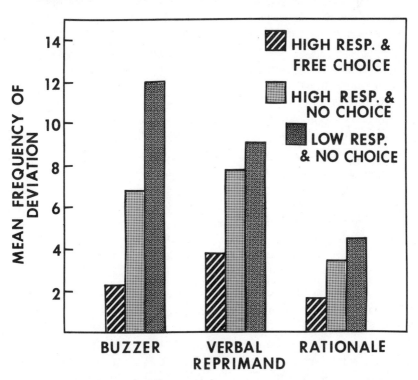

Figure 9. The combined effect of level of rule transmission responsibility and type of disciplinary tactic on response inhibition (Bosserman and Parke, 1973).

133

adults. Also, our findings emphasize the role played by peer-peer interaction in the development of self-control and suggest that opportunities for rule enforcement may be one way to enhance self-control. Although these findings consistently suggest that assuming the role of rule enforcer is effective in promoting self-control, the mechanisms underlying this effect will have to be specified by future research. The contribution of the active rehearsal of a rule to subsequent self-control needs to be examined. Active repetition may increase the salience of the rule and so enhance its recall in the resistance-to-deviation test situation. However, it is unlikely that the effect is caused by rule rehearsal per se. Rather, it is probably owing to rehearsal occurring in the context of rule enforcement. Effects of rule rehearsal that occur independently and in the context of rule enforcement should be assessed.

The experience of executing a responsible role may, itself, contribute to one's subsequent self-control, regardless of the relevance of the rule that is transmitted to the subsequent resistance-to-deviation test; or the effect may be the result of the responsibility in transmitting a rule that is directly relevant to the child's own subsequent test situation. Comparisons between the effects of rules concerning an irrelevant task (e.g., picture sorting) and the effects of rules relevant to toy touching would permit assessment of the relationship between the type of rule and the type of rule-following test.

Although the current findings testify to the importance of structured rule-enforcing opportunities for the development of rule adherence, the role in moral development of spontaneous rule enforcement that occurs during peer-peer interaction deserves renewed attention (Piaget, 1948). Not only is more experimental analysis of this problem necessary but systematic observations are needed of the development of rule-transmitting and rule-enforcing behaviors in natural settings.

The Role of the Child in Shaping Parental Disciplinary Tactics

A question which has been ignored by developmental psychologists is the role of the child in determining the socializing agents' choice of disciplinary techniques (Parke, 1970). Laboratory investigations of punishment, as well as interview studies of child-rearing and disciplinary practices, have been based on a model of unidirectional influence in which it is assumed that adults influence children; but little attention has been paid to the ways in which children can influence adults' behavior. Bell (1968) presented a persuasive case for reconsidering the direction of effects in socialization. Applying this viewpoint to disciplinary tactics, we noted earlier that parental disciplinary tactics vary with the characteristics of the child, and Clifford (1959) illustrated that adults shift their disciplinary practices as a function of the age of the target child. Similarly Dion (1972) reported that adults advocate less intense punishment for females than for males who commit the same severe offense. Rothbart and Maccoby (1966) found that fathers were more lenient with daughters and mothers were less punitive with their sons. Another illustration of the importance of the characteristics of children is provided by Coates (1972) who found that in a learning situation white adult males gave more negative responses to black children than to white children. Even more persuasive evidence comes from studies of excessive use of physical punishment (e.g., child battering) in which it has been found that the same child received very similar batterings in two different homes (Milowe & Lourie, 1964). Certain child characteristics may, in part, be responsible for eliciting extreme treatment from adults. The message of these findings is clear: the characteristics of children do play a role in determining the disciplinary practices that adults choose.

However, there is another analysis that can usefully elucidate the child's role in modifying adult behaviors in a disciplinary context. By this analysis an attempt is made to specify the kinds of responses by children that are effective either in modifying the adult's choice of disciplinary tactic or in modifying adult behavior subsequent to the administration of discipline.

In a recent study (Parke, Sebastian, Collmer, & Sawin, 1974), we explored one aspect of this problem—the manner in which adult behavior following the administration of discipline is altered by the child's reaction to being disciplined. Our aim was to illustrate the role played by the child in modifying adult behavior in disciplinary encounters.

As a first step in understanding this role, we sought to determine whether adults and children can reliably predict adult behavior in a video-taped disciplinary encounter. Specifically we asked both adults and children to judge how an adult disciplinarian would respond to different reactions (e.g., defiance, reparation) of a child to being disciplined. To assess developmental changes in children's perceptions of the effectiveness of different reactions for modifying adult behavior, children of different ages and adults were used as judges.

First it was necessary to determine adult perceptions of what impact child reactions to being disciplined would have on the subsequent behavior of an

135

adult. A sample of 144 adults was shown a single two-minute video tape in which a child misbehaved (deliberately knocked a book off a peer's desk) and a female teacher verbally reprimanded the misbehaving child ("That was bad; you shouldn't have done that. You won't be able to go out for recess"). The child's reaction to being disciplined was varied in one of the following ways: reparation—the child offered to pick up the book; defiance—the child told the teacher, "I don't like recess anyway"; plead—the child protested the punishment, "I wasn't that bad; I really want to go out for recess"; ignore—the child showed no verbal reaction but turned away from the teacher.

There were 24 video tapes on which boys or girls in one of three grades (second, fourth, and sixth) exhibited one of the four reactions. Each adult viewed a single film and then rated on a five-point scale the probability that the teacher would show different positive and negative behaviors. Positive reactions were smiling ("respond positively by smiling") and consolation ("tell the child not to worry, he can go out another day"). The negative reactions were anger ("become angry with the child") and threaten ("tell the child if he doesn't behave, he'll have to stay in tomorrow").

The main results are presented in Figures 10 and 11. Adults who saw the child make reparation (offer to pick up the book) were significantly more likely to predict that the teacher would respond positively by "smiling" than were adults who saw the child react defiantly or ignore the disciplinary agent. Pleading elicited more predictions that the teacher would console the child than did either ignoring or defiance. If the child reacted defiantly after being reprimanded (Figure 11), most adults predicted that this would increase the probability that the teacher would react with anger or threat.

After determining the adult's perceptions, we investigated children's perceptions of the impact on adults of the reactions of children to discipline. A sample of 187 children divided approximately equally into boys and girls at second-, fourth-, and sixth-grade levels participated in this phase of the project. Each child viewer saw a film with a child of the same grade level and sex as himself exhibiting one of the four reactions. The children, like the adult viewers, indicated on a five-point scale their predictions of how adults would respond to these reactions. The children's results are summarized in Figures 12 and 13, and they closely parallel the adult ratings. Children who saw the film child make reparation after being disciplined were more likely to predict that the teacher would respond positively than were children who saw the defiant child. Pleading elicited more predictions of the consoling reaction than

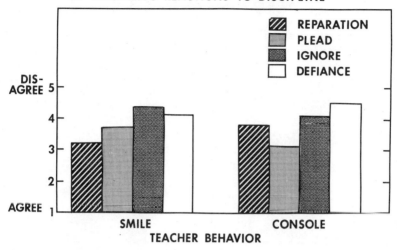

Figure 10. Adult predictions of the relationship between the reactions of children to discipline and the positive responses of teachers (Parke, Sebastian, Collmer, and Sawin, 1973).

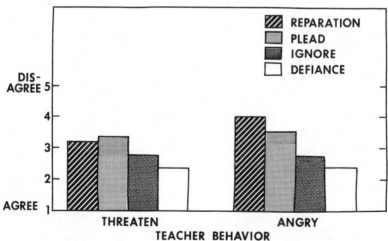

Figure 11. Adult predictions of the relationship between the reactions of children to discipline and the negative responses of teachers (Parke, Sebastian, Collmer, and Sawin, 1973).

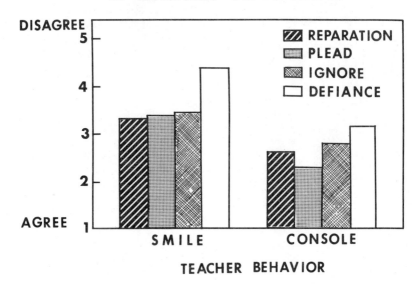

CHILDREN'S PERCEPTIONS OF IMPACT
OF REACTIONS TO DISCIPLINE

Figure 12. Children's predictions of the relationship between other children's reactions to discipline and the positive responses of teachers (Parke, Sebastian, Collmer, and Sawin, 1973).

did defiance, which elicited predictions that the teacher would respond with anger and threat. The fact that the grade and sex differences of the children in the sample did not produce differences in the results suggests that as early as second grade children have well-defined notions about how adults will respond to the reactions of children to being disciplined. In a follow-up study, four- to six-year-old children have been included; the findings indicate that children as young as four years of age are accurate and discriminating predictors of adult behavior.

A related question concerns the impact of children's reactions that occur after misbehaving, but before discipline is administered, on the type or severity of discipline that an adult will select. The same video-tape technique that was used in the earlier studies was employed. Children from four to seven years of age saw a short video tape of a child model of the same age and sex as themselves misbehaving (pushing a peer's books off his desk) and then immediately exhibiting one of the four reactions that were examined in the previous studies. On a five-point scale of punitiveness the children rated the adults' choice of discipline. As the results indicate in Figure 14, ignoring the teacher or behaving defiantly led to predictions of more severe discipline than did either pleading or making reparation. There were no age effects.

In summary, children expect defiant reactions to lead to more severe discipline and more negative responses from adults; reparative reactions are expected to elicit more positive responses and less severe discipline.

What are the implications of these findings? First, children's awareness of the impact of their reactions on adult disciplinary choices and postdisciplinary behaviors suggests that children probably play an important controlling role in modifying adult discipline. Second, child reactions may contribute to inconsistency in the selection and administration of discipline. Moreover it is possible that positive reactions following a disciplinary procedure may dilute the inhibitory value of the discipline. In other words, by reacting positively shortly after administering a reprimand, an adult may undermine the effectiveness of the discipline. Not only is such inconsistency ineffective in achieving suppression of unacceptable behavior in the immediate situation

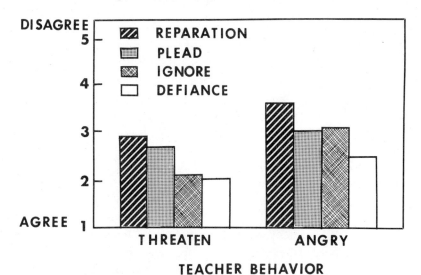

CHILDREN'S PERCEPTIONS OF IMPACT OF REACTIONS TO DISCIPLINE

Figure 13. Children's predictions of the relationship between other children's reactions to discipline and the negative responses of teachers (Parke, Sebastian, Collmer, and Sawin, 1973).

CHILDREN'S PERCEPTIONS OF IMPACT
OF INTERVENTION PRIOR TO DISCIPLINE

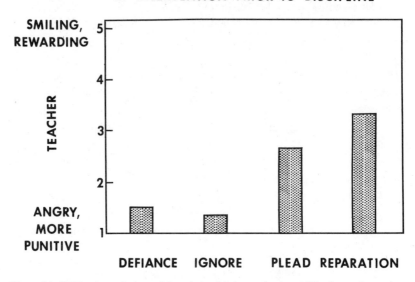

Figure 14. Children's predictions of the relationship between other children's reactions prior to discipline and the disciplinary choices of teachers (Parke, Sebastian, Collmer, and Sawin, 1973).

(Parke & Deur, 1972) but it may also make it more difficult to control the child with this kind of discipline on future occasions. In fact other findings (Deur & Parke, 1970) have indicated that the combination of inconsistent reward and punishment increases resistance to subsequent control either by extinction or by consistent punishment. Possibly a better understanding of the tactics used by children that promote inconsistent discipline will suggest techniques for training socializing agents to increase their consistency.

One word of caution: although the situations used in our study were closely patterned after real-life situations, there are obvious limitations to the findings. They indicate how children expect adults to respond, but it is necessary to determine both by experiments and by naturalistic observations whether parents, teachers, and other socializing agents do respond to children's reactions to discipline as our findings suggest they do. In any case, these findings provide strong support for a bidirectional model of adult-child interaction in which the role· of the child in controlling adult behavior is recognized.

140

ROSS D. PARKE

Conclusion

This overview of our recent research reflects the change in our orientation to punishment, discipline, and self-control. The model of the child as a passive recipient of adult-controlled input is no longer adequate. The child plays an important role in modifying adult behavior in disciplinary contexts and is recognized as an important socializing agent in his own right. As our findings illustrate, children as well as adults function as rule transmitters and rule enforcers. Most important, the evidence reviewed here requires viewing these issues from a developmental as well as from a social learning perspective. An interactive model of response inhibition in which both the cognitive capacities of the child and the social situational factors are recognized would offer the greatest promise for understanding the development of self-control.

The results of these laboratory studies need supplementation by field observations. If this combination of field and laboratory approaches is conducted within a social learning framework in which cognitive development is given proper recognition, it should prove fruitful for further understanding the contributions of punishment and discipline to the socialization of self-control in childhood.

References

Allen, V. L., & Feldman, R. S. Learning through tutoring: Low achieving children as tutors. *Journal of Experimental Education*, 1973, 42, 1–5.

Allen, V. L., & Newtson, D. Development of conformity and independence. *Journal of Personality and Social Psychology*, 1972, 22, 18–30.

Aronfreed, J. Punishment learning and internalization: Some parameters of reinforcement and cognition. Paper read at the biennial meeting of the Society for Research in Child Development, Minneapolis, 1965.

Aronfreed, J., & Reber, A. Internalized behavioral suppression and the timing of social punishment. *Journal of Personality and Social Psychology*, 1965, 1, 3–16.

Bain, K., Milowe, I. D., Wenger, D. S., Fairchild, P., & Moore, L., Jr. Child abuse and injury. *Military Medicine*, 1965, 130, 747–762.

Bandura, A., & Kupers, C. J. The transmission of patterns of self-reinforcement through modeling. *Journal of Abnormal and Social Psychology*, 1964, 69, 1–9.

Bell, R. Q. A reinterpretation of the direction of effects of socialization. *Psychological Review*, 1968, 75, 81–95.

Borishevsky, M. I. Osobeniosti otnoshenie rebenka k pravilam povedenia v igroboi situatsi. *Voprosy Psikhologii*, 1965.

Bosserman, R., & Parke, R. D. The effects of assuming the role of rule enforcer on self-control in children. Paper presented at the biennial meeting of the Society for Research in Child Development, Philadelphia, 1973.

Brehm, J. *A theory of psychological reactance*. New York: Academic Press, 1966.

Cheyne, J. A. Punishment and reasoning in the development of self-control. In R. D. Parke (Ed.), *Recent trends in social learning theory*. New York: Academic Press, 1972.

Cheyne, J. A., & Walters, R. H. Intensity of punishment, timing of punishment, and cognitive

141

structure as determinants of response inhibition. *Journal of Experimental Child Psychology*, 1969, 7, 231–244.

Clifford, E. Discipline in the home: A controlled observational study of parental practices. *Journal of Genetic Psychology*, 1959, 95, 45–82.

Coates, B. White adult behavior toward black and white children. *Child Development*, 1972, 43, 143–154.

Deur, J. L., & Parke, R. D. The effects of inconsistent punishment on aggression in children. *Developmental Psychology*, 1970, 2, 403–411.

Dion, K. K. Physical attractiveness and evaluation of children's transgressions. *Journal of Personality and Social Psychology*, 1972, 24, 207–213.

Gartner, A., Kohler, M., & Riesmann, F. *Children teach children*. New York: Harper, 1971.

Grinder, R. E. Relations between behavioral and cognitive dimensions of conscience in middle childhood. *Child Development*, 1964, 35, 881–891.

Haviland, J. A developmental study of children's beliefs about punishment. Unpublished doctoral dissertation, Michigan State University, 1970.

Hess, R. D., & Shipman, V. C. Cognitive elements in maternal behavior. In J. P. Hill (Ed.), *Minnesota symposia on child psychology*. Vol. 1. Minneapolis: University of Minnesota Press, 1967.

Kamii, C. K. Socio-economic class differences in the preschool socialization practices of negro mothers. Unpublished doctoral dissertation, University of Michigan, 1965.

Kohlberg, L. Development of moral character and moral ideology. In M. L. Hoffman and Lois W. Hoffman (Eds.), *Review of child development research*. Volume 1. New York: Russell Sage Foundation, 1964. Pp. 383–431.

————. Stage and sequence: The developmental approach to socialization. In D. A. Goslin (Ed.), *Handbook of socialization theory and research*. Chicago: Rand McNally, 1969.

LaVoie, J. C. Punishment and adolescent self-control: A study of the effects of aversive stimulation, reasoning and sex of parent. Unpublished doctoral dissertation, University of Wisconsin, 1970.

————. A developmental study of reasoning and its effects on resistance to deviation in children of high and low maturity of moral judgment. Paper presented at the biennial meeting of the Society for Research in Child Development, Philadelphia, 1973.

Lippitt, P., & Lippitt, R. Cross-age helpers. Unpublished research report, Center for Research on Utilization of Scientific Knowledge. University of Michigan, 1968.

Milowe, I. D., & Lourie, R. S. The child's role in the battered child syndrome. *Journal of Pediatrics*, 1964, 65, 1079–1081.

Parke, R. D. Effectiveness of punishment as an interaction of intensity, timing, agent nurturance and cognitive structuring. *Child Development*, 1969, 40, 213–236.

————. The role of punishment in the socialization process. In R. A. Hoppe, G. A. Milton, & E. C. Simmel (Eds.), *Early experiences and the processes of socialization*. New York: Academic Press, 1970. Pp. 81–108.

————. Rationale effectiveness as a function of age of the child. Unpublished research, Fels Research Institute, 1972. (a)

————. Some effects of punishment on children's behavior. In H. W. Hartup (Ed.), *The young child*. Washington: National Association for the Education of Young Children, 1972. (b)

————. Explorations in punishment, discipline and self-control. In P. Elich (Ed.), *Social learning*. Bellingham: Western Washington State Press, 1973.

Parke, R. D., & Deur, J. L. Schedule of punishment and inhibition of aggression in children. *Developmental Psychology*, 1972, 7, 266–269.

Parke, R. D., & Dimiceli, S. The modification of a developmental trend in rationale effectiveness as a function of peer group endorsement. Unpublished research, Fels Research Institute, 1973.

Parke, R. D., & Murray S. Re-instatement: a technique for increasing stability of inhibition in children. Unpublished manuscript, University of Wisconsin, 1971.

Parke, R. D., Sebastian, R., Collmer, C., & Sawin, D. Child and adult perceptions of the impact of reactions to discipline on adult behavior. Unpublished research, Fels Research Institute, 1974.

Piaget, J. *The moral development of the child*. Glencoe, Illinois: Free Press, 1948.

Rothbart, M. K., & Maccoby, E. E. Parents' differential reactions to sons and daughters. *Journal of Personality and Social Psychology*, 1966, 4, 237–243.

Sarbin, T. R., & Allen, V. L. Role theory. In G. Lindzey & E. Aronson (Eds.), *Handbook of social psychology*. Reading, Pa.: Addison-Wesley, 1968.

Walters, R. H., & Parke, R. D. The influence of punishment and related disciplinary techniques on the social behavior of children: Theory and empirical findings. In B. A. Maher (Ed.), *Progress in experimental personality research*. Vol. 4. New York: Academic Press, 1967, Pp. 179–228.

Walters, R. H., Parke, R. D., & Cane, V. A. Timing of punishment and the observation of consequences to others as determinants of response inhibition. *Journal of Experimental Child Psychology*, 1965, 2, 10–30.

+ DAVID ZEAMAN AND BETTY J. HOUSE +

Interpretations of Developmental Trends in Discriminative Transfer Effects

AGE TRENDS have been reported in discriminative transfer effects, but the interpretation of these developmental trends is currently controversial. Older children differ from younger children in the relative difficulty they experience with various kinds of intradimensional and extradimensional shifts, and at least three types of explanation have been offered to account for the developmental differences. One hypothesis is that older children tend to mediate their discriminations to a greater extent than younger children. Another explanation relates shift effects to developmental differences in learning-rate parameters. A third account posits ontogenetic changes in the perception of compound and component aspects of complex discriminative stimuli. These three developmental hypotheses correspond roughly to three traditional and basic issues in learning theory: (1) *how* learning takes place (older subjects tend to mediate, younger do not); (2) how *fast* learning occurs (older subjects learn faster); (3) *what* is learned (older subjects tend to learn components, younger learn compounds). It is our purpose here to review the current experimental and theoretical literature of discriminative transfer and to evaluate the support for the three types of explanation.

NOTE: The preparation of this paper was supported by Grant M-1099 from the National Institute of Mental Health and Research Career Program Award K6-HD-20,325 of the National Institute of Child Health and Human Development, United States Public Health Service. Appreciation is expressed to William Zieger for his help in carrying out the computer simulations.

144

DAVID ZEAMAN

Three Developmental Hypotheses

The Developmental Mediation Hypothesis. Kendler and Kendler are the authors and staunch defenders of this position, which in its simplest form may be stated as: the tendency to mediate discriminative learning increases with age. Younger children solve discriminative problems using "a single-unit mechanism in which responses are under direct control of external stimulation" in contrast to older subjects who make use of "a mediational mechanism in which behavior is controlled by self-generated symbolic cues that represent conceptual categories" (Kendler, Kendler, & Ward, 1972, p. 102). Whether this age trend in conceptual mediation represents a difference in capacity or merely in preference is an issue of importance, but not one on which the Kendlers have taken a clear stand. Yet another related issue of substance is the nature of the developing mediation, e.g., selective attention versus verbal mediation. These subissues are of interest in the context of the present paper only if the developmental mediation hypothesis is true.

The Learning-Rate Hypothesis. Some theorists (e.g., Fisher & Zeaman, 1973; Sutherland & Mackintosh, 1971; Zeaman & House, 1963) maintain that all discrimination learning is mediated by selective attention. To predict performance on a discrimination shift, one must take into account two sources of positive or negative transfer from the original problem — instrumental habit strength and the dimensional mediating response. If there are developmental effects in shift data, it seems reasonable to assume that these may be related to developmental differences in learning rates rather than to qualitative differences in the mechanism. A number of writers have pointed this out, e.g., Campione (1970) and Dickerson, Novik, and Gould, who explicate the hypothesis with great clarity: "The relative rates at which mediating and instrumental choice responses are acquired and extinguished change developmentally" (Dickerson, Novik, & Gould, 1972, p. 117).

The Compound-Component Hypothesis. The ontogenetic changes in discriminative shifting have been attributed to differential attention to, or perception of, stimulus components and compounds. Older humans tend to perceive dimensional components of discriminative stimuli (such as form or color attributes), but young children and nonhumans respond more to undifferentiated, thing-like combinations of stimulus attributes (compounds). The major proponents of this view are Tighe and Tighe (1972; T. Tighe, 1973), and Cole (1973). The distinction between components and compounds is easy enough to exemplify, but it is more difficult to define precisely. For a simple example consider a two-choice simultaneous discrimination with two kinds of trials alternating randomly: a black square versus a white circle (with black square positive) and a black circle versus a white square (with black circle positive). At least two solutions are possible: (1) a component solution (black is correct) and (2) a compound solution (the black square is correct and the black circle is correct).

A variety of descriptions of component and compound solutions has been offered. Tighe and Tighe (1972) equate compound and component solutions with object and dimensional control of discriminative response, respectively. In 1966 Tighe and Tighe described the compound solution as one in which "the subject has not isolated the relevant distinguishing feature, that is, the properties of the stimulus objects are not fully differentiated. He may be distinguishing the stimulus objects on the basis of combined values of the two features on different trials . . ." [p. 366]. They characterize the component solution as one in which "the subject has isolated the relevant distinguishing feature" [p. 366]. Cole (1973) refers to a component solution as "conceptual" in contrast to a compound solution which is achieved "on the basis of particular object-reward relation (S-R associations)" [p. 127]. Earlier proponents of the compound-component hypothesis include Werner (1948), who regarded responses to components as abstract (and characteristic of higher developmental levels) and responses to compounds as concrete (and more immature), and Teas and Bitterman (1962), who described compound solutions as more primitive than component solutions. Although they were led to question the ontogenetic aspects of the problem, House and Zeaman (1963) introduced some experimental designs and theory to measure discriminative control by components and compounds; the latter were described as the combination of two or more aspects responded to as a unitary pattern, different from, and independent of, any of the constituent components.

Data Domains

Reversal and Extradimensional Shift. About a decade ago Kendler and Kendler (1962) demonstrated developmental differences in the relative ease of reversal shift (RS) and extradimensional shift (EDS) discriminations—specifically the probability that RS is learned more quickly than EDS increases with age. (Figure 1 illustrates the two shift designs.) This finding instigated a flood of research reports continuing, although at a reduced rate, up to the present. Extensive surveys of this research have been published by Shepp and Turrisi (1966) and by Wolff (1967); more recently there have been shorter reviews by many investigators. It is not our purpose to review this voluminous literature in its entirety but rather to summarize and to evaluate the evidence for each of the three explanatory hypotheses.

The Mediation Hypothesis. Kendler and Kendler started from the strong position that subjects at the earlier developmental levels were incapable of mediating their discriminative learning. Younger human subjects and rats learned in a single-link fashion, but adult humans mediated their discriminations either verbally or perceptually. The logic relating the RS-EDS comparisons to underlying mechanisms can be stated qualitatively. For subjects not mediating, RS should be harder than EDS because of

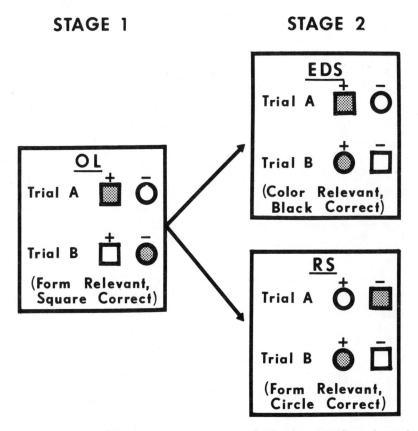

STAGE 1   STAGE 2

Figure 1. Illustrations of EDS-RS comparison. Two types of trial settings, A and B, are alternated randomly with left-right positions of the stimuli varied irregularly. Reward values of the cues are indicated by + and −. OL refers to original learning, EDS to extradimensional shift, and RS to reversal shift.

147

negative cue transfer in RS. For the mediating subject, EDS introduces negative transfer for the mediating response (which is assumed to be dimensional in nature); so the possibility exists that EDS will be harder than RS if, and only if, the negative transfer of the mediating response exceeds the negative cue transfer of the reversal problem; otherwise the opposite will be true. It has been pointed out many times (e.g., Eimas, 1965; Wolff, 1967; Zeaman & House, 1963) that no mediation theory predicts unconditionally that EDS will be harder than RS. Rather, the logic is: nonmediation makes RS harder; mediation is consistent with any outcome of an RS-EDS comparison; therefore if young subjects find RS harder, they are presumably nonmediators. The weakness of this logic is apparent. All that can be asserted is that the relative difficulty of reversals in the young is consistent with their assumed incapacity to mediate.

The original finding of Kendler and Kendler that preschool children find RS harder than EDS has not been replicated under all conditions. Caron (1970) reports that RS is easier than EDS for children as young as three years of age when shift testing is done with an irrelevant dimension variable within trials rather than between trials, as in the Kendler study. His results are consistent with those of three other studies (Dickerson, 1966; Dickerson, Wagner, & Campione, 1970; Mumbauer & Odom, 1967), but Tighe and Tighe (1967) reported the opposite result. Recently, however, Tighe (1973) replicated Caron's experimental procedures closely and got Caron's results. Since the weight of the evidence appears to support Caron and since single-link or nonmediation theory cannot handle these data, the domain of RS-EDS comparisons lends scant support for the developmental mediation hypothesis.

The Learning-Rate Hypothesis. No one has questioned the developmental differences in RS-EDS comparisons with a constant irrelevant dimension, so the problem of accounting for these effects remains. Can the learning-rate hypothesis account for these? The answer is yes, and the logic is as follows: in the RS problem, speed of solution will strongly depend upon two factors, the rates of cue-learning and extinction ($\Theta_{r's}$) and the rates of dimensional acquisition (Θ_{oa}) and extinction (Θ_{oe}). To the extent that the $\Theta_{r's}$ are high (fast instrumental learning and extinction), the RS problem will be solved quickly. To the extent that $\Theta_{oe's}$ are low (slow acquisition and extinction of the mediating responses), RS problems again will be solved quickly. This follows from the fact that RS requires new cue-connections and the maintenance of the existing dimensional responses. If as children mature the

148

Θ_r parameters increase and the Θ_{oe} parameter decreases, the relative speed of RS and EDS should change in the direction observed. The effect can be simulated by any of the existing attention theories of discrimination learning (Fisher & Zeaman, 1973; Lovejoy, 1968; Sutherland & Mackintosh, 1971; Zeaman & House, 1963).

An experiment directed specifically at the learning-rate hypothesis was designed by Dickerson, Novik, and Gould (1972). They had kindergarteners and second-grade children learn three problems in succession. The first required learning a two-choice visual discrimination of either size or brightness with one dimension relevant and the other variable and irrelevant. The second problem had the same stimuli but had a change in the relevant dimension (EDS) so that the previously correct cues were rewarded randomly. The third problem was also an extradimensional shift back to the relevant dimension of the first problem. During the third phase, subjects were divided into two subgroups, one with cue-reward arrangements identical to those in the first phase, the other with reversed cue-reward arrangements. If the random rewards had neutralized the cues during the second task, the two subgroups would have been equal in performance. The results showed that kindergarteners performed more poorly under the reversed cue-reward arrangement than under the nonreversed arrangement, but the second graders found both to be of equal difficulty. The interpretation of these results was that during the second problem (EDS) the kindergarteners switched their attention to the newly relevant dimension before completely neutralizing the cues of the former dimension. For the older children, on the other hand, the cues of the initially relevant dimension must have lost all their differential response attachments before they switched to the new dimensions during the second problem. In terms of the parameters of acquisition and extinction, the most reasonable developmental interpretation of this experimental outcome is that there are higher cue-learning parameters (Θ_rs) for older subjects or that there is a lower extinction rate parameter (Θ_{oe}) for the dimensional mediating response in the older subjects. One aspect of the data of this experiment tends to rule out the Θ_r argument. The speed of original learning of the older children was not faster than that of the younger children, which it should have been if Θ_rs were higher for the older children. This leaves the Θ_{oe} parameter (to which original learning would be relatively insensitive). The final interpretation is that dimensional mediating responses extinguish faster in older subjects.

The Compound-Component Hypothesis. The solution of the simple

149

two-choice discrimination problem illustrated at the left in Figure 1 (original learning [OL]) can take place in at least two ways. For a component solution, the subject approaches the square (or avoids the circle) regardless of color. For a compound solution the subject does not ignore the color and regards the black square as a different stimulus from the white square. The solution in this case is compound (a compound of color and form), which means that the OL problem is solved as two problems: the black square is correct for trial setting A and the white square is correct for trial setting B.

The EDS and RS problems are of differential difficulty for the subjects, depending upon whether they solve on the basis of compounds or components. Consider first the compounder. In the EDS, trial setting A requires no new learning. The reward values for compounds are the same as in OL. The problem on trial setting B is, however, a reversal of that during OL. For the RS, on the other hand, both trial settings are reversals, so the RS is obviously harder for the compounder. Now consider the component solver. In the EDS this subject must now shift his attention from form to color and must also learn the correct cue of the color dimension (black). In the RS, form is still the relevant dimension, and the only new learning to be done is a reversal of the reward values of the black-white cues. It might seem from this analysis that EDS is harder than RS for the component solvers, since they have both dimensional *and* cue learning to do in the EDS; but, as indicated in the previous section, this depends upon learning-rate parameters.

This, then, is the logic: compound learning makes RS harder than EDS; component learning permits either EDS or RS to be harder. If, as development proceeds, subjects tend to use compounds less and components more, then according to the analysis just made younger subjects would find RS harder than EDS and older subjects might find either harder, depending upon the learning-rate parameters. The reported finding that RS is progressively easier than EDS for older subjects is thus consistent with the compound-component hypothesis, but it provides no strong test of it.

OPTIONAL SHIFTS (RS-EDS)

In the major variant of the optional shift method, original training is given with one relevant dimension and one irrelevant dimension, variable within trials (as illustrated in Figure 2). For the optional shift only one of the settings is presented and the reward values of the relevant cues are reversed. As shown in phase 2 of the figure, white is now correct and the size cues become redundant relevant cues. Thus the optional shift can be solved either by

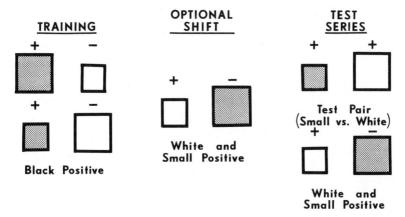

Figure 2. Illustration of the optional shift RS-EDS design. The two settings of training are randomly alternated as are left-right positions of the stimuli. After criterion on the optional shift phase, the two settings of the test series are presented alternately with position variable.

reversing the original habit based on brightness or by learning a new size discrimination. During phase 3, test trials are presented with the other setting from phase 1 to determine which solution has been adopted. Since the correct brightness and size cues during phase 2 are in conflict on the test trials of phase 3, choices will be determined by the stronger of the two tendencies. Generally, the criterion for categorizing subjects as reversal (RS) or extradimensional shift (EDS) is 8 of 10 responses to a particular cue on test trials. Subjects who score between 2 and 8 are classified as inconsistent (I).

The optional shift method has an advantage over the RS-ED shift comparisons because a measure that represents relative strength of reversal and extradimensional shift cues can be obtained for each subject. In general, distributions of test choices tend to be bimodal with relatively few subjects scoring between 2 of 10 and 8 of 10 reversal responses. The percentages of subjects falling into the RS, EDS, and I categories afford a continuous measure of performance change as a function of age, in contrast to the grosser measure of better or worse group performance when reversals are compared with extradimensional shifts.

The percentage of RS subjects increases with age (Kendler & Kendler, 1970; Kendler, Kendler, & Learned, 1962). About 50 percent of kindergarten children chose RS when tested on such dimensions as color, size, or form, but 85 percent of college students given similar training chose RS. A highly discrepant value was reported by Brown and Scott (1972), however, when

151

they tested transfer with two relational dimensions—oddity versus similarity and relative size. In that study 90 percent of the three- and four-year-old children chose an RS.

The probability of choosing an RS over an EDS is strongly influenced by the relative salience of the two dimensions. An extreme example was reported by Kendler, Basden, and Bruckner (1970). They tested rats on an optional shift task in which either color or form was relevant during original learning. All the rats learned color on the optional shift; therefore 50 percent of the subjects were RS and 50 percent were EDS. The color cues had previously been shown to be dominant over the form cues in learning and half-reversal tasks. Degree of learning was an additional factor; form subjects were unable to achieve the same criterion of original learning that color subjects achieved. Tighe and Tighe (1966) compared optional shifts with horizontal or vertical stripes on flat or raised squares. Both rats and children made more RS choices when flat versus raised was the relevant dimension. Children make more RS shifts when assigned to their preferred dimensions (Smiley & Weir, 1966) and also when the physical similarity of the cues of the relevant dimension is greater than the physical similarity of the cues of the irrelevant dimension (Smiley, 1972).

The Mediation Hypothesis. For the RS-EDS optional shift problem the increase with age in the percentage of RS subjects is thought to indicate a transition from single-stage to multistage learning by Kendler and Kendler (1970). This interpretation does not rest on the assumption that choice of an RS shift is a valid index of mediation in an individual subject. Such an outcome for an individual could result from more similar cues on the irrelevant dimension than on the relevant dimension. This effect of dimensional dominance is regarded by Kendler et al. as a single-stage phenomenon. Kendler, Basden, and Bruckner (1970) and Kendler and Kendler (1970) outline a semiquantitative model based on Spence's theory showing that the amount of control exercised by a given dimension is related to the psychophysical similarity of the cues in the positive and negative compounds. This factor was assumed to account for the 50 percent RS rate in the Kendler et al. study. However, in a properly counterbalanced study, each subject would have an even chance of being assigned to his dominant dimension. Thus when the percentage of RS subjects goes above 50 percent, mediational responses are implicated. The rationale is similar to that proposed for facilitation of reversal; without mediation, negative instrumental transfer would produce slower learning of the reversed cues than the old irrelevant cues, resulting in an optional ED shift. The Kendler data are consistent with the developmental mediation hypothesis, but the support is weak, again because mediation theory can account for any outcome of the EDS/RS comparison with free parameters.

The Learning-Rate Hypothesis. The observed increase in RS over EDS subjects can also be explained by assuming differential rates of instrumental and attentional learning in the same manner as for the RS versus the EDS data. Using the multiple-look attention theory of Fisher and Zeaman (1973), we have simulated optional shifts (EDS versus RS) under a few parameter conditions. All parameters but one were fixed at levels within the range of previous simulations that had been found to hold for retarded children; we varied the cue-learning parameter Θ_r from .1 to .7, simulated an optional shift design, and classified the output (statchildren) as RS subjects or EDS subjects using the same 8 of 10 consistency criterion that had been used experimentally (see accompanying tabulation). The RS percentage and the EDS percentage

Value of Θ_r	Children Classified as RS	Children Classified as EDS
.1	5%	67%
.7	38	15

do not sum to 100; the remaining percentage consisted of inconsistent subjects. RS-EDS proportions are clearly sensitive to Θ_r changes.

Simulations were also run with Θ_r held constant (at .4) and variation of Θ_{oe} (extinction-rate parameter for the dimensional mediating response). RS-EDS ratios are also sensitive to Θ_{oe} changes (see accompanying tabulation).

Value of Θ_{oe}	Children Classified as RS	Children Classified as EDS
.1	24%	2%
.4	28	37

Although the results of these two simulations are not quantitatively in close agreement with empirical results (the percentages of I subjects are too high), they do show that mediation theory can, with parameter changes, accommodate the observed developmental differences in the relative probabilities of RS and ED shifts in an optional shift design. The percentages of I subjects can be reduced by varying other parameters such as the starting probabilities of attending to the two dimensions, but we have not yet attempted a thorough parameter search. The major point to be made is simply that developmental differences in EDS-RS optional shift outcomes are consistent with the learning-rate hypothesis.

The effect of dimensional dominance on transfer performance has also been claimed as a consequence of attention theory (e.g., Smiley & Weir, 1966)

153

However, the magnitude of the effect is probably beyond the predictive capacity of a one-look model such as that of Zeaman and House (1963). According to that model, the probability of attending to the relevant dimension approaches 1.00 and attention to the irrelevant dimension is reduced to a near zero value. Original salience, then, would have a minor effect. Lovejoy's (1968) attention model, although similar in some respects to that of Zeaman and House, has a feature that would allow dominance effects to carry over into the transfer phase. In Lovejoy's model the distinctiveness of each dimension is divided into two parts, a fixed base level value and a directable component. The latter aspect allows temporary changes in salience, while leaving the underlying dominance hierarchy intact. The multiple-look model of Fisher and Zeaman (1973) can handle dominance effects in transfer since a complementary relation between attention probabilities to relevant and irrelevant dimensions is not required. The irrelevant dimension might retain sufficient strength to influence transfer performance appreciably.

Compound versus Component Learning. The explanation of the RS-EDS age effect in optional shift designs proposed by Tighe and Tighe (1972) is different from the mediational theories considered above. If the subjects learn the two settings of original learning as independent problems, then reversal on one of the settings during the optional shift phase would not affect performance on the other setting. As a result, children who have learned the problems independently will respond to the test trial settings in the same manner as they did during original learning and will be categorized as EDS subjects.

Jeffrey (1965) tested the theory that compound learning accounts for ED shifting by comparing performances when the original compounds were destroyed on the optional shift trials and when they were left intact. When the same brightness-size compounds appeared during training and shift, the percentage of RS subjects increased from 37.5 at four years to 74 at age ten. In a second experiment, brightness and size were again the variable dimensions, but the constant form dimension was changed on the optional shift trials. If the training stimuli were squares, the shift stimuli were circles, and vice versa. Under these circumstances the percentage of RS subjects among four-year-olds increased to 76.

Although Jeffrey's results weigh strongly in favor of the compound-component hypothesis (and strongly against the developmental mediation idea), other evidence indicates that young subjects do not use *solely* compound solutions. If an organism learned exclusively on the basis of compounds, no dimensional dominance would be expected. It would make no difference which component was considered "relevant" by the experimenter if the subject perceived only undifferentiated wholes. The logic of this assertion can be demonstrated with reference to Figure 2. If the two settings of the original learning stage consist of four unrelated stimuli, then the difficulty of one setting should not be affected by reward assignments on the other setting. It should be as easy to learn with large black and large white correct as to learn with large black and small black correct. The demonstration of dimensional dominance shows that, in fact, difficulty does depend on which stimuli are correct. Wolff (1967) also pointed out the incompatibility of dimensional dominance and compound learning. In a reply, however, Tighe and Tighe (1968) denied any inconsistency between dimensional prepotency and their theory. They appealed to primary stimulus generalization as an explanation of dimensional dominance in subjects who had not dimensionalized the stimuli.

For example, assume that Ss must discriminate between objects varying simultaneously in size (T,S) and brightness (B,W) and that learning is faster when size is relevant than when brightness is relevant. Such a difference in learning is consistent with the assumption that with size relevant, there is positive transfer from trial to trial due to greater generalization from TB to TW than from TB to SB, but that with brightness cues relevant, there is negative transfer from trial to trial under the same mechanism. (p. 759)

This statement implies that even when subjects perceive stimuli as undifferentiated wholes they generalize from one stimulus to another on the basis of common components. This description of discrimination learning is basically Spencean. If children behave according to Spence's theory before differentiation, it is difficult to see differential consequences of the compound-learning and mediational hypotheses. The notion is at variance with the statement of Tighe and Tighe (1966) that the level of perceptual learning "determines what property or properties of the stimulus objects will be related to reinforcement" [p. 366]. The account is also difficult to reconcile with the statement of Tighe and Tighe (1972) that when stimuli are undifferentiated, the settings of a discrimination problem are learned independently. Perhaps a resolution lies in the assertion of Tighe and Tighe (1972) that "the object-reward relations are both facts of the learning environment, and we assume that the two aspects of stimulation are processed in parallel" [p. 139]. This modification reduces the predictive power of the Tighes' theory unless rules relating stimulus processing are provided. However, it presumably allows generalization by partial identity.

EXTRADIMENSIONAL-INTRADIMENSIONAL SHIFTS

The term intradimensional shift (IDS) is used when new cues from the same relevant dimension are introduced in the shift phase. This provides an opportunity for dimensional mediation as in reversal but eliminates instrumental transfer. No one seems to have made a systematic study relating ED-ID shifts (with an independent group paradigm) to age over any appreciable range, and what few data exist support Wolff's (1967) conclusion that there is no evidence of a shift x age interaction. Eimas (1966) compared kindergarten and second-grade children on ED-ID differences and found that IDS was easier for the children than EDS, but he found no age differences. Rather, the factor most frequently reported to affect EDS-IDS performance differences is the nature of the stimulus display. House and Zeaman (1962) found that with retarded children, constant irrelevant stimuli produced negligible ED-ID differences compared to differences with variable irrelevant stimuli. Trabasso, Deutsch, and Gelman (1966) reported that the use of objects rather than two-dimensional patterns as stimuli strongly enhanced ED-ID differences for nursery school children. Stimulus control of ED-ID differences was also found by Shepp and Gray (1971). In their experiment, the use of variable-between and variable-within irrelevant stimuli had a strong interactive effect on ED-ID differences.

Recently a study has been done using an optional shift paradigm to study ED-ID differences over a wide age range (Figure 3). Kendler, Kendler, and Ward (1972) found that the percentage of subjects choosing an ID shift (when ED and ID shifts were optional) increased from 45 percent at age four to 84 percent at age eight, with an additional increase to 100 percent at the college level. But partially conflicting results have also been reported. Campione (1970) found no differences between four- and eight-year-old children in the percentage of ID shifts (63 percent and 65 percent, respectively). The two studies differed somewhat in procedural details, but the source of the discrepancy has not yet been determined. However, since there is little reason to doubt the adult level of ID preference, the question is not whether a developmental trend is present but, rather, when transition from EDS to IDS occurs. It can be concluded on the basis of all available data that there is some, but not strong, evidence for developmental differences in ED-ID shifts in the direction of the increasing ease of ID in relation to ED shifts.

OPTIONAL SHIFT PARADIGM
EDS VS. IDS

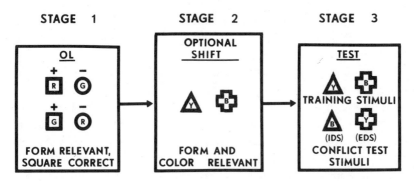

Figure 3. Illustration of the optional shift EDS-IDS design. The two settings of stage 1 are randomly alternated with position variable during OL (original learning). After criterion on the optional shift stage 2, the two settings of stage 3 (test) are alternated with position randomized. The letters R, G, Y, and B refer to the colors red, green, yellow, and blue, respectively.

Developmental Mediation Hypothesis. A strong version of this hypothesis (subjects at low developmental levels are incapable of mediating) is denied by the reports of ED-ID differences (the presumed index of mediation) at the level of nursery school children and even at the level of the rat (Shepp & Eimas, 1964). A weaker version of the developmental mediation hypothesis (age increases the *tendency* to mediate) does receive some factual support from ED-ID experiments, although more data are sorely needed here.

Learning-Rate Hypothesis. If ED-ID differences are to be used to infer dimensional mediation, new cues are generally used during transfer on relevant and controllable irrelevant dimensions. With new cues to be learned for both the ED and ID shifter, there is no obvious reason why higher or lower cue-learning parameters (Θ_r) would change ED-ID differences.

Developmental differences in Θ_{oe}, the mediating response extinction parameter, would, however, change ED-ID differences. Relatively low Θ_{oe} facilitates IDS performance and impairs EDS learning, thus increasing the ED-ID differences. But relatively high Θ_{oe} impairs IDS and facilitates EDS, thus reducing ED-ID differences. In summary, the presence of age x shift interaction is consistent with age changes in Θ_{oe}.

Compound-Component Hypothesis. Subjects solving a discrimination purely on the basis of compounds should show no ED-ID difference, since with new cues during shift all compounds present during learning are

157

destroyed on transfer. We can reason, therefore, that children as young as four years of age do not use compounds entirely. The compound-component hypothesis predicts of course that older subjects would show progressively greater ED-ID differences, and the developmental data in this area, weak though they may be, are consistent with the compound-component hypothesis.

It is possible that all subjects use compounds to some extent or that some subjects at each developmental level use compounds; it is also possible that the observed instances of stimulus control of ED-ID differences have occurred because the compounding tendency is controlled by stimulus factors. Shepp and Gray (1971) have made this argument in accounting for the wide variations they observed in ED-ID differences under various conditions of irrelevant stimulus variability. The possibility of the stimulus control of compounding does not rule out the truth of the compound-component hypothesis; it means only that comparisons of ED-ID differences across age groups must be closely controlled for stimulus factors.

SUBPROBLEM ANALYSIS

Tighe, Glick, and Cole (1971) presented a new method for analyzing ED shift performance that provides a test of compound versus component learning. Figure 1 shows an R and an ED shift design following original learning with a variable-within irrelevant dimension. Note that on the ED shift problem, one of the settings is treated exactly the same as is original learning with respect to reward values of the stimuli. The other setting represents a reversal of reward. In subproblem analysis, performance on the two settings is analyzed separately. Figure 4 shows the pattern of results obtained with lower organisms. There is no decrement in performance for the unchanged setting; subjects continue at 100 percent even though one of the components of the stimulus compound is receiving extinction trials on the changed setting. Performance on the changed setting, in contrast, begins near zero and improves gradually over trials. The pattern suggests that the subjects learned the two settings as independent subproblems. The criteria for independence are (1) little or no decrement on the unchanged setting, and (2) no difference between performance on the changed setting and the standard reversal learning function. The performance of rats, pigeons, and monkeys, as well as turtles, show these signs of independence (Tighe, 1973).

Figure 5 shows the subproblem analyses for four-year-old and ten-year-old children from a study by Tighe, Glick, and Cole (1971). The older children

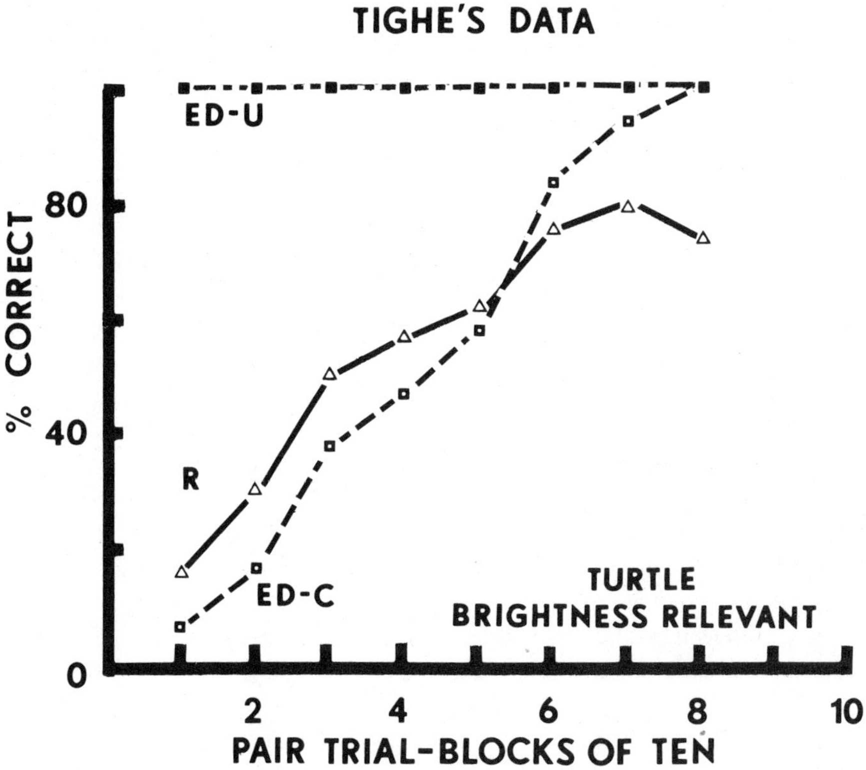

TIGHE'S DATA

Figure 4. Percentage correct as a function of trials for the changed (ED-C) and unchanged (ED-U) settings of EDS and for both settings (R) of RS. The data of this subproblem analysis are from V. Graf and T. J. Tighe, "Subproblem Analysis of Discrimination Shift Learning in the Turtle (Chrysems Picta Picta)," *Psychonomic Science,* 1971, 25, 257–259.

perform similarly on changed and unchanged settings, indicating that they have learned the task as a single problem. Performance on the unchanged setting drops as a result of component extinction on the changed setting. The performance of the four-year-olds, however, falls between the pattern shown by older children and the nonhuman functions in Figure 4. Performance on the unchanged setting does drop somewhat, but there are sizable differences between the two functions. The performance of the younger children is described as relatively independent. Cole (1973) obtained similar age effects with rural Mexican children ranging from age four to age ten.

Tighe (1973) showed that the degree of dependence of subproblems could be increased by adding irrelevant dimensions. In two-dimensional problems with either position or brightness relevant, rats show marked independence whether they were shifted from position to brightness or vice versa. However, when striped versus solid color floors were added as irrelevant cues, the pattern of performance changed. On one of the three sequences tested, position to stripes, evidence of dependent subproblem learning was obtained. Other sequences, stripes to brightness and brightness to position, showed independent patterns. In another experiment the three visual dimensions were variable in addition to position: brightness, stripes versus solid color, and steady versus flickering light. Again the sequence of position to stripes resulted in dependent subproblems. Also the sequence of position to brightness showed mixed results; one rat showed independent solution, three showed dependence, and two were indeterminate. Since position to brightness resulted in strong independence in the two-dimensional problem, this shift toward dependence implicates variability as the causal factor. In another experiment, the performance of four-year-old children became similar to that of ten-year-olds when the number of variable irrelevant dimensions was increased. Origional training was done with brightness relevant and form, height, and position irrelevant. All children were shifted to height relevant. Under these conditions, the performance of the four-year-olds on changed and unchanged settings overlapped as was the case for ten-year-olds.

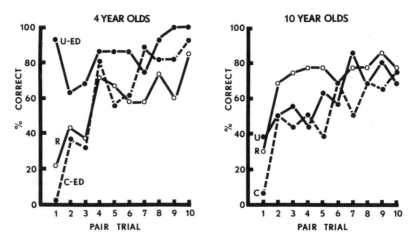

Figure 5. A comparison of the subproblem performance of children four and ten years of age. Percentage correct as a function of trials is shown for the changed (C-ED) and the unchanged (U-ED) settings of EDS. Reversal (R) performance is plotted as the average of both settings. The data are from T. J. Tighe, J. Glick, and M. Cole, "Subproblem Analysis of Discrimination Shift Learning," *Psychonomic Science*, 1971, 24, 159–160.

The Mediation Hypothesis. The results of subproblem analyses do not correspond to expectations based on the theory of Kendler and Kendler (1970). They assume that the behavior of nonhuman subjects and young children with low mediation capacity follows Spencean S-R association laws in which the effective reaction potential of a compound is a function of the weighted sum of the reaction potentials of its components. Response tendencies generalize from one compound to another on the basis of similarity. Although Kendler and Kendler (1962) suggested the possibility that the two settings of a discrimination might be learned as two separate problems, their recent work (Kendler, Basden, & Bruckner, 1970; Kendler & Kendler, 1970) explicates a version of Spencean theory that predicts response to compounds from strength of components. With reference to Figure 1, Spencean theory predicts that an extinction trial on white square would reduce the tendency to approach black square, since there is a common element. Independent subproblem performance indicates a failure to generalize on the basis of partial identity.

Although Spence's theory does not predict subproblem independence as a general rule, Tighe (1973) reports that simulated data from Spence's theory is, in fact, very similar to the independent subproblem pattern over a wide range of parameter values representing the starting weights of the component cues. However, it is not clear from Tighe's report whether independence for both dimensions of a counterbalanced experiment is consistent with Spence's theory. That is, if transfer from dimension A to dimension B shows independence, can the same parameter values predict independence when transfer is from dimension B to dimension A. In a similar demonstration Wolford and Bower (1969) showed that Spence's theory could predict faster reversal than ED shift with some parameters, but the theory could not predict the same direction of results for both dimensions of a counterbalanced experiment. The ability of Spence's theory to predict independence in certain cases indicates that when independence is demonstrated in one direction only, Spencean theory cannot be ruled out. In summary, if the developmental mediation hypothesis is true and young children are following single-link principles, the data of subproblem analyses, taken as a whole, are quite surprising.

Learning-Rate Hypothesis. An attention theory that assumes attention responses that are restricted to those aspects of stimuli generally regarded as "unitary dimensions" (such as size, color, form, brightness, etc.) cannot account for complete subproblem independence. This was demonstrated by

161

Medin (1973). He developed a highly generalized formula, consistent with attention postulates of multiple-look as well as single-look models, to be used as a test of independence. He concluded that such attention models could be rejected for nonhuman subjects but that they "may have been rejected prematurely" [p. 332] for four-year-old children. Using the Zeaman and House (1963) single-look attention model, Medin simulated subproblem data resembling that of both four-year-olds and ten-year-olds. Figure 6 shows that the two simulated functions resemble the empirical findings of Figure 5. The only parameter change necessary was in Θ_r which was set at .15 for the younger statchildren and at .40 for the older children. Thus the learning rate hypothesis may account for developmental differences in humans although not for species differences. However, both Tighe (1973) and Cole (1973) report that a considerable number of four-year-old children made no errors on the unchanged subproblem even though the group curve showed a decrement. Possibly there are some children's data that are also beyond the reach of attention models of component learning.

The developmental differences in the results of subproblem analyses (Figure 5) can be simulated not only by single-look attention theory (with varying Θ parameters) but also by a multiple-look theory that assumes that a subject may attend to one or more component dimensions on each trial. We have used the multiple-look model of Fisher and Zeaman (1973) to simulate the salient features of the human developmental data. In Figure 7 the "4-year" data are simulated with a relatively low Θ_r and a relatively high Θ_{oe}. For the ten-year-old statchildren (Figure 8) the converse holds; Θ_r is relatively high and Θ_{oe} is relatively low. With such parameter arrangements, the points of agreement between children and statchildren are these: (1) younger subjects find RS harder than ED shift; older children find the opposite; (2) the changed and unchanged subproblems follow approximately the same course during most of learning for the older subjects; and (3) the RS and changed subproblems produce approximately the same learning curve for younger subjects.

These results confirm Medin's conclusion that mediation theory (single-look or multiple-look) can handle adequately the observed developmental differences in subproblem analysis data together with one version or another (Θ_r or Θ_{oe}) of the learning-rate hypothesis.

Compound versus Component Learning. Subproblem analyses provide convincing evidence of compound learning in nonhuman subjects and some evidence of compound learning in children. But the finding that independent

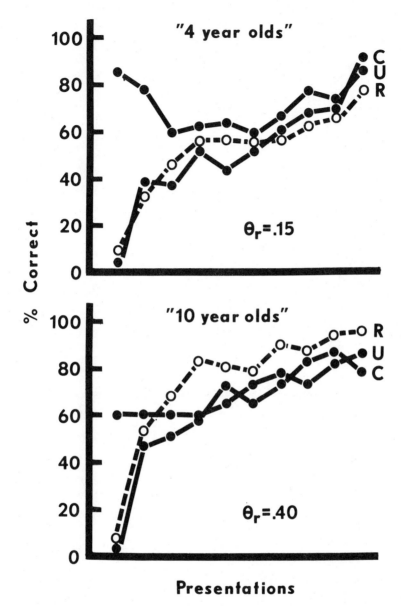

Figure 6. An attention model simulation of subproblem performance with two values of Θ_r. Percentage correct is shown as a function of trials for changed (C) and unchanged (U) settings of EDS and for both settings of RS. The simulations were done by Medin ("Subproblem Analysis of Discrimination Shift Learning," *Behavior Research Methods and Instrumentation*, 1973, 5, 332–336) using the single-look attention model of Zeaman and House ("The Role of Attention in Retardate Discrimination Learning," in N. R. Ellis [ed.], *Handbook of Mental Deficiency*, New York: McGraw-Hill, 1963). The functions resemble data from four- and ten-year-old children.

163

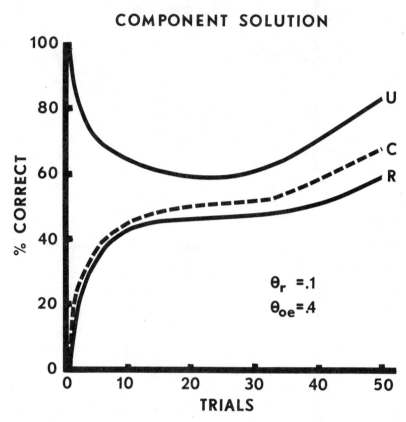

Figure 7. Simulated subproblem performance with relatively low Θ_r and high Θ_{oe}, assumed to be characteristic of four-year-old children. Percentage correct as a function of trials is shown for the unchanged (U) and the changed (C) settings of EDS and for both settings of RS. The multiple-look attention model of Fisher and Zeaman (''An Attention-Retention Theory of Retardate Discrimination Learning,'' in N. R. Ellis [ed.], *International Review of Research in Mental Retardation.* Vol. 6. New York: Academic Press, 1973) was used for the simulation. The curves have been smoothed by the use of rolling averages.

subproblem performance can be reduced by experimental manipulations (such as increasing the number of irrelevant dimensions) suggests that the ability to learn compounds does not necessarily imply an incapacity to learn components. Tighe and Graf (1972) reached a similar conclusion that compound control is not an ''all-or-none matter for a given organism'' [p. 141]. In their study, pigeons were found to learn subproblems independently, whereas in previous experiments using different techniques pigeons had shown a high degree of selectivity of components.

An increase in dependent subproblem learning with increased numbers of variable irrelevant dimensions is consistent with an attention model that assumes that either compounds or components can be selected for attention. Note that when irrelevant dimensions are added in the usual manner, the number of subproblems increases. With one irrelevant dimension, two settings are required; with two irrelevant dimensions, four settings are needed, and so on. As a result, components and compounds have unequal frequencies. The subject has an opportunity to learn about the correct and

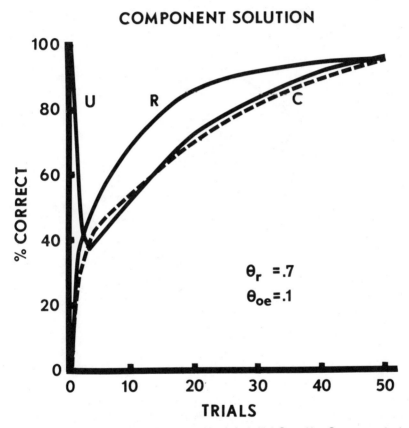

COMPONENT SOLUTION

Figure 8. Simulated subproblem performance with relatively high Θr and low $\Theta \infty$, assumed to be characteristic of ten-year-old children. Percentage correct as a function of trials is shown for the unchanged (U) and the changed (C) settings of EDS as well as for both settings of RS. The multiple-look attention model of Fisher and Zeaman ("An Attention-Retention Theory of Retardate Discrimination Learning," in N. R. Ellis [ed.], *International Review of Research in Mental Retardation,* Vol. 6. New York: Academic Press, 1973) was used for the simulation. The curves have been smoothed by the use of rolling averages.

165

COMPOUNDS IN ATTENTION THEORY

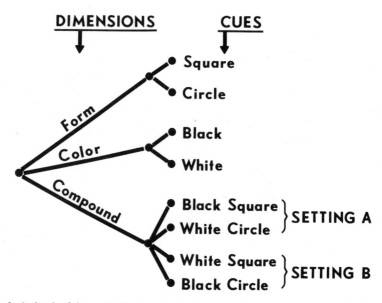

Figure 9. A sketch of the probability tree for the dimensional compounding hypothesis. The discrimination problem is shown at the top. The tree shows the available cues given attention to form, color, or compounds.

incorrect components on every trial, regardless of the number of irrelevant dimensions. But with two variable irrelevant dimensions, for example, each compound cue appears only once every four trials on the average. Even if probability of attending to components were small, the greater number of training trials on component cues might compensate to the extent that instrumental response strength to the component cues exceeds that of compounds at the end of training. Theoretically, such training would increase additional strength so that dependency of subproblems would be expected.

The above analysis assumes that compounds are mediated (House &

Zeaman, 1963) rather than nonmediated as other theorists of subproblem analysis have assumed. Mediated dimensional responding is schematized in Figure 9. The subject's first choice is to attend to component or to compound dimensions; if the compound dimension is selected, the subject is then presented two different compound-cue problems on randomly alternating trials. During ED shift one of these two problems must be reversed. The early trials of reversal bring some extinction of the compound dimensional response which would tend to weaken performance on the unreversed problem. In order to get the pattern of complete independence of subproblems (characteristic of animal subjects), it would be necessary to minimize dimensional extinction. In simulating ED shift dynamics we employed the multiple-look attention model of Fisher and Zeaman (1973) and assumed that subjects finish original learning attending strongly to the compound dimension. Figure 10 shows the results of the simulation with varying, but

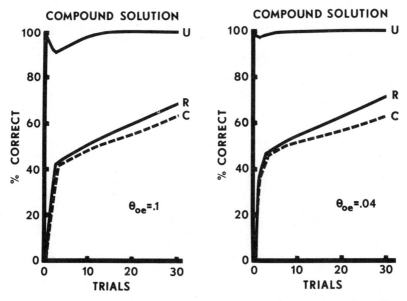

Figure 10. Simulated subproblem performance assuming a compound solution of the problem. Percentage correct is shown as a function of trials for the unchanged (U) and the changed (C) settings of EDS as well as for both settings of RS. The functions on the left were obtained with a somewhat higher value for Θ_{oe} than the functions on the right. The multiple-look attention model of Fisher and Zeaman ("An Attention-Retention Theory of Retardate Discrimination Learning," in N. R. Ellis [ed.], *International Review of Research in Mental Retardation*. Vol. 6. New York: Academic Press, 1973) was used for the simulations. The curves have been smoothed by the use of rolling averages.

167

low, values of the dimensional extinction parameter, Θ_{oe}. These results indicate that it is possible to get as close to the pattern of complete subproblem independence as desired by reducing the Θ_{oe} parameter or as close to the pattern of subproblem dependence (usually assumed to be characteristic of the component responder) by increasing the value of Θ_{oe}.

The conclusion to be drawn from these simulations is that mediation theory can account for just about any pattern of subproblem results by assuming various proportions of compound and component responders and by varying values of the Θ_{oe} parameter.

MINIATURE EXPERIMENTS

Estes (1960) has coined the term *miniature experiment* to refer to designs in which each subject receives only two trials, a training trial and a test trial. This is the *minimum* number of trials necessary for a learning experiment, and great theoretical simplicity arises from such designs. House and Zeaman (1963) adopted this methodology to the study of compound and component solutions of simple discrimination learning and transfer problems. Figure 11 illustrates a test for compound solutions. In this design, subjects responding to components on trial 1 have no obvious basis for an overall suprachance performance on a series of test trials of the kind illustrated, but a compound solution is valid. Figure 12 shows a component testing design. With

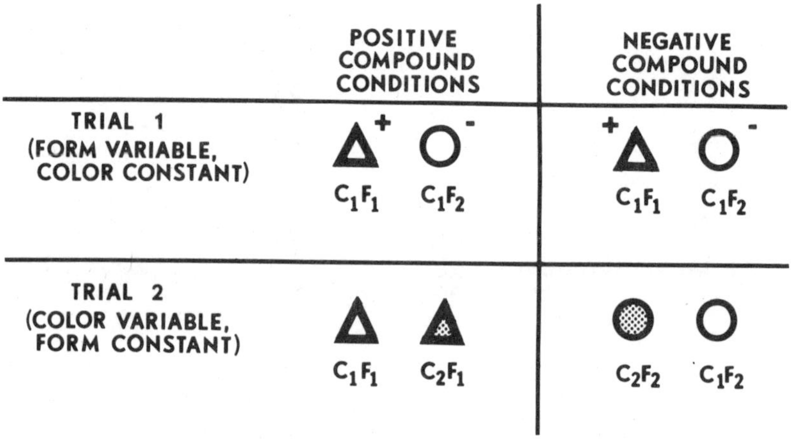

	POSITIVE COMPOUND CONDITIONS		NEGATIVE COMPOUND CONDITIONS	
TRIAL 1 (FORM VARIABLE, COLOR CONSTANT)	$\triangle^+$ C_1F_1	$\bigcirc^-$ C_1F_2	$^+\triangle$ C_1F_1	$\bigcirc^-$ C_1F_2
TRIAL 2 (COLOR VARIABLE, FORM CONSTANT)	$\triangle$ C_1F_1	$\triangle$ C_2F_1	$\circledast$ C_2F_2	$\bigcirc$ C_1F_2

Figure 11. Sample stimulus arrangements on trials 1 and 2 for two experimental conditions. A descriptive notation is introduced beneath each stimulus: C and F represent color and form; the numerical subscripts 1 and 2 denote different component values of color and form. Subjects responding only to components on trial 1 have no basis for responses on trial 2.

COMPONENT TESTS

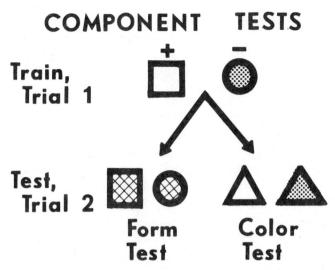

Train,
Trial 1

Test,
Trial 2

Form
Test

Color
Test

Figure 12. Sample stimulus arrangement on trials 1 and 2 for two experimental conditions. Trial 1 stimuli differ in both color and form. On trial 2 the forms for the form test are paired with a new color and the colors for the color test with a new form.

compounds of color and form destroyed on test trials, suprachance performance is attributable to component strengths alone.

A battery consisting of these tests and several variants was administered to a population of retarded children varying in intelligence. The results of this small program of research quite clearly bear a relation to the compound-component hypothesis. The probabilities of attending to both compounds and components increased with mental age over the MA range of four to eight years for retarded children. Both these probabilities can increase with age in a multiple-look model because these probabilities are independent and the subjects are assumed to be capable of looking at more than one dimension on a trial.

The conclusion that retardates in this four- to eight-year mental age range were using both compounds and components increasingly with development is at variance with the notion that components are not used at all by these subjects. The conclusion holds for problems in which components are either optional or are required for solution. It might seem that the developing use of compounds would be inconsistent with the compound-component hypothesis (which predicts the opposite), but in a sense it is not. The program of research described in House and Zeaman (1963), although showing an increase in both

169

compound and component solutions, did not provide controlled comparisons of the rates of growth of each tendency with age. Therefore, the possibility cannot be ruled out that the probabilities of attending to components increase at a faster rate than those of attending to compounds; such a comparison is necessary for a rigorous test of the compound-component hypothesis.

PSEUDOREVERSAL-NONREVERSAL

Some recent studies have cast doubt on the role of dimensional mediation in shift experiments. Bogartz (1965) introduced the technique of presenting reversal-nonreversal tasks with unrelated stimuli. College students learned to associate response A with one set of stimuli and response B with another set. On the transfer shift, either all S-R associations were reversed or only half were reversed. The design is illustrated in Figure 13. Reversal shifts were learned faster. Such designs have been called pseudoreversal-nonreversal shifts (Sanders, 1971), since they share some of the formal properties of traditional RS-EDS experiments without the possibility of dimensional mediation.

Bogartz's effect has been replicated in several studies (e.g., Richman & Trinder, 1968). In a variation, Marquette and Goulet (1968) changed responses on the transfer shift, either maintaining or not maintaining the same stimulus grouping. That is, on a reversal shift all stimuli previously associated with response A were assigned to response C, and response B items were assigned to response D; on half-reversal, response assignments were mixed. For college students reversal was easier than half-reversal whether or not new responses were introduced on the transfer shift. It appeared that stimuli had acquired equivalence on the basis of common learned responses.

Nondimensional transfer has also been demonstrated with school children. Shaeffer and Ellis (1970) found that reversal was easier than half-reversal for eight-year-olds, provided that the original task was overtrained. Goulet and Williams (1970) obtained the same effect in first- and third-grade children. However, unlike the college students of the Marquette and Goulet study, children did not find reversal easier when new responses were introduced during transfer. Goulet and Williams inferred a response-switching strategy in children to account for faster reversal with unchanged response terms, and representational mediation was attributed to adults since they found reversal easier with changed responses as well as with unchanged responses.

Sanders (1971) compared rats, preschool children, and second graders on pseudoreversal and nonreversal shifts. Two settings were presented during

PAIRED-ASSOCIATE PROBLEMS

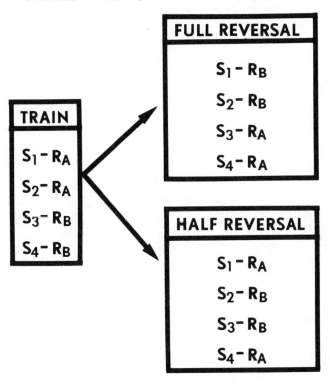

FULL REVERSAL

$S_1 - R_B$

$S_2 - R_B$

$S_3 - R_A$

$S_4 - R_A$

TRAIN

$S_1 - R_A$

$S_2 - R_A$

$S_3 - R_B$

$S_4 - R_B$

HALF REVERSAL

$S_1 - R_A$

$S_2 - R_B$

$S_3 - R_B$

$S_4 - R_A$

Figure 13. A diagram of a pseudoreversal-nonreversal design using paired-associate items. During the training period, four different, unrelated stimuli are paired with response A or response B. All pairings are reversed on full reversal; half are reversed on half reversal.

original learning with four unrelated stimuli. The design is shown in Figure 14. The positive stimuli designated A and C do not have a common relevant component. Thus dimensional transfer is ruled out. During transfer, reward values were reversed for either one or both of the settings. Pseudoreversals were learned faster by second-grade children, but pseudo-nonreversals were easier for rats and preschool children. Sanders also noted spontaneous response shifting on one setting following a reversal trial on the other setting by the older children. In another experiment, Sanders found that a change of instructions caused preschoolers to behave like second graders. Instead of saying simply "No, that is the loser," the experimenter also said "That was the winner before, but now I've changed it so that that's the loser card." The result was spontaneous shifting and faster reversal than nonreversal.

Cole (1973) tested both pseudoreversal-nonreversal shifts and the traditional RS-EDS design with rural Mexican children from ages four to ten. Simultaneous versus successive presentation was another variable. Overall, RS shifts were faster than ED shifts when dimensional mediation was possible and pseudo-nonreversals were learned faster than pseudoreversals. Although no age effects were obtained for the trials-to-criterion measures, subproblem analyses of simultaneous discriminations revealed important differences as a function of age. Among children below the age of nine, pseudo-nonreversal performance indicated independent subproblem learning and dimensional nonreversal showed some tendency toward dependence. For children aged nine to ten, however, both types of nonreversal shifts revealed dependent subproblem performance. Thus there was evidence of dimensional transfer in the younger children, and the older children revealed "conceptual learning in the absence of dimensions" [p. 143]. With successive presentation, dimensionality was less important and the age effects were less

DISCRIMINATION PSEUDOREVERSAL-NONREVERSAL

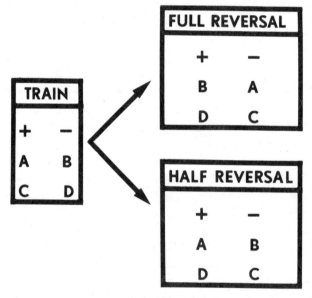

Figure 14. An illustration of a pseudoreversal-nonreversal discrimination transfer task. Stimuli A, B, C, and D are unrelated and randomly assigned to reward conditions. During training, the two settings are randomly alternated and left-right positions of the stimuli are also varied irregularly. On a full reversal, all reward contingencies are reversed; on half reversal, one setting has the reward values reversed but the other does not.

172

clear than with simultaneous presentation. Cole also found that spontaneous shifting increased with age in both dimensional and nondimensional conditions.

The data of this section have no obvious relevance for the learning-rate hypothesis or for compound versus component learning, but they do have implications for the mediation hypothesis. The mediation demonstrated in these studies is highly general in that it operates on arbitrarily selected sets and not just on dimensionally related stimuli. Two types of explanation have been suggested. One is a response-switching strategy (e.g., Goulet, 1971; Sanders, 1971); the other is acquired equivalence by the association of common responses or outcomes to the experimental stimuli. Mechanisms such as acquisition of "novel stimulus dimensions" (Richman & Trinder, 1968) and the imposing of "conceptual order" (Cole, 1973) probably belong in the latter category.

These demonstrations are significant because some transfer shift experiments may confound at least two sources of mediation. Nondimensional mediation can affect RS-EDS comparisons, optional shifts, and dependence of subproblems on EDS tasks. Two questions are suggested: How large is the contribution of nondimensional mediation to shift data? How much of the age effect can be attributed to the development of new sources of mediation?

With respect to the first question, it is clear that nondimensional mediation cannot be the exclusive source of transfer in shift experiments. Decisive evidence comes from ID-ED shift experiments in which all new cues are presented and dimensional mediation is the only source of transfer. There is also some evidence that dimensional mediation is stronger than nondimensional mediation when the two are placed in conflict. Kendler, Kendler, and Sanders (1967) trained adults on a paired-associate task with stimulus words belonging to two categories, e.g., vegetables and insects. Assignment to one of the two responses was by mixed categories; half of each category was associated with one response and half with the other. On the half-reversal shift, all words belonging to the same category were assigned to the same response. Under these circumstances, half-reversal was easier than reversal, revealing the dominance of pre-experimentally acquired conceptual mediating responses. Richman (1973) showed that the direction of results could be reversed with overtraining; that is, categories determined by experimental response assignments became dominant and reversal was superior to half-reversal.

173

It appears that nondimensional mediation increases with developmental level, although there is some discrepancy in estimates of its earliest appearance. Goulet and Williams (1970) reported that six-year-olds showed such mediation, but Cole (1973) did not observe such mediation in rural Mexican children until they reached the age of nine. Dimensional mediation appeared earlier than nondimensional mediation in the Cole study. Preschool children did not show nondimensional mediation without special instruction in Sanders's (1971) study. Thus it seems likely that changes in reversal behavior with age may be influenced by the development of nondimensional mediation; but the extent to which this occurs cannot be determined with available data. Changes in ID-ED shift behavior with age cannot, of course, be explained by nondimensional mediation.

Summary

This section summarizes the evidence and arguments for each of the hypotheses under consideration in relation to some competing theoretical orientations.

Developmental Mediation Hypothesis. The idea that subjects at lower developmental levels are incapable of mediating their discriminations is no longer tenable because it has been demonstrated that three-year-old children show ED-ID shift differences and because of the monumental amount of evidence amassed by Sutherland and Mackintosh (1971) indicating that subhuman animals employ selective attention in discriminative learning. We agree entirely with Cole and Medin (1973) in their conclusion that this is a dead issue. They say, "It is urged that investigators lay aside demonstrations of the existence of mediation in young children as a focus of research, substituting a search for the conditions of its occurrence" [p. 353].

Mediational Tendency. Kendler and Kendler have moved away from their initially strong views on mediational capacity to a version of the developmental mediation hypothesis which holds that children become increasingly likely to mediate as they mature (Kendler & Kendler, 1968). These writers leave open the question of whether the increased tendency to mediate is the result of cumulative experience or of some underlying maturational variable. If younger subjects have the capacity to mediate and do not do so spontaneously on tasks in which mediation is optional but do mediate on tasks in which mediation is required or mediate after special training, then the law implied here is not developmental (in the maturational sense) but rather is an instance of transfer of training or more broadly reflects a law of learning. If, on the other hand, there are maturational differences in susceptibility to mediational training, this may be a developmental law, although it would imply some form of learning-rate argument, which we consider elsewhere. In summary, any form of the developmental mediation hypothesis that speaks merely of a maturing tendency to mediate leaves us in doubt about the nature of the developmental law implied.

Even if the developmental significance of a mediational tendency hypothesis is questionable, we may still ask, how well supported is this hypothesis in the data domains being considered? The answer, in summary, is that the EDS-RS data (including the optional shift variants) are at least consistent with the hypothesis, although the experiments were not well controlled for competing interpretations. The ED-ID shift data (including optional shifts) are mixed, providing some positive evidence and some negative evidence. The subproblem analysis data generally are consistent with the hypothesis, although the behavior of the younger subjects, who presumably are nonmediating (the single-linkers), does not conform easily to expectations of single-link theories, especially the recent one of Kendler and Kendler (1970). The results of pseudoreversal experiments support a mediational tendency hypothesis insofar as they show age changes in mediational tendencies; however, the kind of mediation which is developing is not dimensional. Finally, the data of the miniature experiments area are consistent with the hypothesis if responses to both compounds and components are assumed to be dimensional in nature; otherwise these data are weakly relevant or inconsistent.

The data of the pseudoreversal experiments can be summarized easily: (1) nondimensional mediation apparently increases with age but at a slower rate than does dimensional mediation; (2) the two kinds of mediation are confounded in experiments on EDS-RS, on optional shift (EDS-RS), and on subproblem dependence but not in ED-ID shift experiments.

At the empirical level there is a large body of experimental evidence, most but not all of which is consistent with the idea that "something" mediational may be increasing with age. That the something is not a capacity seems clear; that it is a tendency to mediate appears to us to be a proposition that begs the question of developmental significance.

Learning-Rate Hypothesis. The EDS-RS data are consistent with either the Θ_r or Θ_{oe} variants of this hypothesis, as is the evidence on age trends in optional shift (EDS-RS) experiments. The ED-ID shift and optional shift data provide no test of the Θ_r hypothesis and partial evidence for the Θ_{oe}

175

version. Perhaps the strongest support for the learning-rate hypothesis comes from the domain of subproblem analysis. Single-look attention theory can successfully simulate the human developmental effects using Θ_r variation; multiple-look theory can handle the same data with a combination of both Θ_r and Θ_{oe} manipulation. The other data domains we have considered provide no test of this hypothesis. In summary, there is some but certainly not conclusive evidence in these areas of discriminative transfer for developmental changes in learning-rate parameters.

We criticized the mediational tendency hypothesis on the grounds that it had uncertain developmental significance. This criticism does not apply to the learning-rate hypothesis. We adhere to the distinction drawn by Atkinson and Shiffrin (1969) between control processes and structural features. With respect to theory, the former refers to parameters that change with factors such as experience, training, or instructions; the latter refers to parameters characteristic of the organism which are not readily changed by factors such as experience, etc. It seems to us that developmental laws should be concerned with structural features rather than with control processes. A learning-rate parameter is, we believe, a candidate for structural feature status, and maturation of learning rates, if it occurs, is a developmental law. There are difficult problems of control in separating transfer (control process) and learning-rate (structural feature), but the separation is, we believe, possible in principle. However, the evidence is only suggestive.

The Compound-Component Hypothesis. This hypothesis can account adequately for the age trends in EDS-RS comparisons with standard or optional designs as well as for developmental differences in the results of subproblem analyses. What evidence there is for age trends in ED-ID shift comparisons is in a direction consonant with this hypothesis, but the data are inconclusive. Results from the miniature experiments do not show an absolute decline with development in indices of compounding, but these data are indeterminate with respect to a decline of component tendencies. In summary, the compound-component hypothesis accounts for as much of the data of discriminative transfer as does either of the competing hypotheses, and there are no strong disconfirming data. Thus this hypothesis is very much alive.

The meaning of a developmental trend toward an increasing use of component solutions as compared to compound solutions depends upon the theory of compounding used for interpretation. In this section we will consider some current conceptualizations of compounds and components and the theories that are associated with each conceptualization.

176

Tighe and Tighe (1966) relate their version of the compound-component hypothesis to the differentiation theory proposed by Gibson and Gibson (1955). However, the Tighes' definition of differentiation as applied to discrimination learning adds assumptions to the Gibsons' view that make the behavioral consequences quite different. The description of differentiation offered by Gibson and Gibson is that "a stimulus item starts out by being indistinguishable from a whole class of items in the stimulus universe tested, and ends by being distinguishable from all of them" [1955, p. 38]. Thus differentiation decreases generalization among stimuli; a given identifying response comes to be made to a specific stimulus rather than to a broad class. The definition of differentiation given by Tighe and Tighe (1972) is the isolation and independent utilization of the relation between a dimensional attribute and reinforcement across settings. The objective indices of differentiation are opposite for the two theories—ability to discriminate, according to the Gibsons and ability to generalize according to the Tighes. That is, the Gibsons infer differentiation from the ability of the subject to judge correctly that two stimuli are different. In contrast, Tighe and Tighe infer differentiation when subjects treat certain unlike stimuli as though they were the same. It is not clear how the same concept can be consistent with such different behavioral manifestations.

The developmental trends implied by the two theories are also quite different. According to Gibson and Gibson (1955) young children overgeneralize. That is, they are more likely to make errors of judging stimuli to be the same when they are different than are older children. Age and experience increase the ability to discriminate. But Tighe and Tighe predict the opposite trend—from overdiscrimination to ability to generalize. Young children "are likely to discriminate on the basis of the specific object-reward relations of the task while the perceptually pretrained subjects are likely to discriminate on the basis of dimension-reward relations" [Tighe & Tighe, 1972, p. 138]. Responding to specific objects requires more discriminations than responding to dimensions. To illustrate this point, let us consider the data of a subject classified as a compound learner on the basis of independent subproblem performance. Such subjects respond to a white square (+) versus a black circle (−) as a completely different problem from a black square (+) versus a white circle (−); the white square is not "the same" positive stimulus as the black square, nor is the black circle "the same" negative stimulus as the white circle. Given that each positive stimulus is also discriminated from each negative stimulus, there is a total of four discriminations. The more sophisticated subject, however, generalizes from white square to black square and is said to have isolated the form dimension. In summary, according to Gibson and Gibson, differentiation implies a trend from broadly generalized to more specific responses. But Tighe and Tighe predict the opposite trend for discrimination learning—from highly specific object-reward responding to generalization along component dimensions. Thus the relation between the compound-component hypothesis and the differentiation theory of Gibson and Gibson is far from clear.

If we reject Tighe and Tighe's identification of compounds with Gibson's concept of undifferentiated stimuli and if we accept their description of a compound as a response to a combination of two or more dimensions, then the developmental sequence implied by the compound-component hypothesis is an instance not of a progression from overgeneralization to discrimination but of a progression with age from overdiscrimination to a greater generalization. Some data supporting this interpretation come from a study by Saltz and Sigel (1967) in which it was found that as children get older they are less likely to "overdiscriminate," that is, to regard stimuli as different when they are really alike.

The data of subproblem analysis showing a failure of generalization (instances of relatively complete subproblem independence) also support Tighe and Tighe's definition of a compound, but at some theoretical cost. The existence of pure compound learning entails some awkward consequences. The pure compound learner would show: (1) no ED-ID differences; (2) no dimensional dominance effects in learning or transfer; and (3) no differences in difficulty of discrimination problems with variable-within and variable-between irrelevant dimensions. The logic behind the first two predictions was given in the sections on extradimensional-intradimensional shifts and optional shifts. To derive the third prediction, observe that the change from variable-within to variable-between is made by simply re-pairing the stimuli. With reference to Figure 2, in order to change the variable-within problem shown here to a variable-between problem, the two large stimuli could be paired in one setting and the two small stimuli in the other setting. If the subject perceives these stimuli as four specific compounds, the manner of pairing would not affect speed of learning. Since there is evidence contradicting all three predictions, even at the animal level, we are left with a somewhat paradoxical state of affairs. Subproblem independence indicates total use of compounds by some subjects at a lower developmental level; other data indicate the use of components. This paradox might be resolved by a theory which allows a subject to look at both compounds and components, with probabilities dependent upon stimulus conditions and previous training.

Tighe and Tighe (1968) introduce a distinction between two kinds of compounds that bears on the present discussion. For the first kind, "stimulus compounding may indicate response to stimulus objects as more or less undifferentiated wholes . . . In its most primitive form such discrimination would be based upon response to the difference between one object perceived as a whole and another object perceived as a whole. . . . A second sense in which the term stimulus compounding may be used is to indicate a response involving the combining of distinguishing features which Ss are *capable* of using independently, as when mature Ss make exact matches between multidimensional stimulus objects" (Tighe & Tighe, 1968, p. 760). Tighe and Tighe call the latter type of compounding "combining abstracted features." The distinction between the two kinds of compounds is based upon whether or not the subjects have the *capacity* to use the components (in some other situation) which are combined to make the compound. There is great difficulty with this distinction because just about all of the subjects used in this literature seem to be capable of using components in discriminative tasks requiring components for solution (i.e., where compounds are made irrelevant). Also the specification "perceiving objects as a whole" is inadequate in not telling us what aspects of a stimulus to include in the "whole." If, for instance, position and temporal order were included in the whole, no two objects would ever be perceived as the same. No such difficulties accompany the definition of compounds as a combination or pattern of specified aspects of stimuli, independent of the component aspects.

With this definition, the compound-component hypothesis makes the interesting prediction that as development proceeds some discriminative tasks will become more difficult. These tasks will have compounds relevant and components irrelevant. A good example of such a task is shown in Figure 15. In the simultaneous conditional problem, the subject who perceives only compounds should have no great difficulty. There are simply two different problems to be solved on randomly alternating trials. However, the subject who perceives components will have trouble, since each color and form component is reinforced randomly over trials. If the compound-component hypothesis is true, younger subjects (compounders) should find this problem easier than older (component) subjects find it. To our knowledge no one has tested this contraintuitive prediction directly. Some data, indirectly relevant, have been reported by Warren (1964), who found that sophisticated monkeys

CONDITIONAL SIMULTANEOUS PROBLEM

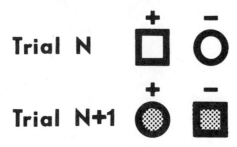

Figure 15. An illustration of a conditional simultaneous discrimination problem. The two settings are randomly alternated and left-right positions of the stimuli are also varied. One solution can be stated as follows: if white, choose the square; if black, choose the circle.

could solve the simultaneous conditional problem quite easily (less than five errors to criterion). Our guess is that subjects of a higher phylogenetic or developmental level may have more trouble than this. Gollin (1964, 1965, 1966) studied a variant of the simultaneous conditional problem. He reported that children found his variant very difficult (older children less so than younger), but Gollin used a background stimulus as the conditional cue rather than the arrangement shown in Figure 15. Gollin's arrangement presumably reduces compounding tendencies and provides a poorer test of the compound-component hypothesis than do Warren's stimulus arrangements. Some direct developmental comparisons on this problem are needed.

The final theoretical implications of compounding to be considered are derived from our multiple-look attention theory (House and Zeaman, 1963). The major feature of this formulation that distinguishes it from those of other compounding theorists such as the Tighes, Cole, or Spiker is the assumption that compounds are dimensional and are mediated by selective attention in exactly the same way in which components are dimensionally mediated. The attentional dynamics have been diagrammed in Figure 9. The probability of attending to compound and component dimensions may vary independently, but if a subject focuses on a compound dimension (through training or preference), then the solution of a new compound problem (new cues on the same compound dimension) will be facilitated. This is, in effect, a prediction

180

of an intradimensional shift within a compound dimension. In contrast, the negative transfer of extradimensional shifts would obtain for the solution of a compound problem following prior focusing on a component dimension. Although the demonstrations of ED-ID shift differences can be regarded as defining operations for the inference of dimensional mediation, we have been unable to find any reasonably direct experimental demonstrations of such transfer effects that use both compound and component dimensions. For this reason we ran a small pilot study designed to demonstrate ED-ID shift effects with respect to compounds and components. Such a study requires subjects to learn two discriminations: the first is either a compound or component problem and the second is a new problem, either compound or component. This yields two ID shift conditions (compound-to-compound and component-to-component) and two ED shift conditions (compound-to-component and component-to-compound). To make shift comparisons, the first requirement is a problem solvable only on the basis of compounds. For this we chose the simultaneous conditional problem illustrated in Figure 15. In this problem, color-form compounds are relevant; color and form components are variable and irrelevant. The second requirement is a component problem that would have components relevant and compounds variable and irrelevant. This can be achieved using a standard two-choice discrimination with form components relevant and color varying unsystematically from trial to trial (i.e., with new color cues introduced on each trial).

For convenience and speed (we thought of the experiment while writing this paper), we used college student subjects, and instead of multivariable color cues we employed just two variably irrelevant color cues in a standard form problem because there is strong evidence that adult subjects attend to the form component dimension in such problems to achieve solution. Sample stimulus settings for these component and compound problems are shown in Figure 16. We arranged two ED shifts: compound-to-component (C_1-to-S_2), and component-to-compound (S_1-to-C'_2). Only one ID shift was run (compound-to-new compound, C_1-to-C_2) because of a floor effect on errors in a component-to-component (S_1-to-S_2) condition. Too few errors were made on S_1 to permit ID shift facilitation of S_2.

The results for three groups of ten subjects each who had been randomly assigned to conditions are shown in Figure 16. The negative transfer of ED shifting can be assessed by looking at the relative difficulty of a compound solution *before* component solution (C_1) and *after* a component solution (C'_2) or by comparing the difficulty of a component solution before and after a compound solution (data points S_1 and S_2, respectively). Both comparisons show reliable decrements in performance with shifts in the relevant dimension. Some insight into the subjective mechanism of this negative transfer from compound-to-component shift can be gleaned from the answer of one subject to the question (asked at the end of the experiment), "How did you solve the last problem?" The response was: "When the black triangle was with the white cross, the black triangle was correct; for the other

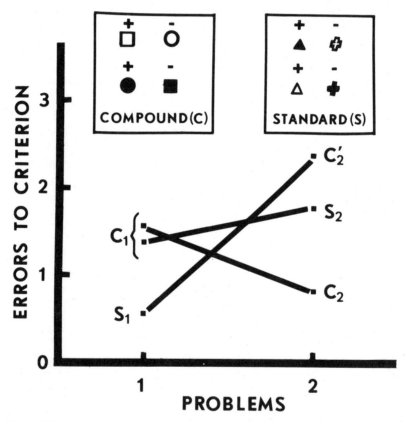

Figure 16. Results of a pilot study showing transfer relations of ED and ID shifts of compounds and components. Two trials of the compound problem (C_1) are illustrated at top left. These two kinds of trials were presented in irregular alternation. New color-form cues were used for the second compound problem (C_2 and C'_2). The component problem (or standard) is illustrated at top right. Subjects were run to a criterion of 10 successively correct responses. The errors-to-criterion measure excludes the first trial. The left-right position of the positive stimuli was irregularly alternated; the trials were subject-paced; the two problems for each subject were run in immediate succession; and the specific color and form cues were changed for each problem.

arrangement the white triangle was correct.'' We interpret this to mean that a component problem (triangle is correct) was solved by this subject as two independent compound subproblems. In terms of the compound-component hypothesis, we had caused this adult (component) subject to regress to a lower developmental level of a compound subject simply by focusing his attention on compounds in the first problem. The positive transfer of ID shifting is measured by the compound-to-new compound (C_1-to-C_2) difference which was also reliable. These pilot data are completely consistent with a model that assumes that compounds are dimensional and mediated by selective attention. These results pose a challenge for other views of compounding.

Of course our results were obtained with adults and our conclusions may be different when we run subjects who are at a lower developmental level with this experimental design. Whatever the answer with respect to the dimensional nature of compounds in younger subjects, the compound-component hypothesis still predicts that the relative difficulty of the compound problem in relation to the component problem will *decrease* with age.

Our last theoretical comment concerns the developmental significance of compounds in any theory that treats these merely as dimensions with varying probabilities of controlling attention. If the probability of attending to compounds decreases with age (and the probability of looking at components increases), then the observed age trends in discriminative transfer would be accounted for. But we are left with a question of developmental significance: is the shift in attention probabilities a result of learning or maturation? Because attentional probabilities are easily changed in value by even brief training procedures, they are examples of control process parameters. But one alternative possibility should not be overlooked: attention probabilities (or saliencies) may have a fixed (or unlearned) component as well as an adjustable or learned component. Lovejoy's (1968) attention model has a theoretical feature that makes this distinction: fixed saliencies of dimensions have a measure D, and learned or directable saliencies have a measure $\triangle$. These two measures combine additively to determine the attentional probability of a dimension. The D parameters may be structural features that change not with experience but with maturation. Component dimensions for older subjects may have a higher fixed salience than compounds, and the reverse may be true for younger subjects. Conceivably this could be a fundamental developmental law not derivable from principles of learning. If it is true, then all attention models, both single look and multiple-look, would include a theoretical mechanism such as Lovejoy's to include the distinction between learned and unlearned saliencies.*

Conclusions

There is modest empirical support for some version of each of the three hypotheses in the data domains examined. Most experiments reviewed provided confounded tests of two or all three of the hypotheses, so there are currently no strong grounds for deciding among them. In this sense, all three are still alive. Thus there may be developmental differences in how we learn, how fast we learn, and what we learn. In our view, the developmental mediation hypothesis receives the least support and may be a special example of the learning rate hypothesis. For optimal test, the learning-rate hypothesis requires quantitative models yielding parameter estimates of learning and attention probabilities; but very few of the studies in discriminative transfer have provided such tests. The compound-component hypothesis (what we learn) is for us the most interesting of the three hypotheses, carrying strong implications for both developmental psychology and theory construction in discriminative learning.

References

Atkinson, R. C., & Shiffrin, R. M. Human memory, a proposed system and its control processes. In K. W. Spence and J. T. Spence (Eds.), *The psychology of learning and motivation*. Vol. 2. New York: Academic Press, 1969. Pp. 90–197.

Bogartz, W. Effects of reversal and nonreversal shifts with CVC stimuli. *Journal of Verbal Learning and Verbal Behavior*, 1965, 4, 484–488.

Brown, A. L., & Scott, M. S. Transfer between the oddity and relative size concepts: reversal and extradimensional shifts. *Journal of Experimental Child Psychology*, 1972, 13, 350–367.

Campione, J. C. Optional intradimensional and extradimensional shifts in children as a function of age. *Journal of Experimental Psychology*, 1970, 84, 296–300.

Caron, A. J. Discrimination shifts in three-year-olds as a function of shift procedure. *Developmental Psychology*, 1970, 3, 236–241.

Cole, M. A developmental study of factors influencing discrimination transfer. *Journal of Experimental Child Psychology*, 1973, 16, 126–147.

Cole, M., & Medin, D. On the existence and occurrence of mediation in discrimination transfer: A critical note. *Journal of Experimental Child Psychology*, 1973, 15, 352–355.

Dickerson, D. J. Performance of preschool children on three discrimination shifts. *Psychonomic Science*, 1966, 4, 417–418.

Dickerson, D. J., Novik, N., & Gould, S. A. Acquisition and extinction rates as determinants of age changes in discrimination shift behavior. *Journal of Experimental Psychology*, 1972, 95, 116–122.

Dickerson, D. J., Wagner, J. F., & Campione, J. Discrimination shift performance of kindergarten children as a function of variation of the irrelevant shift dimension. *Developmental Psychology*, 1970, 3, 229–235.

*Sutherland and Mackintosh (1971), following Lovejoy, have also included in their attentional model a measure of fixed as well as of adjustable saliencies.

DAVID ZEAMAN

Eimas, P. D. Comment: Comparisons of reversal and nonreversal shifts. *Psychonomic Science*, 1965, 3, 444–446.

———. Effects of overtraining and age on intradimensional and extradimensional shifts in children. *Journal of Experimental Child Psychology*, 1966, 3, 348–355.

Estes, W. K. Learning theory and the new "mental chemistry." *Psychological Review*, 1960, 67, 207–223.

Fisher, M. A., & Zeaman, D. An attention-retention theory of retardate discrimination learning. In N. R. Ellis (Ed.), *International review of research in mental retardation*. Vol. 6. New York: Academic Press, 1973. Pp. 171–257.

Gibson, E. J. *Principles of perceptual learning and development*. New York: Appleton, 1969.

Gibson, J. J., & Gibson, E. J. Perceptual learning: differentiation or enrichment. *Psychological Review*, 1955, 62, 32–41.

Gollin, E. S. Reversal learning and conditional discrimination in children. *Journal of Comparative and Physiological Psychology*, 1964, 58, 441–445.

———. Factors affecting conditional discrimination in children. *Journal of Comparative and Physiological Psychology*, 1965, 60, 422–427.

———. Solution of conditional discrimination problems by young children. *Journal of Comparative and Physiological Psychology*, 1966, 62, 454–456.

Goulet, L. R. Basic issues in reversal-shift behavior: A reply to Kendler and Kendler. *Psychological Bulletin*, 1971, 75, 286–289.

Goulet, L. R., & Williams, K. J. Children's shift performance in the absence of dimensionality and a learned representational response. *Journal of Experimental Child Psychology*, 1970, 10, 287–294.

Graf, V., & Tighe, T. J. Subproblem analysis of discrimination shift learning in the turtle (Chrysemys picta picta). *Psychonomic Science*, 1971, 25, 257–259.

House, B. J., & Zeaman, D. Reversal and nonreversal shifts in discrimination learning of retardates. *Journal of Experimental Psychology*, 1962, 63, 444–451.

———. Miniature experiments in the discrimination learning of retardates. In L. P. Lipsitt & C. C. Spiker (Eds.), *Advances in child development and behavior*. Vol. 1. New York: Academic Press, 1963. Pp. 313–374.

Jeffrey, W. E. Variables affecting reversal-shifts in young children. *American Journal of Psychology*, 1965, 78, 589–595.

Kendler, H. H., & Kendler, T. S. Vertical and horizontal processes in problem-solving. *Psychological Review*, 1962, 69, 1–16.

———. Mediation and conceptual behavior. In K. W. Spence & J. T. Spence (Eds.), *The psychology of learning and motivation*. Vol. 2. New York: Academic Press, 1968. Pp. 198–244.

Kendler, H. H., Kendler, T. S., & Sanders, J. R. Reversal and partial reversal shifts with verbal material. *Journal of Verbal Learning and Verbal Behavior*, 1967, 6, 117–127.

Kendler, H. H., Kendler, T. S., & Ward, J. W. An ontogenetic analysis of optional intradimensional and extradimensional shifts. *Journal of Experimental Psychology*, 1972, 95, 102–109.

Kendler, T. S., Basden, B. H., & Bruckner, J. B. Dimensional dominance and continuity theory. *Journal of Experimental Psychology*, 1970, 83, 309–318.

Kendler, T. S., & Kendler, H. H. An ontogeny of optional shift behavior. *Child Development*, 1970, 41, 1–28.

Kendler, T. S., Kendler, H. H., & Learned, B. Mediated responses to size and brightness as a function of age. *American Journal of Psychology*, 1962, 75, 571–586.

Lovejoy, E. *Attention in discrimination learning*. San Francisco: Holden-Day, 1968.

Marquette, B. W., & Goulet, L. R. Mediated transfer in reversal and nonreversal shift paired-associate learning. *Journal of Experimental Psychology*, 1968, 76, 89–93.

Medin, D. L. Subproblem analysis of discrimination shift learning. *Behavior Research Methods and Instrumentation*, 1973, 5, 332–336.

Mumbauer, C. C., & Odom, R. D. Variables affecting the performance of preschool children in intradimensional, reversal, and extradimensional shifts. *Journal of Experimental Psychology*, 1967, 75, 180–187.

185

Richman, C. L. Role of overtraining in reversal and conceptual shift behavior. *Journal of Experimental Psychology*, 1973, 99, 285–287.

Richman, C. L., & Trinder, J. Effect of a novel stimulus dimension on discrimination learning. *Journal of Experimental Psychology*, 1968, 77, 163–165.

Saltz, E., & Sigel, I. E. Concept overdiscrimination in children. *Journal of Experimental Psychology*, 1967, 73, 1–8.

Sanders, B. Factors affecting reversal and nonreversal shifts in rats and children. *Journal of Comparative and Physiological Psychology*, 1971, 74, 192–202.

Schaeffer, B., & Ellis, S. The effects of overlearning on children's nonreversal and reversal learning using unrelated stimuli. *Journal of Experimental Child Psychology*, 1970, 10, 1–7.

Shepp, B. E., & Eimas, P. D. Intradimensional and extradimensional shifts in the rat. *Journal of Comparative and Physiological Psychology*, 1964, 57, 357–361.

Shepp, B. E., & Gray, V. Some effects of variable-within and variable-between irrelevant stimuli on dimensional learning and transfer. *Journal of Experimental Psychology*, 1971, 89, 32–39.

Shepp, B. E., & Turrisi, F. D. Learning and transfer of mediating responses in discrimination learning. In N. R. Ellis (Ed.), *International review of research in mental retardation*. Vol. 2. New York: Academic Press, 1966. Pp. 86–122.

Smiley, S. S. Optional shift behavior as a function of dimensional preference and relative cue similarity. *Journal of Experimental Child Psychology*, 1972, 14, 313–322.

Smiley, S. S., & Weir, M. W. Role of dimensional dominance in reversal and nonreversal shift behavior. *Journal of Experimental Child Psychology*, 1966, 4, 296–307.

Sutherland, N. S., & Mackintosh, N. J. *Mechanisms of animal discrimination learning*. New York: Academic Press, 1971.

Teas, D. C., & Bitterman, M. E. Perceptual organization in the rat. *Psychological Review*, 1962, 59, 130–140.

Tighe, L. S., & Tighe, T. J. Discrimination learning: Two views in historical perspective. *Psychological Bulletin*, 1966, 66, 353–370.

Tighe, T. J. Subproblem analysis of discrimination learning. In G. H. Bower (Ed.), *Psychology of learning and motivation*. Vol. 7. New York: Academic Press, 1973.

Tighe, T. J., Glick, J., & Cole, M. Subproblem analysis of discrimination shift learning. *Psychonomic Science*, 1971, 24, 159–160.

Tighe, T. J., & Graf, V. Subproblem analysis of discrimination shift learning in the pigeon. *Psychonomic Science*, 1972, 29, 139–141.

Tighe, T. J., & Tighe, L. S. Overtraining and optional shift behavior in rats and children. *Journal of Comparative and Physiological Psychology*, 1966, 62, 49–54.

———. Discrimination shift performance of children as a function of age and shift procedure. *Journal of Experimental Psychology*, 1967, 74, 466–470.

———. Differentiation theory and concept-shift behavior. *Psychological Bulletin*, 1968, 70, 756–761.

———. Stimulus control in children's learning. In A. D. Pick (Ed.), *Minnesota symposium on child development*. Vol. 6. Minneapolis: University of Minnesota Press, 1972.

Trabasso, T., Deutsch, J. A., & Gelman, R. Attention and discrimination learning of young children. *Journal of Experimental Child Psychology*, 1966, 4, 9–19.

Warren, J. M. Additivity of cues in conditional discrimination learning by rhesus monkeys. *Journal of Comparative and Physiological Psychology*, 1964, 58, 124–126.

Werner, H. *Comparative psychology of mental development*. (rev. ed.) New York: International Universities Press, 1948.

Wolff, J. L. Concept-shift and discrimination-reversal learning in humans. *Psychological Bulletin*, 1967, 68, 369–408.

Wolford, G., & Bower, G. H. Continuity theory revisited: Rejected for the wrong reasons? *Psychological Review*, 1969, 76, 515–518.

Zeaman, D., & House, B. J. The role of attention in retardate discrimination learning. In N. R. Ellis (Ed.), *Handbook of mental deficiency*. New York: McGraw-Hill, 1963. Pp. 159–223.

LIST OF CONTRIBUTORS

List of Contributors

R. ALLEN GARDNER and BEATRICE T. GARDNER are both professors in the Department of Psychology, University of Nevada. R. A. Gardner studied at New York University, Columbia, and Northwestern. Under the influence of B. J. Underwood, he became interested in learning and problem solving. Before Washoe, the subjects of his research had been rats and human beings. B. T. Gardner majored in psychology at Radcliffe and at Brown, then went on to study with Niko Tinbergen, and received her doctorate in zoology from Oxford. Her research interests are in the integration of behavior sequences, and she had worked with spiders, fish, and humans, before Washoe. The Gardners met and married while R. A. Gardner was a research psychologist and B. T. Gardner was teaching psychology at Wellesley College. They came to Nevada a few years later and have been living there ever since.

ELEANOR J. GIBSON is the Susan Linn Sage Professor of Psychology at Cornell University. She received her Ph.D. from Yale University in 1938 and taught at Smith College until 1949 when she moved to Cornell. She was a research associate there until 1965. During this time she was a Fellow at the Institute for Advanced Study at Princeton and at the Center for Advanced Study in the Behavioral Sciences at Stanford. She was a Guggenheim Fellow in 1972–73. Her research interests include perceptual learning and development, and the reading process.

I. I. GOTTESMAN is a professor of psychology in the departments of psychology, psychiatry, and genetics, and director of the Behavioral Genetics Center at the University of Minnesota from which he also received his Ph.D. in clinical child psychology. He has taught at Harvard University and the University

189

of North Carolina School of Medicine. He was an NIMH Special Fellow in psychiatric genetics at the Maudsley Hospital in London (1963–64) at which time he began his enduring collaboration with Eliot Slater and James Shields. In 1972–73 he was a Guggenheim Fellow at Kommunehospitalet and the University of Copenhagen. His research interests include human behavioral genetics and developmental psychopathology. For five years he was a consulting editor to *SRCD Monographs*.

P. HERBERT LEIDERMAN is a clinical and research psychiatrist who has worked on problems at the interface between biology and behavior. His early research dealt with sensory deprivation and social isolation in adults and was extended to the applied problems of the premature infant nursery in his work on mother-infant separation in the neonatal period. Through this research he became involved in issues on the development of social bonding — and its subsequent influence on the cognitive and social development of the child. He received his M.A. degree in psychology from the University of Chicago in 1949 and his M.D. degree from Harvard Medical School in 1953. He has held teaching and research appointments at Harvard and Stanford medical schools. Currently he is professor of psychiatry in the Department of Psychiatry, Stanford University School of Medicine. GLORIA F. LEIDERMAN is a developmental psychologist who combines her research work in early infant cognitive and social development with applied work in a center for disturbed and learning disordered children. She received her Ph.D. from Radcliffe in 1953 and has held teaching and research positions at Harvard and Stanford universities. Currently she is clinical assistant professor in the Department of Psychiatry, Stanford University School of Medicine, and acting director of Peninsula Children's Center in Palo Alto.

ROSS D. PARKE, a University of Waterloo Ph.D., is currently chief, Social Development Section of the Fels Research Institute and Fels Clinical Professor of Research Pediatrics at the University of Cincinnati College of Medicine. Until 1971, he was professor of psychology at the University of Wisconsin. He is an associate editor of *Child Development*. His research interests involve various aspects of social development, including the development of aggression and self-control, and recently the role of the father in infancy.

DAVID ZEAMAN is professor of psychology at the University of Connecticut where he has been for the last 25 years. Before that he was an instructor at

Brown University for two years, after having received his doctorate in experimental psychology at Columbia University. In 1963 he received a Lifetime Research Career Award from NIMH to study mental retardation, and since that time he has devoted his research efforts to the study of the relation of intelligence to such behavioral processes as attention, learning, transfer, and memory. BETTY HOUSE received her M.A. in experimental psychology at Brown University and her Ph.D. at the University of Connecticut in 1953, where she is currently professor in residence. Her research interests have been concentrated in the experimental psychology of mental retardation.

INDEX

Index

INDEX

Mother-infant interaction
  and attachment, 91–92
  and cognitive development, 81, 83, 99,
    106
  cross-cultural comparison of, 82, 106–107
  in nuclear families, 81–82, 99
  in polymatric families, 83, 86–89, 90, 99
  and social development, 81, 82–83

Peer group influences
  cross-age tutoring, 126–127, 129–130
  on discipline techniques, 121
  and inhibitory rule transmission, 121–126
  on resistance to deviation, 118, 123–124
Phenotype
  effects of genotype and environment on,
    57–62, 72
  and reaction range, 58–62
Prohibitory rationales
  and classical conditioning, 119
  developmental changes in response to,
    115–117, 118
  effectiveness of, 112–114, 119, 123, 125–
    126, 132–133
  effects of peer endorsement, 118, 123,
    124
  and moral judgment, 115, 117
  and observational learning, 119–120
  and punishment, 112–114, 119
  and rule transmission, 121–126
  and social learning theory, 120
Psychopathology: and genetics, 70–77
Punishment, physical
  and agent-child relationship, 114
  effectiveness of, 112–114, 119, 123
  intensity of, 114
  role in socialization, 111–112
  timing of, 114
  and verbal rationale, 112–114, 119

Reaction range: and gene-environment interaction, 58–62

Reading
  and attention, 31–37
  cognitive processing in, 37–52
  and development of meaning, 26–31
  and perceptual differentiation, 26–31
  and semantic structure, 48–52
  stimulus information in, 31, 34–35
  use of orthographic rules in, 39–48
Role playing: and moral judgment, 127, 134
Rules
  enforcement and self-control, 126–134
  peer transmission of, 121–126
  and type of discipline, 130–134

Scanning
  age differences in rates of, 32–34, 40,
    42–43
  and attention, 32–35
  effects of interfering stimuli on, 33–34
  effects of orthographic structure on, 42–43
  role of meaning in, 34–35
Schizophrenia: genetic aspects of, 71–77
Self-control: and rule enforcement, 126–134
Social development. *See also* Attachment
  maternal role in infancy, 82–83
  in polymatric setting, 105–106, 109
Socioeconomic status
  and cognitive performance, 98–99, 106,
    108–109
  and discipline techniques, 120

Verbal behavior: of infants, 103. *See also*
  Language acquisition; Language, sign

Word recognition
  age differences in, 40, 42–43
  of deaf subjects, 40–41
  effects of bimodal presentation on, 44
  morphological features, 41–42
  orthographic features, 39–48
  and pronounceability, 40–41
  stimulus information for, 31

197